Food and
Multiculture

SENSORY STUDIES SERIES

Series Editor: David Howes
ISSN: 2052–3092

As the leading publisher of scholarship on the culture of the senses, we are delighted to present this series of cutting-edge case studies, syntheses and translations in the emergent field of sensory studies. Building on the success of the *Sensory Formations* series, this new venture provides an invaluable resource for those involved in researching and teaching courses on the senses as subjects of study and means of inquiry. Embracing the insights of a wide array of humanities and social science disciplines, the field of sensory studies has emerged as the most comprehensive and dynamic framework yet for making sense of human experience. The series offers something for every disciplinary taste and sensory inclination.

Published Titles:

Ian Heywood (ed.), *Sensory Arts and Design*

Luca Vercelloni, *The Invention of Taste*

Michael Bull and John P. Mitchell (eds), *Ritual, Performance and the Senses*

François Laplantine, *The Life of the Senses: Introduction to a Modal Anthropology*

Forthcoming Titles:

Constance Classen, *The Museum of the Senses*

David Le Breton, *Sensing the World*

Rupert Cox, *The Sound of the Sky Being Torn: A Political Ecology of Military Aircraft Noise*

Food and Multiculture

A Sensory Ethnography of East London

Alex Rhys-Taylor

Bloomsbury Academic
An imprint of Bloomsbury Publishing Plc

B L O O M S B U R Y

LONDON · OXFORD · NEW YORK · NEW DELHI · SYDNEY

Bloomsbury Academic

An imprint of Bloomsbury Publishing Plc

50 Bedford Square	1385 Broadway
London	New York
WC1B 3DP	NY 10018
UK	USA

www.bloomsbury.com

BLOOMSBURY and the Diana logo are trademarks of Bloomsbury Publishing Plc

First published 2017

© Alex Rhys-Taylor, 2017

Alex Rhys-Taylor has asserted his right under the Copyright, Designs and Patents Act, 1988, to be identified as Author of this work.

British Library Cataloguing-in-Publication Data

A catalogue record for this book is available from the British Library.

ISBN:	HB:	978-1-4725-8116-7
	ePDF:	978-1-4725-8117-4
	ePub:	978-1-4725-8118-1

Library of Congress Cataloging-in-Publication Data

A catalog record for this book is available from the Library of Congress.

Series: Sensory Studies

Cover image: Brick Lane market, London, England © Scott E. Barbour/Getty Images

Typeset by RefineCatch Limited, Bungay, Suffolk

To find out more about our authors and books visit www.bloomsbury.com. Here you will find extracts, author interviews, details of forthcoming events and the option to sign up for our newsletters.

For Odysseus

CONTENTS

ACKNOWLEDGEMENTS

Any work engaging in 'the social' is, to one degree or another, a collaborative effort. This is all the more so when there are so many years of research behind the book, across which the collaborators have piled up. In the first instance I would like to extend my thanks to every market trader, restauranteur and shopkeeper entrepreneur that allowed me to lurk around their businesses; notably Irene and Mashun at Tomos Japanese Food, and the staff of Al Badar Fried Chicken. Special thanks to Paul Simpson for the laughs, and the rich insights into the historical East End that I discovered while chewing on a cup of cockles. Thanks go to all my peers at the NYLON seminars with whom I shared early drafts of this work, including occasional partners in crime Hannah Jones and Emma Jackson, along with the responsible adults in the group, Fran Tonkiss, Richard Sennett, Michael Bull and Vic Seidler. Among my peers, Shamea Mia, Vanessa Arena, Anamik Saha, Tomoko Tamari and Paz Concha have all also provided invaluable feedback and tip-offs. I am deeply grateful to David Howes for taking a punt on this monograph, and for the rigour of his feedback. Thanks also to my colleagues at Goldsmiths Sociology and the Centre for Urban and Community Research; it is a privilege to be surrounded by such simultaneously sharp minds and warm hearts. Among my colleagues, the most gratitude ought to be extended to Les Back, whose capacious sociological imagination opened the space for this study to be conceived, and whose encouragement kept it moving along. The biggest debt of all, however, is owed to Natasha Polyviou. As I sit here writing these last pages at home, Natasha is literally wrestling our son to the ground trying to make sure he doesn't disturb me. Your efforts are priceless and there are no words to express how grateful I am for that. One more sentence to go and I'll be able to cook dinner. Or maybe pick up a pizza.

1

Coming to Our Senses

Halfway along Whitechapel Road on a warm early October evening in 2015. A congested patchwork corridor of clothing wholesalers, budget hotels, homeless hostels, high-street retailers and a street market packing up for the day. Shutters are pulled down as the daytime businesses close. Bassy dance music pummels through the panelling of a low-riding hatchback as it passes through the thick traffic. Yogic exhalations of vanilla 'e-cig' vapour intermingle with beedi and tobacco trails of pedestrians hurrying – back home, to the cinema, to the doctor, to the shop for dinner ingredients. The sweet rose and frankincense of a mirror-lined Arabic fragrance retailer, open for evening trade, competes with the high street choices of the emerging party crowd. Powdery, citrus, jasmine, lilies and rose for her. Woody, grassy spices and herbs for him.

Whitechapel sits to the immediate east of 'The City', London's central business district. Looking east along Whitechapel Road, the apricot setting sun catches the glass curtains draped over buildings towering on the horizon – 'The Gherkin,' 'The Cheesegrater' and a cluster of several other less savoury sounding offerings. During the day, the white noise of riveters, buzz-saws and jackhammers accompanies the smell of concrete, sawdust, solvents and fresh paint; the sensory signatures of The City's eastward creep. Paving the way for the new towers of luxury are the milky and nutty air of white-tiled coffee shops and a fog of herbs – stoned baked pizza and nouveau pan-Asian cuisine. The new constellation encroaches on the aromatic environs of fried chicken shops and curry canteens. An evening chorus of default ring tones and message alerts chirrups away. Plans for the final hours of the week are laid out.

Moving westward, approaching Brick Lane, once best known for its Bengali curry houses, a smoky fog of charred lamb and chicken (emanating from newly opened Turkish restaurants) catches the nose and refracts the light. Passing through the mist of meat fumes is a German couple, mother and daughter. Their hair glistens with the synthetic bergamot of budget hotel shampoo. '*Es riecht nach Kreuzberg,*' says the mother to the daughter. It smells like Kreuzberg.

What, in a twenty-first century city like London, is the social significance of the transnational flow of ideas and materials that pass through it? How to conceptualize the city's cultures, without recourse to crude and ill-fitting caricatures of ethnicity, class, the 'local' and the 'global'? How to express the significance of an individual's dreams and fears, while attending to the contingencies and histories that shape her sensibility? How to get beyond the ways in which we *talk* about both ourselves and each other, to the significance of the ways in which we *feel*? The following chapters argue that answers to each of these questions lie in a close attention to the sensory ambience of the city, and the everyday life that underpins it. More precisely, through honing a sensorial attention to a series of the spaces between 'The City' and the East End – over an eight-year period stretching from the immediate aftermath of the financial crisis, through the 2011 riots and the Olympics, to the present day – the following book highlights experiences, artefacts and relationships that help understand early millennial London. The hope is to present the reader with an appreciation of the role that oft-overlooked multisensory experiences might play, within the key sociological processes of our age.

The Insensible Urban

Cities are sonorous, smelly and full of both delectable and stomach-churning things. As part of everyday life, urbanites' evaluations of city's sensoria inform an array of decisions. Where to sit on public transport? Next to a young woman guzzling a burger and fries? Next to the teenage boy whose personal soundtrack is spilling loudly out of his leaky headphones? Or next to the middle-aged man, who despite spreading his legs inhospitably, is wearing the same aftershave as a favoured uncle? Which way to get to work? Through the maelstrom of the high street, or through the shaded and notably quieter side streets? Who to approach for directions? Where to go for dinner? Where to buy a house? As Richard Webber demonstrates in correlations of housing choice and lifestyle type, the visual appearance of a given locale certainly plays a pivotal role in guiding like-minded city dwellers to the same neighbourhoods (Webber 2013). Although 'big data' on the matter is a long way from being gathered, the research upon which this book rests suggests the same seems true of the soundscapes and aromatic ambiences of neighbourhoods. Particular atmospheres seem partly to correlate with particular sensibilities. As the following chapters will demonstrate, there are a great many ways in which the visual, the sonic, the gustatory and olfactory landscapes of cities shape movements through urban space; drawing people towards that which they desire, providing comfort and reassurance while also alerting them to both real and imagined threats.

Whether luring, reassuring, or alerting, the senses – as this book demonstrates – inform many decisions of sociological significance. Much of the work of the senses, however, happens at a relatively microscopic, interpersonal level, invisible at the scale of the whole city. So microscopic, in fact, that such experiences are often felt to be of barely any sociological significance for the individual, let alone the broader mass of cities or societies.

Yet, it is this book's contention that, when aggregated, these experiences, and the sensibilities they are part of, often have significant consequences for the city and society of which they are part.

In this respect, this book works against the cautions offered by a number of influential urban theorists warning against trying to understand the contemporary city from amidst the thick, sensuous clamour of urban life. The sensuous experiences of the city dweller, it was once compellingly argued, are simply too microscopic, myopic, self-involved and localized to lend anything to our understanding of supra-personal processes shaping cities; processes that for the main part, operate at an increasingly global scale (Soja in Westwood and Williams 2003: 21). Accordingly, for macro theorists of pre-millennial urban space, the preferred means of representing cities, and understanding the life evolving therein, was to set up a lens – at least 20,000 feet, but ideally around 450 miles – above an urban form (Soja 1996: 152). Elevated out of the clamorous urban miasma, the 'zenith view' (Boeri in Koolhaas et al. 2000: 358), produces a spatio-temporal gestalt through which gargantuan, globe-spanning flows in capital, commodities, labour and information became clearly visible. Free of the transient clamour of urban life's sounds, smells and textures, the position previously reserved for angels reveals 'macro spatial' maps delineating the apparent 'organizing principles' of contemporary cities (Soja 1996: 153). As seen from above, global cities such as London were revealed as centralized 'command centres', integral to the integrated global economy and as such, driving the becoming-one-none-place of the world – a world in which serially monotonous ghettos of affluence are surrounded by the undifferentiated squalor of slums (Harvey 1989: 23–43; Davis 2006, 2007). In both the centres and the margins of cities, and in both central and marginal cities, global urbanization visible from on high is credited with 'overriding . . . history and culture' (Sassen 1993: 22–34).

Doubtless, the tools and abstractions of macro-spatial urban theory have helped identify geographies of resource control, capital accumulation and environmental impact, of which today's global cities are a central part. The global sprawl of suburban McMansions, luxury flats and the simultaneous processes of dispossession and the growth of 'slums' undoubtedly lend to the appearance of an increasingly divided yet homogeneously urban planet. Zooming out to a view of the city from 450 miles up does not, however, mean 'more' is subsequently encompassed within the 'frame'. While revealing certain aspects of reality, such generalized representations of urban life are as vulnerable to hypermetropia as the perspectives of the city dweller are to myopia. That is to say, they reveal little of the actual corporeal experience of city dwellers and their relationship to the political economy of the city. Which is shame, for while, from certain angles, many twenty-first century cities look increasingly alike, rarely do they smell, sound, feel or taste like the same place. Or if they do smell or sound like somewhere else, it is not always the same somewhere else to which a city 'appears' to be similar. If nothing else, the discontinuity between relative visual homogeneity and the landscapes sensed by the other senses, ask serious questions of the extent to which today's cities are successfully overriding local histories and culture (Sassen 1993: 22–34). At worst, the lack of attention to the actual experiences of city dwellers is of significant detriment to our understanding of the problems faced by today's cities and the solutions to those problems.

Following these critiques, I want to argue that to understand properly the relationship between everyday urban lives and globe-spanning processes, urban scholarship needs to develop methodological tools, and analyses, that are sensitive to the specific textures *on the ground* of contemporary life. In particular, drawing on a range of pioneering and sensorially attuned scholarship (Classen, Howes and Synnott 1994; Seremetakis 1996; Stoller 1997; Sutton 2001; Howes 2003; Vannini, Waskul and Gottschalk 2011; Back and Puwar 2012; Howes and Classen 2013), I argue that an understanding of the pressing social questions of the twenty-first century city is significantly enhanced by a sensitivity to the multisensory ambience of its everyday life.

Sensoria and Sensibilities

Beneath the city captured in aerial images and maps is a panoply of materialities (*sensoria*) – volatile aromatics, sonic vibrations, distributions of heat and cold – that, combined, serve to distinguish different urban spaces, as well as the types of activity that take place there. Consider, for instance, the aforementioned bassy beats, glowing lights and synthesized perfumes that create the atmospheres of the city's night-time economy. Or, if you prefer something more genteel, consider an early morning autumn walk through one of London's Royal Parks – the rustling branches of trees that accompany the sweet composting scent of fallen leaves decaying on an asphalt path while a woollen sweater scratches at the nape of your neck. These are just some of the many *sensoria* that fill a city.

A tree falling, or even rustling in the autumn breeze, only makes a noise if somebody is there to hear it. In other words, sensoria are only of sociological importance if somebody is there to experience them as a *sensation* (rustling branches, a portend of seasonal change, decaying leaves evoking memories of childhood walks home from school). But of course, such sensations are deeply personal and are often related to biography. For the purposes of this book, what marks one individual's experience of *sensoria* from another, is understood as their *sensibility*. It is through sensibilities, a biographically, culturally and, to an extent, biologically specific filter, that *sensoria* become *sensations*. An individual's sensibility is, as mentioned, partly a facet of the biological body – its ability to hear, see or touch to varying degrees. Sensibility is also, however, highly plastic, shaped by both individual life experience as well as broader social histories in which biographies are nestled, each of which work to determine how a particular sensation is evaluated. It is because of sensibility, the matrix through which sensoria are rendered into sensations, that London's most expensive flat ends up being No.1 Hyde Park, deriving its value precisely in part because of its proximity to a romantically bucolic landscape of rustling trees, ornamental lakes and grassy lawns. It is because of sensibilities, that cheaper flats can be found above bars and pubs of the city's night-time economy. Accordingly, alongside an attentiveness to the myriad sensoria that colour urban space, the book also aims to approach an understanding of the countless sensibilities through which sense is made of the materialities of urban space.

A Critique of Perspective

From Charles Booth's illuminating maps (Booth and Argyle 1902), through Park and Burgess' bird's-eye representation of the concentric city's ecology (Park and Burgess 2012), to the contemporary urban theorists' preference for satellite images (Soja 1996; Longley 2002; Florida, Mellander and Gulden 2012), the zenith view has come to dominate representations of the modern city. That is not to say that other perspectives have been absent. The sociological and anthropological interest in urbanism has, in fact, given rise to a number of distinctly more human perspectives on the city, which have taken the analytical lens from on high, re-angling it closer and parallel to the ground. From the second generation of Chicago school urbanists rallying against the broad brushstrokes of their predecessors (Anderson 1961; Becker 1963; Whyte 1993; Cressey 2008; Goffman 2008), through increasingly close-up studies of urban British culture (Cohen 1997; Cohen 1998; Willis 1981; Young and Wilmott 2013) to the globally attuned urban ethnographies of the new millennium's cities (Hannerz 1980; Back 1996; Alexander 2000; Bourgois 2003; Keith 2005; Wacquant 2007; Venkatesh 2009; Goffman 2015), urban scholars have provided rich insights into the social processes covering the last century of urban life.

Even the richest ethnographic representations of urban life, however, fall short of recording and representing the full range of forces carving the social morphology and cultural texture of cities. Urban ethnography's historic shortcomings seem, in part, rooted in the inherently textual nature of ethnography itself. In recent years a number of ethnographers have started drawing on the opportunities afforded by increasingly accessible audio-visual technologies to develop a range of non-textual forms of analysis and representation. As a result, 'visual sociology' and 'visual ethnographies' of urban environments have made significant strides in addressing the erstwhile blind-spots generated by an over-reliance on reproducing spoken words and textual descriptions. A clear antidote to the totalizing vision of high-flying spatial theorists, reconstructed urban ethnographies have opened our eyes to the visual perspectives of the city's homeless communities (Knowles 2005; Harper 2006), street booksellers (Duneier and Carter 2001), migrant domestic workers (Knowles and Harper 2009) and spectacles of consumption (Penaloza 1998), as well as revealing new angles on the infrastructure of cities (Dorrian and Rose 2003).

However, if the dominant way of understanding life in global cities has been to take the disembodied view from 450 miles up, and the critical response has been to privilege the optics of city dwellers, a significant portion of experience 'down below' (Certeau 1988: 92–93) is still missing from contemporary sociological investigations of urban life. Writing in 1882, Gustav Teichmuller developed a critique of the dominant 'perspective' deployed by science and philosophy. Noting that 'all philosophies are [. . .] perspectival images of reality from a certain standpoint', Teichmuller cautioned sternly against adherence to any one 'perspective' (Teichmuller in Ten 2003: 183). Teichmuller's critique of perspective was not just a critique of the 'angle' with which the analytical lens had been set up. Rather, it was, above all else, a critique of the use of a 'perspectival lens' in the first place. 'Lens', here, is not simply a metaphor for how we 'look' at things. Rather, it points toward the ways in which a particular sensory modality came to dominate the production of modern knowledge. In short, Teichmuller wrote, '[p]hilosophy has been dominated by a bias in favour of sight' (Teichmuller in Ten 2003: 183). This bias, we now know, is very real and skews not just Western philosophy but also the social scientific disciplines that emerged out of it. From Aristotle to Kant, through Freud and Foucault, big thinkers have made no bones of placing the visual at the top of a hierarchy prioritized for serious thinking and explorations of truth (Jay 1993; Korsmeyer 2014: 11–31). Vision is preferred for its purported objectivity, for the ability to see at a distance without being emotionally moved. Conversely, at the very bottom of the sensory hierarchy are taste, olfaction and touch, the 'animalistic' senses that have been thought to result in more visceral, emotional responses to sensoria. The result of this sensory hierarchy in Western thought, as Teichmuller and others since have argued, has been a very partial account of reality and is of significant detriment to our wider understanding of the world (Jay 1993; Pallasmaa 2005; Howes 2005; Korsmeyer 2014). Teichmuller's solution to perspectival bias was 'to over-throw this dictatorship and establish a kind of *democracy of the senses*' (Teichmuller in Ten 2003: 183, emphasis added.) Yet despite a minor literature critiquing the 'ocularcentrism' (Jay 1993) of twentieth-century thought, the dictatorship of the eye shows no sign of abating. If anything, the new millennium has seen a proliferation of optical technologies, visual practices, theoretical lenses and points of view. There is then, more than ever, a pressing need to ask 'what of the other senses?' What of hearing, smell, taste and touch, let alone heat-sensitivity, balance and pain? There is, is there not, a great deal more to the formation of subjectivities and social forms in cities than 'meets the eye'?

The Senses in Critical Thought

It is not that critical thinking about modernity and metropoles has been completely numb to 'the other' senses for the last two hundred years. As mentioned, modernity's key thinkers – including, Nietzsche, Simmel and even Karl Marx – made serious efforts to theorize the relationship between the senses and epochal processes of industrialization and urbanization. Karl Marx, for instance, noted explicitly that, 'The forming of the five senses is a labour of the entire history of the world up to the present' (Marx 2012a: 108).

Neither Marx nor Engels sustained a consideration of the senses as a distinct theme in itself. But in Marx's vivid descriptions of the mills and factories of the nineteenth century (Marx 2012b: 275, 286, 290, 325) or in Engels' bleak trudge through the congested streets of east London and Manchester (Engels 2012: 23–24), it is clear that both related to the distribution of sensory experience, and specific sensibilities, to the capitalist city's social structure. Engaging more explicitly and consistently with the senses as part of his broader reflections on modernity, Georg Simmel channelled Teichmuller when he asserted that '*every sense* delivers contributions characteristic of its individual nature to the construction of sociated existence' (Simmel, Frisby and Featherstone 1997: 110, emphasis added). Relating this theme to cities more specifically, in *The Metropolis and Mental Life*, Simmel also famously predicted the impact that the ongoing bombardment of sensory experiences had upon urbanites. He did so, in part, to account for the emergence of a newly *blasé* disposition (Simmel, Frisby and Featherstone 1997: 174–187), a phenomenon later dissected in more detail by mid-century urban social psychologists (Goffman 2008).

The reworking of Marx by mid-twentieth-century cultural theorists of the Frankfurt School also implicitly placed the sensory experiences of mid-century city dwellers at the heart of their interest in modernity's accumulating catastrophes (Benjamin 1968; Benjamin and Tiedemann 1999; Adorno 2002; Horkheimer, Adorno and Noerr 2002; Benjamin 2009). From the palid 'muzak' that drifted around 'places of amusement' (Adorno 2002: 289) to the razzle-dazzle of the advertising industry and the warm glow of neon lights reflecting on wet asphalt (Benjamin 2009: 86), metro-sensory experiences were thought of, by these scholars at least, as both symptoms and causes of twentieth century society's rapid transformation. In the decades following the Second World War, structuralist anthropology also sought to delineate the hidden organizing principles beneath culturally specific tastes. Again, never referring to the senses, sensibilities or sensoria as such, many of the last century's most cited anthropological texts of the era are concerned with the ways in which human sensory experiences relate to the reproduction of social order (Douglas and Nicod 1974; Bourdieu and Nice 1984; Caplan 1992; Lévi-Strauss et al. 1992; Lévi-Strauss 1997). However, following the post-structural backlash against anthropology, phenomenology and the 'subject' at the centre of both, came two decades of desensitized critical thought enamoured instead with discursive analysis and word games. It was only in the final decade of the second millennium that critical thought returned with any seriousness to more fleshy concerns. Inspired in part by a return to Simmel (Featherstone, Hepworth and Turner

1991) and re-evaluation of mid-century phenomenology (Crossley 1995; Vasseleu 1998; Crossley 2001; Diprose 2002), progressive critical thinking at the turn of the millennium reinstated 'the body' firmly at the centre of the new millennium's moral and intellectual questions.

In terms of urban theory, the attention to 'embodiment' yielded new understanding of the relationship between desire and space (Pile 1993, 2013), as well as the spatialization of gender, sexuality (Braidotti 1994; Grosz 1995; Cresswell 1999; Hemmings 2002), race and class, by way of the body. Importantly for this book, the 'corporeal turn' also nurtured an emerging literature engaging in the relationships between food, the body and accelerated processes of globalization (Lupton 1996; Bell and Valentine 1997; Atkins and Bowler 2000; Warde 2000a; Ritzer 2004).

Building on the accumulating critiques of ocular-centrism, textual introspection and linguistic fetish, more recent years have seen the emergence of a program of research that engages explicitly, as Teichmuller called for a century before, in a 'democracy of the senses,' (Berendt 1992; Bull and Back 2003). This 'the sensory turn' (Howes 2012) has emerged from two distinct fronts. First, the ground-breaking social and cultural *histories* of the sensory experience (Corbin 1988, 1998; Camporesi 1989; Classen, Howes and Synnott 1994; Smith 2003, 2006, 2014; Sterne 2003; Classen et al. 2014); second, a collection of studies exploring the role of smell, taste, touch and sound in an assortment of contemporary cultural and geographic contexts (Seremetakis 1996; Feld 1996; Sutton 2001; Stoller 2002; Degen 2008; Drobnick and Fisher 2008; Waskul, Vannini and Wilson 2009; Wise 2010; Low 2013; Obasogie 2013; Howes and Classen 2013; Riach and Warren 2014).

Despite the occasional fetishization of the 'affective' and 'non-representational' aspects of the senses (Lorimer 2008; Thrift 2008), the main objective of this 'sensory turn' has not been to do-away with a theoretical concern for language or the visual. Nor has the intention been to ignore the power dynamics that ocular-centric abstractions have revealed. Rather, the sensory turn has been at its best exploring the middle ground opened up by a century of oscillation between mind and body, language and emotion. What it has also revealed is that, notwithstanding the relatively late arrival of an explicitly sensory focus, the last century of social scientific and critical thinking hosts abundant resources for theorizing the sensuosity of twenty-first century city life.

Given the advance of social theory through the senses, this is far from the first book to bring a sociological attention to the role of the senses in a twenty-first century city. In recent years scholars have honed their attention on a range of specific areas of city life including enquiries into the production of urban soundscapes (Bull 2000; Raimbault and Dubois 2005; Adams et al. 2006; Adams et al. 2008) and probes into the tactile city (Sasaki 2000; Devlieger et al. 2006; Iida 2010; Devlin 2011). Paying serious attention to the most denigrated of the senses, a small collection of ground-breaking studies has also started exploring the place of smells within cities. Notable amongst those are the pioneering studies, maps and smell walks compiled by the late Victoria Henshaw (Henshaw 2011, 2013; Henshaw and Mould 2013). Equally of note, although less themed around any one sensory organ, are studies into the role of the senses within immigrant's experience of cities (Stoller 2002; Manalansan 2006; Low 2013a), within the production of everyday multiculture (Wise and Velayutham 2009; Wise 2010; Rhys-Taylor 2013a), and in driving urban tourism (Edensor 2006, 2014). These studies complement a growing interest in the role of the senses with regards to urban regeneration of city life (Parham 2005; Degen 2008, 2014; Edensor 2014). The work of Degen and Edensor especially, has significantly broadened our understanding of the ways in which the senses mediate, and are mediated by, the shifting social, economic and physical terrain of major cities.

It is true that the pages of the following book have been inspired by what remains a relatively anaesthetized mainstream of urban theory. However, in light of the remarkable work that has taken place as part of the sensory turn, this book is in no way the sensory 'awakening' that was once called for (Stoller 1997: xii). Its purpose, rather, is to relate the insights that have amassed from the sensory turn, and in particular the urban focus of the sensory turn, to a specific consideration of the relationships between an inner-city's culture, its economy and its social forms. As you will discover, a sensorially attuned attention to the everyday life of the city reveals, with remarkable granularity, the ways in which the city's social morphology is both sustained, and transformed, across time.

Mouth and Nose

Heartened by calls for social science engaging in a 'democracy of the senses', what follows feeds into an argument for a broadly multisensory set of research methods, analyses and representational practices. However, it should also be noted that while the book argues for a multisensory engagement with everyday life, the argument is made, primarily, through a focus on the interrelated senses of taste and smell – particularly in relation to food. To be precise, each of the following chapters centres on specific gustatory sensations and ingredients scattered through the everyday life of the city, from the heat of chilli peppers, the brackish tang of jellied eels and the warmth of Japanese curry sauce to the oily herbs and spice of fried chicken takeaways. This narrower sensory focus draws inspiration from other single-sense studies into the social life of ears, eyes, hands and noses. Therein, the narrowed focus allowed authors to reveal, 'the contributions [. . .] characteristic [of each sense's] individual nature to the construction of sociated existence (Simmel, Frisby and Featherstone 1997). However, as important as it might be to understand each sense, on its own, for its own sake; above all else such an understanding seems crucial to finally understanding how the senses shape sociality *together*.

On the subject of senses 'working together', smell and taste are described throughout this book as interrelated primarily because a considerable percentage of what we experience as 'taste', or rather 'flavour', is – anosmia aside – the product of smell. As we realize when pinching our noses while eating, it is the nose that helps distinguish the taste of a raw potato from that of an apple (Philpott and Boak 2014). In fact, without smell, taste and flavour are a narrow combination of bitterness, saltiness, sourness and sweetness. Compared to other senses – touch, vision and sound for instance – taste alone is ill adept at sensing difference. Combined with olfaction, however, taste becomes *the most* sensitive of the senses, primarily because smell itself is sensitive to the slightest molecular variations in any given material. Even more important than the specificity of these senses, although related, are their relationship to emotion. It is almost a cliché amongst biologists to assert that 'smell reaches more directly into [. . .] emotions than other senses (Gibbons 1986: 337; Ehrlichman and Bastone 1992: 410). The nose's capacity to sense the specific atmosphere of a given moment, alongside aroma's tendency to tap straight into the body's emotional mechanics, are also crucial to the role that the senses of smell and taste play in episodic memory. As the architect Juhani Pallasmaa notes in his advocacy of a fully multisensory architecture for the city, 'A particular smell makes us un-knowingly re-enter a space completely forgotten by the retinal memory; the nostrils awaken a forgotten image, and we are enticed to enter a vivid day-dream. The nose makes the eyes remember' (Pallasmaa 2005: 54).

A century before the sensory turn within the social sciences, Marcel Proust (2006) demonstrated to his readers that entire biographical memories, complete with sound, texture and emotions, can be rekindled through the olfactory encounter with the most dilute substance from the past. Many cultures had, in fact, already inadvertently harnessed olfaction and gustation's ability to conjure meaningful memories of emotional states. From Hindu weddings, to Greek Orthodox Easters and Northern European Christmases, a particular combination of smells and flavours have had an enduring utility in reproducing and transmitting the meaningfulness of cultural and religious rituals. Even in secular contexts, olfactory and gustatory sensoria, often incorporated into specific cultural rituals, have been crucial to shaping who 'we' think 'we' are (Howes 1987; Classen 1990; Caplan 1992; Sutton 2001). Phillip Vannini and his colleagues have referred to each cultural event's specific combination of smells, flavours and sounds as part of that culture's 'sensory order' (Classen 1990; Geurts 2002; Howes 2006; Vannini, Waskul and Gottschalk 2011). Through the ritualized transmission of a culture's 'sensory order' (its sensoria), along with the somatic rules (sensibilities) by which the sensoria acquire their meanings, culture itself is sensorially reproduced.

That taste and smell are the dual focus of this book, is not to say they are entirely the same senses. Even if we recognize that taste involves the sense of smell, there is no denying that gustatory taste only works in direct contact with the item concerned, and only with the permission of the jaw. As such, and as denoted by the use of 'taste' to denote a preference, taste is much more likely associated with sensations that we have already sought out and serves often to satisfy and shore-up pre-established attachments. In contrast to taste, smell on its own, works in both proximity *and* at a distance. This renders smell a notably spatial sense, working with sight and sound to imbue the body with a relationship with its broader environs. Moreover, while we can close our mouths, we cannot close our nostrils, which, like the ear, are 'indefensible' portals into the body (Schwartz 2003). As such, our sense of smell is susceptible to unpredictable stimulation from the world outside our bodies. This makes nostrils not just tools for hunting down the 'tastes' we desire, but a sort of 'look-out' for threats to the body and the culture that lives through it. Each of the chapters that follows emerges out of a consideration of these specific senses' qualities, as well as the ways in which they work together to inflect the city's social formations. In singling out the interrelated senses of smell and taste, however, the intention is not to place these senses at the top of an inverted sensory hierarchy. Rather, the intention is to foreground the very specific role that these senses play within the life of the city, so as to contribute to a broader understanding of the role, and potential, of the senses in the city.

Looking at the history of the city, there is every reason to believe that these senses play an important, if overlooked role, within its twenty-first century urbanism. For instance, from the Roman London that emerged at the start of the first millennium, right up to industry's flight from the city at the end of its second millennium, a mixture of symbolic lowly smells and genuinely toxic miasma were kept downwind from the seat of power (West London) in the East End. As time passed, these smells shifted from those of beef boiling, tanneries, burial pits and soap making, to factories churning out sulphurous matchsticks, burning sea-coal, boiling vats of plastic and chemicals (Brimblecombe 1987; Fenger, Hertel and Palmgren 1998). Identified for centuries as a threat to both the spiritual and physical health of the city, such smells also marked bodies associated with them as dangerous. As Henry Mayhew notes, even those 'working class smells', smells that weren't actually a toxic product of their industrious environment, such as the smell of the herring, consumed routinely by the working classes up until the early twentieth century, were feared amidst upper class homes for their mere association with 'dangerous' classes (Mayhew 1861: 285).

If bodies marked by the odour of their dwelling were stigmatized, people who were stigmatized for other reasons – their political or religious beliefs, for example – were also historically relegated to parts of the city that smelled 'bad'. The city's new arrivals and heretics in particular, were regularly found living 'down-wind' amidst the 'stench industries', wherein they were doubly stigmatized by the odours that accumulated in their neighbourhoods. West London, by comparison, has historically been a protected environment of sensory refinement, with several large parks serving as the city's lungs (Windham, 1808 in Smith 2012: 285), and streets such as Regents Street designed specifically to keep the miasmic masses of the east at bay. This history of olfactory zoning, of course, is an aspect of other cities' histories besides London. A recently unearthed 'stench map' prepared by the New York's Metropolitan Board of Health reveals how important mapping 'nuisance' smells was to interventions in Manhattan's street scape (Kiechle 2015). As Kiechle recounts, while these maps were produced by health officials, and monitored by chemists, regulation built upon lay conceptions of what a nuisance smell was. While most of these were industrial smells, we know from historical work elsewhere that often the value attached to specific smells was largely arbitrary and symbolic. We also know that, in the US, the senses of smell and taste were integral to the ways in which race and racial divides were constructed and mapped (Smith 2006; Obasogie 2013).

It should go without saying that the sense-scapes of London or New York today are vastly different from those of earlier centuries. The development of sophisticated sewerage systems, and the off-shoring of industry in particular, have removed many of the most genuinely dangerous smells from the public spaces of the city. The chemical revolutions of the late nineteenth century also made cleaning products universally available, vanquishing many of the remaining stigmatized olfactory markers associated with individual dwellings. What is more, the paradigmatic shift from miasma theories of disease transmission to germ theory ostensibly lessened the threat posed by noxious aromas. In the realm of taste, the planetary connections forged through the last two centuries of London's history, as well as the multitude of materials and ideas flowing through them, has also increased the variegation of Londoners' palates. As we shall see in the coming chapters, despite these changes to the sensoria and sensibilities that suffuse the city, they still play a crucial role within the broader morphology of the city's social life. Not least, smell and taste are still important to both individual and collective senses of identity, and both continue to play a central role signifying a broader aura of connotations and values ascribed to the city's 'other' people and places (cf. Classen 1992; Manalansan 2006; Low 2013a).

Senses, Culture and Space

As bodily as they are, processes of socio-sensory attachment have not, historically, taken place outside of space. Rather, connection between people, culture and the senses has often been intimately related to geography. In most instances, the 'sensory orders' or sensibilities that typify various incarnations of culture are also the product of discrete territories and their specific histories. Since their ossification at the tail-end of the Enlightenment, national cultures, for instance, have often had their own sensibilities to which nationals are attached and through which they recognize each other. More often than not, it seems, these sensory orders have been shaped quite deliberately by the distribution, or broadcast, of sensations across a particular territory. Building on Benedict Anderson's account of communities imagined through synchronous acts of reading and recitation (Anderson 1991), Howes and Classen (2013: 84) point to ways in which national communities are not just imagined but actually 'sensed' through the sensoria distributed across a specific territory. The examples Howes and Classen offer are the daily radio broadcasts to which portions of Japanese population perform synchronized aerobics. Similarly, in Gottschalk's analysis of the 'sensory order' of Israel a sense of a national community is produced through the daily radio broadcasts and the culinary rhythms of the territory (Vannini, Waskul and Gottschalk 2011: 103).

Sometimes related, but also often distinct from the sensory orders of nations and territorial regions, are the sensoria and sensibilities that characterize specific cities and the cultures within them. For instance, despite the city's overt cosmopolitanism, a Parisian's domestic *habitus* was, for a long time, entirely coextensive with the smells and flavours of *la terroir Parisienne*. Today, Paris' public atmosphere of burnt rubber, cigarette smoke, butter and urine is still accompanied, domestically, by the taste of 'mackerels in white wine, vegetable *macedoine* salad or the humble *jambon-beurre*' (Wyatt 2003). As the 'central place' of inland France, with a command over the economy of its terrestrial region – and a responsibility for reproducing cultures and traditions across it – the sensoria suffusing Paris were, and to an extent remain, indebted to the territory surrounding the city (Redfield and Singer 1954). Maritime metropolises such as London, New York, Amsterdam and even Venice, on the other hand, have historically had as close a relationship with other cities overseas as they had with their terrestrial neighbours (Hohnenberg and Lees 1995: 70). Thus, while efforts are constantly made to identify the indigenous cuisine of indigenous Londoners (see Chapter 5), the sensibilities underpinning the city's cultures have had more to do with the global networks that the city's ports opened onto, than they have with the terrain at its back door. The relationships between different urban typologies and their concomitant sensoria and sensibilities are discussed further in the conclusion of this book. Regardless of whether the city has been more of a 'central place', or a node in a maritime network, the smells and flavours found within it were always central to the embodied praxis through which geographically distinct senses of 'home' were produced.

But how many of us are at home anymore? It is here, in the hyper-mobility of the twenty-first century, wherein bodies, culture and commodities are increasingly unanchored from discrete territories, that taste and smell appear to be taking on a special geographical significance. One of the consequences of the mobility that contemporary urban living engenders is that the 'embodied praxis', out of which a home is made, is so frequently 'dissembled' according to the absence of 'sensory familiarities' in new locations (Edensor 2006). It is when faced with the alienating experience of dislocation that new arrivals to the city first seek out the imported aromas and flavours of 'home' (Matt 2007; Rhys-Taylor 2013a; Stott 2013). This, it seems, is precisely because the encounter with the smells or flavours from the past or elsewhere – a biscuit, a fruit, a herb, an aftershave, a spice – enable the body to rekindle the embodied praxis out of which a sense of home was first made (Seremetakis 1996; Sutton 2001; Waskul, Vannini and Wilson 2009). It is through smells and flavours that the inhospitable terrain of a new home is first made hospitable.

Thus, while London's culture has always borne traces of its maritime connections, the more recent history of post-colonial migration, global labour markets and geopolitical conflict have seen London's various neighbourhoods host an increasingly varied assortment of sensoria. Today these include the sensorium of urban Jamaica, with fogs of jerked meat and marijuana punctuating the boroughs of New Cross, Brixton and Hackney. Elsewhere, the toffee and anise of Hanoi's stews and grills osmose from around The City's northern fringes. A summer's night in Dalston is distinguished by its atmospheric allusions to the Mediterranean, the air coloured by the charcoal-grilled lamb and oregano operated by a mix of both the Turkish and Greek Cypriot diaspora who live overseas in comparative peace (Bertrand 2004). Consider also the sensoria that have endured throughout the rapacious changes on London's famous Brick Lane: the steamy baked dough of Brick Lane's bagel bakeries on an early Sunday morning, present for well over a century following the arrival of Jewish refugees from eastern Europe. On the same street but 250 metres north is 'Banglatown', with its breezes of cumin, garlic and cardamom, originally anchors for the homesick lascar, nowadays an olfactory overture to parties of tourists and petite-bourgois omnivores. In the midst of urban life, wherein both individual and social life is always on the brink of 'melting into air', the nose and taste-buds continue to create moorings for identities and communities, often out of the most vaporous of materialities.

Planetary History of the Senses

The ways in which the nose and taste-buds are enrolled into the reproduction of urban identities and cultures is largely unintelligible from the angel's-eye view favoured by many contemporary urbanists, strategists, planners and architects. Yet this book's explicitly corporeal focus is by no means a distraction from 'the structuring of the city as a whole [and] the political economy of urban process' (Soja in Westwood and Williams 2003: 21). Spurning the disembodied view of angels in no way necessitates adopting a position that assumes those living the everyday life of cities are somehow better positioned to expound upon processes that shape their lives (Duneier and Carter 2001; Back 2007: 9–10). Rather the main purpose of *zooming in* to the level of the street scape is precisely to reveal the extent to which the globe-spanning political economy of urban process discernible from on high – the apparent 'hardware' of urban life – is in fact entirely coextensive with the ephemeral sensoria and embodied sensibilities of city dwellers.

As discussed previously, efforts to relate the experiences of city dwellers to broader historical, political and economic processes have a good pedigree.

As already mentioned in the work of Marx and Engels, everyday sensory experiences are regularly mentioned and implicitly related to the global procession of History (Marx and Engels 1975: 301). The tradition of figurational sociology (for an overview, see Featherstone 1987) also went to great lengths to relate the visceral 'micro-worlds of everyday life' to the structuring and political economy of the whole. As part of his magnum opus, *The Civilising Process*, for instance, Norbert Elias (Elias et al. 2000) convincingly relates the emergence of particular forms of disgust, taste and embarrassment (particularly around bodily functions and table manners) to shifts in Europe's social and political structures following the Renaissance. Similarly, Stephen Mennell has developed a compelling historical account of the ways in which European distinctions between town and country, rich and poor, were produced, and reproduced, through the long evolution of gastronomic practices (Mennell 1996). In an analogous vein, Italian historian Piero Camporesi paints a vivid picture of linking the gradually shifting social landscapes of pre-enlightenment Italy, to the culinary fears and desires of medieval aristocracy (Camporesi 1989). Perhaps most notable, however, are Alain Corbin's efforts to join the dots between the political, economic and social upheaval within early modern France and emergent olfactory and auditory landscapes (Corbin 1988, 1998). Although focussing intensely on the micro-worlds of everyday life, each of the above authors relates micro-worlds of sensory atmospheres to far larger shifts in social structure and power.

There are, however, limits to these socio-sensory histories' ability to cast light on both the fine grain detail and the global scale of the processes shaping a twenty-first-century city such as London. Most obviously, the limits of these histories' utility for this project lie in the conspicuous occidentalism of the processes they describe. In Elias, civilized regimes of disgust and taste originate solely amidst the power struggles of aristocratic Europe and radiate outwards. In the work of both Corbin and Camporesi an epistemological debt to the avowedly euro-centric Annales school (Wallerstein 1979; Braudel 1992) leaves their analyses focussed on developments indigenous to European geographies. Yet, as figurational sociology's anthropological interlocutors have argued (Goody 2002, 2003), the sophisticated sensibilities, tastes and dispositions that sociologists saw emerging out of the European Renaissance were not peculiar to Europe. Nor did they solely blossom at that particular point in time. Rather analogous regimes of taste and distaste can be seen emerging out of renaissances, efflorescence and civilizing processes everywhere from West Africa (Liston and Mennell 2009; Goody 2009), to the Islamic World, through India to ancient China (Goody 2009).

More than a planet of disparate efflorescences – as material histories of tea, paper, silk, dates, iron, cod and salt demonstrate – the sensibilities and sensoria of one continent, have routinely been tied to the fate and fortunes of others elsewhere (Curtin 1984; Kurlansky 2000, 2003, 2011). In fact, for as long as camels and boats have made it possible, 'civilization', where ever it has emerged, has been nourished by the cross fertilization of both sensoria, and sensibilities, from the disparate-yet-networked territories that connected one hemisphere to the other. As post-colonial scholars have demonstrated particularly forcefully, there is even more reason to develop a planetary historical perspective today. Most obviously, as demonstrated in Sidney Mintz's *Sweetness and Power* and Gary Okihiro's *Pineapple Culture*, the foods and flavours of the early modern plantation system were, and remain, embroiled in the asymmetrical relationships between the economies of 'temperate' and 'tropical' latitudes (Mintz 1986; Okihiro 2009). As we will see from the attention paid in Chapter 2 to the sixteenth-century culinary transformations around the Indian Ocean, or in Chapter 5 to the interconnected port cities of twentieth-century Japan, North America and England, trans-regional histories of the senses become particularly important when trying to understand the culture and social life of a twenty-first century city. Suffice to say that in the contemporary era, in which disparate continents and histories are becoming more tangled than ever, the bounded geographies of the last century's socio-sensory history offers, at best, a partial account of the longer term processes pertinent to the city.

While sea-faring and camel caravans have long linked up many of the planet's most disparate locations, maritime metropolises in particular, seem to have played a crucial role in hosting interactions between different regions' sensoria and sensibilities (Redfield and Singer 1954; Braudel 1982; Curtin 1984; Hohnenberg and Lees 1995; Landa 1997). This is particularly discernible when considering their culinary cultures. As Luce Giard notes, 'Every alimentary custom makes up a minuscule crossroads of histories. In the "invisible everyday" under the silent and repetitive system of everyday servitudes that one carries out by habit ... there piles up a montage of gestures, rites and codes of rhythms and choices, of received usage and practiced customs' (Certeau, Giard and Mayol 1998: 171).

Doubtless, nearly all cultures, whether local, regional or national, are built upon innumerable 'minuscule crossroads' and 'invisible' histories. In the case of the globally networked city, however, these are not simply the invisible histories of the region or nation. Rather, in such cases, the 'invisible non-histories' of the planet frequently come into play. Not least, these multi-lateral histories have significant consequences for how we theorize the city's local culture. As the Cuban anthropologist, Ortiz noted in the 1930s (Ortiz 1995), in situations wherein the confluence of histories and culture is so multi-directional, it made no sense to talk of one group's acculturation or assimilation to another's culture. As is the case of the zones of contact between the new and old worlds recounted by Ortiz, London is – and has long been – a site of *'transculturation'*, wherein histories of the Swahili Coast, Western Atlantic Sea Board and the South China Sea have as significant a bearing on the cultural events that unfold therein as do the specific histories of the city itself.

Giard chooses the term 'invisible' to describe the historical trajectories of the materials, habits and customs that accrete in everyday life, primarily because these influences are generally in*sens*ible within the temporal and empirical frames of orthodox enquiry. However, while these mundane histories are doubtless invisible, they need not remain in*sens*ible. Through the application of a multisensory attention to the flavours and aromas of contemporary urban life, the planet's 'non-histories' – or what Paul Gilroy refers to as the 'primal histories' of modernity – become more sensible, tangible and delectable (Gilroy 1993: 55). Importantly, by paying attention to such histories as they play out through contemporary sensory experience, we witness the monolithic processes of 'global homogenization', meeting the irrepressible eddies, under-tows, counter currents and cross winds of myriad alter-modernities.

Researching and Writing the Senses

In the early twenty-first-century urban scholars have witnessed an increasingly broad range of representational practices and methods admitted as part and parcel of rigorous research practice (Back and Puwar 2012; Lury and Wakeford 2012). Urban ethnography in particular has seen an array of multimedia research tools – including video, cinema, still photography, sound recording and infographics – utilized in efforts to represent and interrogate the mechanics of city life. The emergence of audio and visual modes of ethnography was, of course, significantly helped by the promulgation of technologies for recording, interrogating and representing these particular sensory modalities. The growing number of studies deploying phone cameras as 'mobile probes', for instance, typify the depth and breadth of the data capture and representational practices available for even the lowest budget research projects (Hulkko et al. 2004; Raento, Oulasvirta and Eagle 2009; Büscher and Urry 2009). Yet amidst the barrage of new data and representational practices, there remains an absence of studies pertaining to as-yet-unrepresentable – but nonetheless potentially significant – realms of urban experience (such as olfaction and gustation).

If the emergence of visual and sonic ethnographies has been aided by the democratization of the technologies associated with them, the relative absence of gustatory and olfactory orientated forms of enquiry might be partly related to the fact that no such equivalent technologies exist for flavours or aromas. If they do exist, they remain within very exclusive, and expensive, fields of expertise: branding agencies, pharmaceutical companies, chemical producers, transnational beverage companies, commercial perfume houses and all but the best funded artists and scientists. The lack of accessible recording and recoding techniques for taste and smell is, in many respects, a mixed blessing. On the one hand, the lack of such technologies has, so far, saved these senses from the 'computer based metastasis' that Jean Baudrillard argued had colonized both sight and sound in the twentieth century (Baudrillard and Turner 2003: 103). It does, however, mean that when it comes to practising ethnography, representing and recording the nuances of experience requires careful consideration.

Methodologically speaking, the lack of recording devices ensures that the researcher 'being there,' and having all senses 'switched on' is an important aspect of a multisensory research, allying multisensory research primarily with ethnography. This is not a bad thing. Some researchers have been so bold as to claim that multisensory researcher's necessary dependence on shadowing research participants lives, gives the researcher a unique ability to 'imagine how others might be emplaced in the world' (Pink 2008: 175). Somewhat more reflexively, but nonetheless significant, Paul Stoller notes that the researcher's own 'experience . . . is the key to reducing distances between universes of meaning. As experience expands with time, the boundaries of universes may begin to intersect' (Stoller 2008: 30).

Slowly-intersecting universes of meanings, or fragmentary translations across sensory experiences, however, are still of negligible help when it comes to systematically recording, and evocatively representing the sensory life of the city. That is not to suggest that there are no ways to both record and represent the multisensory 'texture' of the 'sensory ethnographic field'. A number of scholars, for instance, contend that audio-visual film and video provide the best ways to stimulate an embodied form of understanding in the reader/viewer (MacDougall 2006; Pink 2009, 2012; Bates 2014). Likewise, although often thought of as mono-sensory media, still photography also has a limited utility as a poly-sensory recording device and representational practice. After all, as Goethe argued in his lusty meditations on Italian sculptures and women, humans were endowed with an ability to 'see with an eye that feels' and to 'feel with a hand that sees' (Goethe and Hamburger 1996: VII). For this, if no other reason, this book adheres to Steven Feld's (1996) insistence that multisensory ethnography should not become 'anti-visual' ethnography. However, this book contends that if it is to address the 'other senses', multisensory research also needs to work harder to develop less visual or aurally stimulating recording devices and representational practices; tools capable of communicating and evoking the complexities of the field.

As poets, wine tasters and perfume reviewers know well, the most obvious tool for the recording and re-presentation of these sensuous experiences remains the written word. In his essay *The Grain of the Voice* Roland Barthes meditates on the activity of transcribing sound into text. Although a linguistic translation is possible, the semiotician suggests, language tends to do 'very badly' (Barthes and Heath 1988: 179). As hard as transcribing sounds and audition into text might be, the difficulty would seem to be compounded when trying to translate the experiences of gustation and olfaction into words, of which most modern languages are especially ill equipped to talk. For instance, the only English words immediately available for describing the experience of taste and smell, are either emotive and clumsy adjectives – repulsive, fragrant, pleasant, pungent – or un-descriptive nouns-cum-adjectives that identify the object being considered: 'This orange both tastes and smells very . . . orangey'.

However, there are, still 'good reasons for writing' (Pink 2009: 136). For a start, the conventions of ethnographic writing are well understood by you, the reader. Moreover, some of the apparent limitations of text can also be significant advantages. For example, indexical noun-cum-adjectives, as impressionistic as they are, can – as any wine or food writer knows – be effective linguistic tools for translating the materiality of a given sensory event into an intelligible form, and for translating specific experiences across diverse biographies. This all depends, of course, on any sensory description being written up with reference to the likely sensory repertoires of their readers. But when it works, it works. Naturally, language still falls short of accurately representing the full multisensory nuances of the ethnographic field, and the complexity of personal responses to it. Yet despite what Michel Serres notes as the apparent lack of sensuosity in much scholarship on embodied experience (Serres et al. 2008), text can still provide a medium for representing both the materiality and experience of various sensory stimuli. As will be discussed further below, ethnographic writing in particular, sitting as it does in the interstices between literature and science, is ideal for inculcating an embodied understanding of the ways in which socio-sensory processes shape both our own lives, and those of others.

Given its commitment to 'evoking' sensations, parts of the writing that follows this chapter might fittingly be described as ethnographic. But ethnography is more to this project than simply a way of writing. It also denotes a set of methods that were integral to how the research was carried out. Thus, even when the prose departs from ethnographic vignettes into theoretical discussion (as it does in every chapter), the discussion is tethered to data generated by ethnographic methods; the hallmark of which is 'being there'. Which is to say that the inspiration for the following chapters emerges out of a sustained and ongoing ethnographic immersion within the culture, everyday life, social networks and political struggles of inner-east London; my home for the last fifteen years. As with everyday life, at times I was simply an observer (often looking out of a window). At others, I was a more active participant (for instance, when scraping out the detritus from under a food trailer as a favour to a participant, or otherwise gulping down a bowl of cold jellied eels). Sometimes I was merely note taking. A lot of the time I was conversing. The lines between these modes of engagement are far from clear. Suffice to say that, with chapters that cover local developments over nine years, this is not – despite the fleeting nature of the 'events' each chapter describes – a hit and run study. All of the topics, and the vignettes that give way to them, emerge out of the repetitious and sustained process of 'hanging out' in various locations around the London boroughs of Tower Hamlets, Hackney and their immediate environs. This is not to say that the examples used here cover all aspects of everyday life in these boroughs. On the contrary, these are but tiny samples of the city's everyday life.

Some locations, such as the seafood stand featured in Chapter 6, or the international grocer's in Chapter 2, I visited regularly; two to three times a week for a number of years. As such, the 'sensory events' that I have foregrounded have been selected, deliberately, for their pertinence to the broader set of social features and processes that I want to discuss in that location. Many other moments from within these locations, and many other locations I routinely visited besides these, have been edited out, adding to the partiality of these accounts. Other locations, such as the fried chicken takeaway featured in the introduction to Chapter 5, were one of several locations I visited less frequently (sometimes as little as once every month), but which nonetheless were selected as representative of similar locations and situations. Although the chapters focus on a range of specific spaces within the city, it should also be noted that the analyses draw on observations, conversations and texts collected across many locations, from council meetings and architects' practices, to radio shows, hairdressers, and pubs and is, as such, a 'multi-sited' ethnography.

Each chapter opens with a vignette foregrounding an 'event' or 'events' in the everyday life of the city. These events, which would otherwise fade into the background of everyday life, have been selected for the possible parts they play within the urban assemblage. The decision to start each chapter with an 'event' as opposed to, say, a focal object or a person, emerges out of a commitment to an 'anti-reductionist project that seeks to describe the relations between actual things, bodies, and happenings and the independent reality of these events in themselves' (Fraser 2006). As such the analysis of each chapter touches on the various economic, cultural, historical, social and political contingencies that shape the event, as well as the 'fall-out' of the event itself. Most of the individuals and locations featured in the events have *not* been anonymized. Exceptions include the grocery shop, its owner and his fiery customer in Chapter 2, each of which have been renamed. Moreover, in an effort to disclose something of the process by which 'data' become 'findings', it also serves to mention that one of the characters in Chapter 4, 'Charlie', is actually a composite of three different individuals. In my time 'hanging around' the Japanese takeaway stall and speaking to its customers, a number of points – cuts to expenses budgets, the journey from The City into the East End, a need to avoid 'odorous' food for lunch – were raised consistently by different individuals, but never all at once by the same person. Without loss of any important details, these narratives have been reduced to an 'ideal type', called Charlie. Doubtless, the resulting story, that of 'Charlie', the city trader, going for lunch, provides a more coherent and evocative narrative than the cluster of narrative fragments would otherwise have done. Whether this renders the chapter more of a work of sociology or fiction, remains a moot point. As mentioned above, ethnography, as a form of writing rather than a mere research method, has historically filled the gap between science writing and fiction writing. In fact several ethnographers have, in the wake of ethnography's rehabilitation (Clifford and Marcus 1986), made compelling arguments for greater use of literary techniques across *all* social scientific writing (Richardson 1988, 1990; Rinehart 1998; Kress 1998). Certainly, any sociological reader will have read sociological texts stuffed with fictions, as well as encountering fictions brimful of sociological data (Stewart 1989; Knab 1997). In both cases, the result is, more often than not, a more effective communication of sociological processes than any text claiming to objectively present 'raw findings' might otherwise achieve. Accordingly, along with this one conspicuous synecdoche, the following text draws on several other literary devices – poetic prose, metaphor, lyricism, dialogue, third person descriptions, first person monologues, as well as shifting in between past and present tenses – in its effort to communicate more effectively with the reader. And it does so unabashedly.

The Senses and the Metropolitan Paradox: A Taste of Things to Come

This book's focus on the conjoined senses of smell and taste leaves it well disposed to consider key aspects of the 'social' city. The focus on taste and smell open directly into consideration of the role of biography and cultural inheritance in shaping individual identities, as well as the ways individuals organize themselves in relation to others. In a global city such as London, this involves a consideration of the ways in which the senses work to shore up distinct cultural identities, but also means considering the ways in which the senses might work to shore up senses of commonality across apparent differences. Conversely, the empirical foci of this book also leave it well placed to explore the forces of repulsion, estrangement and misanthropy that seemingly inhibit sociality in the city. In focussing on both estrangement and association, the subject matter for the following chapters oscillates between both sides of what Les Back refers to as 'the metropolitan paradox': the coexistence of transcultural and transnational social formations with entrenched senses of social distinction and separation (Back 1996).

Following this introduction, Chapter 2 explores the role of sensation in repairing micro fissures in the city's social fabric, particularly those that emerge out of the cramped economic, spatial and social confines of the city's poorer neighbourhoods. More specifically, the chapter focusses on a heated exchange at a grocery stall that was, in part, resolved through a shared understanding of the sensations that accompany the consumption of hot peppers. Merely a fleeting moment in the everyday life of an unremarkable location, the chapter nevertheless points towards the ways in which sensibilities and sensoria – especially artefacts with transglobal histories – might help shore up transcultural 'senses of community'.

Chapter 3 explores the significance of transglobal ingredients further in an effort to pick apart legacies of the tangled culinary biographies of early-modern port cities (London and Tokyo in particular). Scratching beneath the surface of London's new 'street food scene', the chapter details sixteenth-to twentieth-century journeys between Japanese, American and European ports feeding into contemporary economic circumstance to imbue particular sensations (crispy bread-crumbed fillet with sweet, mild curry sauce) with notable economic viability. Beyond helping explain the surging popularity of specific types of food in the contemporary city, the chapter also serves to foreground the historical routes of the city's millennial cultures.

The first two empirical chapters, as described above, seek to explore the planetary histories manifest in embodied tastes and sensibilities, as well as the ways in which these might afford transcultural affinities through the senses. In some respects, these two chapters are part of an effort to explore the ways in which the senses transcend the work of language and discursive meaning to establish visceral 'senses' of identity and 'senses' of transcultural community. Chapter 4, however, seeks to explore precisely what the previous two chapters 'frame out': the relationship between textual media, discourse and 'gut feelings'. Specifically, it considers the ways in which media-driven 'moral panics' about abject meat (horse meat and bush-meat) reflect and reinforce the racism that is enduringly articulated as part of the everyday life of the city. They do this, the chapter argues, by anchoring their racist 'rationales' in 'gut feelings' elicited by narrative framing of abject practices. The focus on the discursive construction of abject sensations and gut feelings is then carried through into the following chapter. Rather than focussing on an acute bout of media-driven panic, however, Chapter 5 takes as its focus London's perceived 'fried chicken problem'. Starting with a cold winter's evening in a busy, family friendly, chicken takeaway, the chapter zooms out in an effort to trace short genealogies of the various discourses that shape the 'meaning' ascribed to the sensoria of inner-London's fried chicken takeaways. Moving through an assortment of ecological ethics, biological risk calculations and histories of racism, the chapter reveals exactly why this particular food and its consumers are so overly determined as an abject 'problem'. In conclusion the chapter also notes that the abjection of this inner-city institution and its youthful patrons comes at the expense of recognizing the more remarkable multicultural conviviality that often lies at the heart of the inner-city's rapidly disappearing working-class neighbourhoods.

The final empirical chapter, Chapter 6, reiterates themes of its predecessors: first, it traces the transcultural history of an everyday dish; second, it reveals the convivial multiculture that convenes around that dish; third, it touches upon the articulation of exclusive identities and social forms through this dish; and last, it maps the historical abjection of the city's working-class cultures through attitudes to this dish. The dish in question is jellied eels, the research on which was conducted across the final five years of one of London's last jellied eel and seafood stands. With the stand now closed, the chapter is also a testament to the loss of a particular type of space, and a particular type of sociality. As the concluding chapter to the book argues, such spaces are increasingly lost to the city's increasing role as a command centre of transnational finance.

Combined, the chapters demonstrate the variety of processes of affiliation and estrangement that the sensoria of the city are embroiled in. The senses are revealed as the cement binding social strata together, as well as the solvents evaporating the boundaries between hitherto distinct life worlds. Beyond dissecting the sensory mechanics of the 'metropolitan paradox', the book finally argues that an attention to the fine grain detail of the city's everyday smells, flavours and textures, can tell us as much, if not more, than the abstractions of macro-spatial theory. In conclusion, the book argues that an attention to the sensations that fill everyday life is in fact an ideal corollary of macro-spatial theory, revealing the ways in which particular sensoria, and especially sensibilities, mediate the ways in which a 'global city' is actually global. By the end it will be clear that if we are to fully understand the significance of the transnational flows that pass through the city, if we are to understand the city's cultures without recourse to ill-fitting caricatures, if we are to explain the endurance of arbitrary prejudice in the cosmopolitan city, it is imperative that we come to our senses.

2

Heat of the Moment: Transcultural Sensations and Urban Multiculture

For the last fifteen minutes I have been standing in the International Superstore off Commercial Street, investigating the recent new arrivals to fruit and vegetable shelves, and listening to Mo, the shop's owner, and his plans to shut down his retail business to focus on wholesale. In his mid-fifties and a local resident for thiry-five years, Mo appears, to most of his customers, as eternally optimistic, despite the evident slow death of his retail business. As I listen to his complaints about the arrival of two corner shops nearby, run by major supermarkets, I note that Cypriot potatoes and Brazilian mangoes are the only new additions in the increasingly sparse store. As I am about to leave, sack of potatoes in hand, the heavy glass door clatters open against the empty red plastic crates stacked behind it. Wearing skinny jeans, a technicolor shawl and large hooped earrings, in storms Ilhaan. In her hand, the nineteen year old Londoner is waving a metallic blue aerosol can of fly killer. She is pacing straight toward Mo. I decide not to leave, but to witness whatever is about to unfold.

'This doesn't work!' Ilhaan exclaims, dramatically palming her forehead. She pushes the button on the aerosol cap demonstratively. The lid makes plasticky clicks and a brief gassy hiss. But nothing comes out. 'You shouldn't sell stuff like this. I want my money back.'

'Give it to me,' Mo says, beckoning Ilhaan.

Ilhaan reaches forwards and with equal amounts of caution and hope, places the can into Mo's open plan.

He turns it over slowly in his hand as he inspects it. Mo shakes it sharply and fiddles with the lid before turning the nozzle away from himself, and pressing the cap. A plume of toxic aerosol fills the area around the shop counter. Ilhaan steps back.

'I don't want you to fix it. I need a refund,' Ilhaan insists.

'It works.' he says, handing the can back across his till 'Sorry. No money back.'

'It'll break again,' insists Ilhaan, her shoulders tensing.

'It works,' repeats Mo. No money back.' Mo puts the can down on his counter, perhaps goading Ilhaan by sliding it towards her. She steps back and pulling her feet to attention.

'You. Owe. Me.'

'No,' insists Mo one more time.

Lurching back towards him, Ilhaan snatches the can off the counter, turns and paces towards the exit. One step away from the exit, she swings back around toward Mo, using the turning motion to hurl the can over arm at the shop keeper's head. Mo ducks. The can rattles into the shelves behind him, knocking a box of water balloons, some bubble gum and assorted cigarette papers to the floor. By the time he rises – in amused, wide-eyed disbelief – from behind the counter, Ilhaan has gone. A small bell rings as the heavy door hisses back into place on its pneumatic hinge.

'Did you see that?' Mo asks me, an amused astonishment on his face. 'All the time I put up with this.' He collects his stock from the floor and re-stacks it.

Still a little shocked I ask, 'That happens a lot?'

Mo is Bengali, and Ilhaan had struck me as appearing characteristic of London Somali. All summer Tower Hamlets' papers had been running stories about violent clashes between 'gangs' of second and third generation Bengali and Somalis in East London. In the first instance I could not help but see the incident through the prism of the tabloid taxonomies. Mo suggested otherwise.

'People always come in here. Buy something. Take it home. Use it. Bring it back and ask for their money. They expect me to say, "Yes, have your money!" They don't like it when I say no.'

Before I can ask which people Mo is referring to, the air pressure in the shop momentarily leaps as Ilhaan kicks the door back open. The crates clatter again. No fly killer in her hand this time, she strides straight to Mo's counter again.

'You owe me. You got your spray back.'

'No, I don't.'

'I'll have these then.' She leans over and prods her finger into a plastic Tupperware box of dried dark green naga chilli peppers kept beside the till for individual sale. Fifty pence for each of the wrinkly spearhead shaped berries, or three for one pound twenty.

Mo is amused. 'Are you sure?'

Ilhaan swaps melodramatic indignation for equally affected nonchalance. She plucks a pepper from the scuffed plastic box and, holding the stalk between her thumb and forefinger, she pokes the chilli into the very corner of her mouth. Biting off the tip, Ilhaan chews laterally with her mouth open for a couple of seconds before swallowing cartoonishly.

Ilhaan grins smugly at Mo. The smile lasts two seconds. Despite having swallowed the peppery morsel, the nerves around the roof of her mouth are starting to sense the residual oils left by a strain of *Capsicum chinense* that was once a contender for the world's hottest pepper.

The heat of chilli peppers, unlike more subtle flavours, is not detected in the olfactory bulb. Nor is it really sensed on the salty, sweet or sour sensitive taste buds of the tongue. Rather, the heat of chilli, derived from a chemical called capsaicin, is felt by the same nerve system that responds to threats posed to the face, the trigeminal nervous system. With the trigeminal nerves converging at the front of her skull, the naga pepper punches Ilhaan at the bridge of her nose. Her eyes crinkle shut before opening wide at the same time as her mouth.

'Phooooo!' Ilhaan's brow jumps in an effort to throw the sensation from her face, but crumples in defeat. Her hand rushes to fan her mouth. Exhalations morph into a string of breathy curses 'Ffff. . .! Aaa. .ba. . . Ff. . .Shh Wsss!' Ilhaan's eyes are now streaming, her skin flushing. As the heat builds further, she stamps her feet into the ground.

'Hoooh! See! See!' chuckles Mo.

Ilhaan looks up at Mo, still puffing, her eyes red, physically irritated but also seemingly annoyed. She scans the shop for something to cool her mouth down.

'Milk?' I suggest, revealing myself as an observer to the exchange.

'I'm not getting any more until tomorrow,' replies Mo, glancing at the lonely litre bottle of fizzy orange in his otherwise empty fridge unit.

To the right of his till is Mo's vegetable display stand. Ilhaan strides forward, dropping the nibbled chilli pepper back on shop counter. She grabs a cucumber from the display shelf, ripping through its cellophane sheath with her teeth.

Ten seconds pass as Ilhaan hypnotically crunches through the cucumber, gasping between gulps.

Noting the addictive quality of chilli's heat, seemingly derived from the body's doping response to the 'threat', psychologists have noted that, the 'eating of chilli,' like 'riding on roller coasters, taking very hot baths, and many other human activities can be considered instances of thrill seeking or enjoyment of "constrained risks"' (Rozin and Schiller 1980). Finally, Ilhaan pauses, looking up and formally recognizing her audience, she starts laughing, beaming, glowing and clearly exhilarated.

'Whoooa. Phew. That's hot! I mean. That! Is! Hot!'

'That'll be seventy pence for the cucumber. You can have the chilli. I told you it's hot.' retorts Mo.

Smiling now, with a cucumber still clasped in one hand Ilhaan flicks long nails through her tight pockets feeling around for change. She pulls out a pound coin and places it on Mo's counter. He opens his till and slides her her change, smiling back at her.

Ilhaan scrapes up the change, thumbing the coins into her pocket and turns towards the door, opens it gently with her free hand, and saunters out. Thanks, she waves, looking over her shoulder. Ilhaan continued to use Mo's shop frequently for another five years until, its shelves nearly completely bare, it closed in 2013.

Commonality, Conflict and the City

For a small number of Tower Hamlets' young men, the summer evenings of 2008 and 2009 were spattered with what was narrativized as inter-ethnic conflict (Huntley 2009). Hardly out of the ordinary, the masculine territorialization of the East End's wards by second generation Bangladeshi and Somali Londoners was part of a tradition that runs, at the very least, back to the late nineteenth century. The Bessarbains and the Odessians, the Green Gate Gang, the Blind Beggar Gang, the Vendetta Mob, the Titanic Mob, the Hoxton Mob, Brilliant Chang's China Town boys and, of course, most famously, the Krays and their antagonists, all physically clashed with their competitors in street fights in and around Tower Hamlets (Morton 2001). In some cases the violence was over control of the informal economies radiating from the city's eastern ports. At other times skirmishes had more social roots; misunderstandings, shame, disrespect and envy. In each instance, whatever the cause, the conflict was amplified by the pressure that built up in the densely populated streets of the city's margins. Things have, however, changed. The East End's docks are many decades since decommissioned. Vestigial traces of the formal and informal economies once associated with the docks endure. But they are only residues, trickling from hubs of activity elsewhere.

Although the machinery of the working class city has been shipped overseas, the boroughs it was at the heart of remain London's poorest and, partly by virtue of their maritime history, its most ethnically diverse. It was this diversity that British historian David Starkey infamously identified as the cause of the unrest swept through London in 2011 (see also Chapter 5 of this book). 'The whites have become black' and thus inherently violent, claimed Starkey (Newsnight 2011). Given the local and national tendency to write off the inner-city's scuffles as a consequence of problematic identities, it was little surprise to hear the tabloid press reduce the fracas of 2008's summer evenings again to culture and ethnicity. Even those close to the summertime scuffles of 2008, such as those recorded in Sanchita Islam's remarkable anthology of East End Bengali and Somali youth voices, incorporated ethnicity into their explanations. 'Bengalis have been in this country for longer,' argues Hirsi (in Islam 2007: 28). Despite having had a visible presence in east London since the 1860s, 'they [the fighting Bengali youths] feel Somalis', who appeared in larger numbers in the late nineteen eighties, 'are stepping on their territory' (Hirsi in Islam 2007: 28). This particular account of the role of ethnicity in fostering conflict is, however, vastly different from explanation that the street skirmishes arose out of mere identity politics. In contrast, Hirsi's insightful explanation identifies the roots of youthful conflict in the distribution of resources within some of the most socially, economically and physically cramped space in the city. It is also true that as grounded in material circumstance as these conflicts are, they very easily piggy-back on the symbolic differences of 'heritage'. Yet as much as scarcity precipitates conflict and exacerbates senses of difference, it is also true that the cramped confines of city life have also always necessitated that people find ways to get along. In such situations, identity and culture do more than simply separate. The linguistic skills that come with 'culture', and the beliefs, practices and tastes bequeathed through biography can, in fact, go a long way to 'repairing' the tears in fragile social fabrics opened up by malice.

Language

If any cross-cultural communication takes place in the city then it is sensible, first, to consider the role of language. In twenty-first-century London, the specific language bridging differences varies from case to case. Formal English, of course, plays an important role. But so too do French, Spanish, German, Greek, Swahili and Arabic, all fostering communication between distinct individuals and groups within the global city. More pertinent to the case at hand, however, is the particular argot shared between the city's newest and youngest residents (Hewitt 2003: 192). Identified in recent years as a new dialect of English, Multicultural London English or 'MLE' is grounded in 'innovations' peculiar to the 'situation in which at least half the population is undergoing group second-language acquisition' (Cheshire et al. 2011). Distinct from mid-Atlantic drawl of London's transnational technocrats, and oceans away from the estuarine twang and stunted consonants of the previous century's inner-city, MLE indexes the most recent decades of the demographic flux in the inner city. With audible traces of Caribbean dialect, Arabic intonation, Mediterranean grammar, West African melody, Olde English emphases and mid-century American slang, the vernacular bears myriad traces of London's late modern history. More importantly, it provides a medium for communication between individuals and groups with distinct yet tangled cultural histories. Taken by some to index the 'becoming' of new 'creolised' social forms (Alleyne 2003), MLE, as a linguistic form, could be credited with destabilizing ethnicity and related forms of taxonomy and hierarchy, creating bridges between distinct cultural milieus (Hewitt 1990, 2003; Rampton 2014).

There are, however, a number of well-rehearsed critiques of multicultures that are seemingly grounded in language and evidenced by 'what people say' (Taylor 1991; Scollon, Scollon and Jones 2011). For Taylor in particular, 'assimilating' the language of the 'host community' gives merely the semblance of acculturation and assimilation out of which intercultural affinities might be born. Behind the words, Taylor argues, deep attachment to the signs, symbols and material culture of an immigrants' 'heritage' culture remain. The result is that, despite linguistic unity, multicultural social contexts remain, at their core, collections of ethnic enclaves. As if to prove the point, in an article searching for the vital signs of multiculture in London, ethnographer Susan Wessendorf noted a distinct lack of intercultural affiliation masked by a preponderance of primarily 'corner-shop cosmopolitanism' (Wessendorf 2010). People in corner shops and at school gates, Wessendorf argues, were very happy to chat to each other in a shared language, maybe even about a shared culture. Once the public-facing part of the day is done, however, 'cosmopolitan' urbanites apparently abandon intercultural exchanges and scurry home to their own social enclaves. Thus, for critics of corner-shop cosmopolitanism, the inner city might *sound* like a multicultural meshwork. Backstage, however, urban communities appear locked in a mosaic of tightly sealed ethnic identities. In this sense, while language might be credited with potentializing inter cultural affiliation, it is presumably the recalcitrant unchanging *body* of the migrant, or rather the migrants '*sensibility*', that are seen to close down that potential.

Sensory Signs and Group Formation

To an extent, Taylor (1991) might be forgiven for questioning the degree to which a new culture can really be embodied, even if the language is learned. Heritage is, after all, a deeply embodied phenomenon that remains largely intact despite linguistic proficiencies. The senses of taste and smell in particular, have been shown to be integral to anchoring specific 'heritage' cultures in the body. Virtually every variation of human culture on the planet has quietly harnessed the mnemonic power of smell to reproduce culture and its meanings regardless of how 'its people' speak or write (Howes 1987; Stoller 1989; Classen 1990; Caplan 1992; Waskul, Vannini and Wilson 2009; Low 2013). Taken together, the sensoria people surround themselves in, migrants or otherwise, can be understood to be keynotes in culturally specific 'sensory orders' (Classen 1990; Geurts 2002; Howes 2006; Vannini, Waskul and Gottschalk 2011). As demonstrated in Nadia Seremetakis' (1996) and David Sutton's (2001) groundbreaking work, through the experience of migration, the keynotes of home become particularly important anchors for those with little other foothold in their new locality. It is perhaps these types of more sensory and symbolic attachments to heritage culture that Taylor has in mind when he speaks of migrant's enduring recalcitrance vis-à-vis integration into their new 'host community'.

What I want to consider, however, is the possibility that, like a native language that contributes to a new polyglot vernacular, embodied cultural attachments and tastes can also serve as points of translation through which intercultural associations take place, and through which 'transcultural' identities and cultures emerge (Ortiz 1995; Berg 2010; Rhys-Taylor 2013a). None of this is to diminish the role that inner-city argot plays in sustaining ties between the mixed urban population. It is to suggest, however, that neither shared language, nor even belief system or civic identity, are the extent of the channels through which transcultural understanding, exchange and affiliation take place. The senses also, play a very important role.

Transcultural Sensations

In terms of understanding the relationship between embodied experience and transcultural affiliation, the hebdomadal rhythms of inner East London play home to what might be a particularly relevant case study. Every Friday at lunch time, synchronized by the ascetic melodies of the call to prayer, a confluence of Nigerian, Somali, Bengali, Iraqi, Pakistani, Afghani, Saudi and British-born Londoners arrive at The Brune House Masjid, for prayers. Therein, second and third-generation hyphenated Londoners, some working in the curry houses, other crisply suited City boys, line up alongside elders in the car park surrounding the community-centre-cum-mosque. Facing east, down the Thames, the congregations undertake a synchronized procession of movement: raising hands, lowering hands, bowing, standing, kneeling, sitting, turning and chanting.

For Benedict Anderson, it was through practices such as the recitation of *The Book of Common Prayer* that he saw a 'contemporaneous community' of the British being first 'imagined' (Anderson 1991: 145). Drawing on Howes and Classen's reworking of his concept, we might say that through the shared movements of Friday prayers in Tower Hamlets, a community is not just imagined but is also, by virtue of the physicality of prayer, literally 'sensed'. A 'sensed community' (Howes and Classen 2013: 84).

This is not, it should be noted, a 'sensed community' in the sense of a national community as discussed by Anderson, as well as Howes and Classen. Rather, in this instance, the movements and their meaning feed into a 'sense' of a distinctly *transnational* faith community. As Daniel DeHanas notes in his study of young people in Tower Hamlets, the vast majority of young people he canvassed ranked faith as the bedrock of their identity, above being a Londoner, British or Bangladeshi (DeHanas 2013: 76). If 'Islam provides an all-encompassing identity for Bangladeshi youth [in Tower Hamlets], connecting them to others around the world' (DeHanas 2013: 73), there is every reason, sociologically speaking, to suggest that the physical sensations of collective prayer and meanings ascribed to it, play a role in forging this sense of connection.

Profane Botanicals

Sociologically speaking, the sacred are but one category of sensations through which group formations are incarnated. Consider the famous study conducted by Howard Becker that culminated in his book 'Outsiders'. Therein exists one of the first sociological accounts of a community imagined and bound through shared sensations. As Becker notes, the taste for [the marijuana] experience is a socially acquired one, not different in kind from acquired tastes for oysters or dry martinis. The user feels dizzy, thirsty; his scalp tingles; he misjudges time and distances. Are these things pleasurable? He isn't sure. If he is to continue marijuana use, he must decide that they are. [Eventually] a person will feel free to use marijuana to the degree that he comes to regard conventional conceptions of it as the uninformed views of outsiders and replaces those conceptions with the 'inside' view he has acquired through his experience with the drug in the company of other users (Becker 1963: 53, 78).

As Becker recounts, in order to be an 'insider' amongst the 'outsiders', an initiate has to learn to experience a particular set of sensations, along with specific ways in which they ought to respond to and evaluate them. Importantly here, the 'in group' grounded in these sensations has the potential to cut across various social distinctions – class, gender and ethnicity in particular – in important ways. We know from many sources for instance that 'getting stoned' has been crucial to many instances of (not always symmetrical) intercultural affiliation and exchange. From early twentieth-century moral panics centred on the interracial jazz scene (Sloman 1998), to Barack Obama's reflections on toking with a mix of white college classmates, black gym buddies and Hawaiian drop-outs 'everybody was welcome into the club of the disaffected' (Obama 2008: 94). The point being, that an embodied understanding of the affective aspects of a particular plant's consumption – the sensations it provokes and the meanings ascribed to them – has been an important part of a number of modernity's most remarkable transcultural assemblages. This, incidentally, was as much the case in Becker's and Obama's twentieth-century North America, as it was when the dreadlocked mystics from the Ganges first took their sacred medicinal plants to the plantations of the Caribbean (Mansingh 1979; Mansingh and Mansingh 1985, 1999).

This nod to the global history of botanical narcotics is not incidental. As part of the European colonization of the Americas, various plants (marijuana, mangoes and sugarcane amongst them) were uprooted from the foothills of the Himalayas and forests of India and China. From there they were conveyed, along with the blood and tears of slaves and indentured labourers, along Earth's tropical girdle, through Africa, eastwards into the Americas. Through a variety of means, these uprooted botanicals would become integral to the agricultural, industrial and urban assemblages of the American continents' post-Colombian cultures. At the same time as these trees, shrubs and grasses were moving from the global east to the west, another assortment of seeds, saplings, tubers and berries were being transported in the opposite direction. Caravels moving from the tropical to the temperate Americas, then south on the Atlantic's Aeolian gyro carried an array of botanicals from the pre-Colombian Americas to the sixteenth-century soils of the African and Asian continents. Amongst these new arrivals were obvious star players: tobacco, chocolate, tomatoes and potatoes. Nestled in between the bulkier vegetables arriving in Asia and Africa, however, was the smaller cousin of tomatoes and potatoes: the chilli pepper.

From the moment that the military muscle of Portuguese traders first navigated around the horn of Africa to the continent's eastern coast, the burning mouth, watering eyes and glowing gullet that had accompanied meals on the slopes of the Andes for millennia, became steadily intertwined with culinary cultures along the Indian Ocean's Swahili coast (Andrews 1992: 86–87). From there, the Portuguese sailed on the monsoon winds, used for centuries previously by the wooden Dhow Boats of Islamic traders (Sherrif 2010) on a journey across the Indian Ocean to Goa, Surat, Mangalore and Kochi. With the introduction of newly global Europeans into the southern hemisphere's equivalent of the Mediterranean basin in the fifteenth and sixteenth centuries, the relatively settled cultures of the region also started changing according to the maritime traffic cutting across it. This is particularly reflected in the range of new ingredients and culinary practices entering into the circuit between the Arab peninsula, East Africa and India. Of all the new imports, it was a small Bolivian berry, the chilli pepper, that became the most obviously entangled in the Indian Ocean's regional cuisines (Christie 1911; Achaya 1994; DeWitt 2014: 297–343).

In 2015, alongside the assortment of potatoes, cucumbers, garlic, kafir lime, fresh coconut, mango sugar cane and pomegranate, typical of many independent supermarkets of inner East London, are always at least two different choices of fresh chilli for use in cooking, alongside a range of chilli-based sauces, chutneys and spice blends. Perhaps more significantly for young people, the fried chicken shops frequented by the young East Enders (see Chapter 5), are characterized by their offering a conspicuously spicier-than-mainstream green chilli sauce.

There is clearly a very long pre-colonial history of dialogue across the Indian and Atlantic Oceans (Sherrif 2010) that informs the cultures being constituted in contemporary British cities. Combined with the later movement of flavours and sensations across oceans by European imperialists, it is clear that many of the cultures of twenty-first-century London already share cosmopolitan histories. None of this cosmopolitan material history, however, necessitates that anyone actually *senses* a cosmopolitan *community* in the culture and sensations derived from it. Not least, this is because Benedict Anderson's 'imagined communities', like Classen and Howes 'sensed communities', are clearly strengthened by narratives that make sense of culturally specific sensations and give meaning to them. As Les Back argues, community is, in many respects, a 'narrative achievement' (Back 2009: 4). Without stories about modernity's 'primal histories', a conscious sense of the intertwined inheritances bequeathed by the past is kept at bay. Instead, everyday sensations, which arise out of conspicuously global histories, are readily enrolled into twenty-first century nationalisms.

Consider, for a moment, the sensation of eating a mango. While once specific to the shaded foothills of south east Asia, over the course of the eighteenth and nineteenth centuries, specific cultivars were made emblematic of an array of different national cultures – St Lucia, Jamaica, the Philippines, China, Pakistan, Malaysia, Sumatra – many of which are thousands of miles from the fruit's erstwhile home (Rhys-Taylor 2014). The chilli pepper has a similar story: not, as yet, an icon of modernities' intertwining but instead the fruit and its heat have been taken as a markers of various Latin American, South East Asian and African cuisines, wherein conspicuously nationalized senses of meaning are enduringly attached to the rushes and flushes of the pepper's heat.

Oceans Away, Around the Corner

Despite its involvement in specific 'heritage' cultures, there is also a sense in which the global history of the chilli pepper is a part of the contingencies through which the heated exchange between Ilhaan and Mo was repaired. An insignificant episode in itself, this is far from the only instance wherein the heat of the chilli pepper has bridged cultural divides and expanded horizons of possibility. Two hundred metres south of the site at which Ilhaan and Mo settle their small differences, is located Tubby Isaac's seafood stand (for more on the seafood stand see Chapter 6). There, an old East Ender with tight grey curly hair, thin rimmed spectacles and a beige overcoat sidles up to dine alfresco at the white food trailer. Dennis – a senior trader at a major investment bank – orders his normal early afternoon snack, the quintessential East London fare for at least the last couple of centuries: a small bowl of jellied eels and a pot of cockles. The stand's owner, Paul, hands Dennis the eels in their porcelain bowl, and his cockles in a small polystyrene cup. Placing the two dishes in front of him, Dennis grabs his usual condiments from atop the steel and glass display cabinet. First, a sprinkle of salt. He shakes the perennially blocked shaker vigorously to ensure he gets something out. Dennis then reaches for a large bottle sitting beside the salt – a re-used gin bottle filled to the brim with murky malt vinegar in which float over a hundred pickled red chilli peppers. As Dennis starts tucking into his late lunch the seafood stand's proprietor tries to reach back over the counter to retrieve his large chilli vinegar bottle but cannot quite get his hand to it.

'Could you pass me that please, mate? Thanks.'

The proprietor takes the bottle and proceeds to douse his own bowl, a good five or six slugs of the spicy sauce over his own bowl of mixed mussels, whelks and eels. 'Got to keep myself warm. It makes you sweat a bit. And my hands and feet go a bit numb for a minute, but then I warm up. I'm probably addicted to it,' he half jokes.

In northern France, and increasingly in London's Francophilic farmers markets, the preferred dressing for oysters and assorted shellfish is shallot vinegar. In London, however, from at least the early 1980s, the street seafood has been routinely offered with chilli-based sauces. First, Tubby Isaac's proprietor introduced Tabasco Sauce. Then in the 1990s, with the increasing availability of large quantities of dried peppers, the family behind the stand started brewing up their own piquant vinaigrettes. In recent years, Tubby Isaac's Seafood also offered a number of increasingly hot guest chilli sauces.

The evolution maps neatly onto the gradual 'crossing over' of an array of hot sauces, associated with both the Americas and Asia, into the main-aisle of British culture (Cook and Michelle 2003). Using the chilli pepper heat 'scoleville scale' a 2010 newspaper report claimed that the food on the shelves of British supermarkets was 400 times hotter than forty years ago (Quinn 2013). As insignificant as supermarket condiment aisles might seem, the changes therein reflect a genuine change in the sensibilities inhabited by Britons, a change that has likely social correlates: both a more cosmopolitan outlook amongst Britons, but also a more diverse community in general. Both of these facts were in evidence when, on occasion, West African Londoners shopping for colourful fabrics at Petticoat Lane, drifted towards Tubby's seafood trailer for a polystyrene cup of cockles (shellfish is popular in West Africa also). Notably, these women sometimes brought with them their own homemade mixture of fermented fish, oil and searing peppers. And they would eat it, even on one occasion sharing it, with the Essex-born cab drivers and elderly Chinese women they were dining beside at the seafood stand. Even when they are not conversing, the mere acting of eating together, the 'social heat' (Chau 2008) it generates, speaks to the social significance of histories that bequeath us with overlapping tastes.

The history of chilli is one that cuts across cultures and geographies. That is not to say that it is a story about the gradual 'browning out' of difference with generic global culture. In each cultural and geographic assemblage that the pepper took root, it acquired its own set of cultural and biographical meanings. As such, its role in the global city *could* be limited to one of 'inter-semiocity', a point of material overlap between the sensoria of disparate, ascribed different meanings according to culturally and biographically specific sensibility. But, as disparate, isolated and lonely as city dwellers often seem, they do not simply run in parallel to one and other. As Paul Gilroy (1993) has forcefully demonstrated in his accounts of the 'Black Atlantic,' when disparate cultures with interrelated histories converge in the global city, the result is often of great, if under-acknowledged, sociological significance: multicultural conviviality.

Consciously Cosmopolitan?

In the consecutive Julys of 2013 and 2014, the 'Festival of Heat' took place at East London's Spitalfields Farm, a three-acre home to an assortment of pigs, cows, donkeys and chickens on the fringe of The City. The choice of the farm as the location for the festival related, not least, to its 'Coriander Club' – a collective of Bengali women who have, for the last twenty years, worked to transpose Bengali village agriculture (including searing hot chillies) into London's raised soil beds. More than just a celebration of these women's annual harvest, the event's curation of a global cohort of

London's chilli enthusiasts quietly imparted a sense of the significance of this 'heat' to the 'local culture' of the twenty-first century city. Far from a naive 'saris and steel drum' celebration of difference typical of many of London's municipal summer festivals, the Festival of Heat brought together an assortment of food producers, foodies and local residents, around what they shared in common: a borderline addiction for the flushes and rushes induced by chilli.

Among the hot sauce producers and importers present at the festival in 2014 were a Hertfordshire-based company started by an entrepreneur who had picked up the taste for chilli when his father lived in New Mexico. Another vendor made extensive use of Aztec imagery on their promotional material, a choice that followed their foodie tourism in Latin America and which is intended to reflect their subsequent (flimsy) claims to 'authenticity'. A few stalls down stood a London-born woman who imported the sauces and chutneys that her Sri Lankan father used to bring back from his trips 'home'. And the farm's own Coriander Club also presented their locally grown produce. The extent to which the taste for the pepper is forged through very specific biographical incidents and powerful familial memories and associations, is incredibly tangible in the stallholders' own accounts of why they do what they do. The extent to which these biographies emerge out of wider transcultural history, however, is made explicit when a group of gardeners from a Hackney-based farming charity presented a map of the world with different chillies scattered over it, demonstrating the various cultivars that flourish in different climes.

Around the map, shawled Bangladeshi Londoners rubbed shoulders with young foodie yuppies and fumbled through cartons of luminous peppers while horticulturalists answered their questions. At the nearby stalls selling sauces, chutneys and pastes, customers scooped up samples of sauce on bread or corn chips, and – breaking the general behavioural codes on non-contact – warned complete strangers off overly hot sauces, while encouraging others to try whatever they had just sampled, and standing by to watch as they plunged their fingers into small sample pots of sauce.

'Eating the Other'?

The exaggerated conviviality of events such as the Festival of Heat, and the 'passion for chilli' that lie behind it, are far from unproblematic. As well as regularly reifying race and ethnicity, cross-cultural interaction around food risks the reproduction of asymmetrical distributions of power in a number of ways. For instance, symbolizing the city's post-colonial heritage through food – and through chilli in particular – plays into a wide number of racial stereotypes about heat and various races' inherent (in)sensitivity to it. Such discourse has very clear roots in the racist science of the eighteenth to twentieth centuries. Therein researchers have frequently drawn upon the idea of 'innate' capacities for pain and heat in their efforts to construct essential racial others (Home 1821; Woodworth 1910; Chapman and Jones 1944; Baker 1958). As discredited as they are, folkish versions of such beliefs still abound. For instance, in the wake of one his group's violent incursions into the East End, the leader of the English Defence League (a muscular Islamaphobic hate group), Tommy Robinson, belittled the area's curry houses, insisting later that even 'flaming hot Monster Munch [a popular children's maize-based snack] are too hot for English taste buds' (Hopkins 2015). Therein Robinson directly sought to make a tolerance for the heat of a chilli pepper a measure of racialized outsider status.

That distaste for the heat of capsicum serves as a prop in muscular racist rhetoric is not to say that a *taste* for chilli is any less problematic. As Elizabeth Buettner eloquently demonstrates in her critique of 'going for a curry,' a mastery of 'exotic' tastes is part of the way in which relationships between the ancestors of both the colonizer and the colonized are maintained (Buettner 2008). Demonstrating Buettner's point eloquently, the Festival of Heat also hosted a defiantly 'British Made' collection of hot sauces, offering, if nothing else, an option for the English Defence League's chilli enthusiasts. Branded so as to negate association with anywhere other than 'Great Britain', each bottle had a Union Jack emblazoned in the corner of their labels. The real appeal to muscular Britishness, however, came in the names of the various sauces – 'Satan's Blood', 'Black Mamba Extreme' and 'Who Dares Burns' – each tapping into a symbolic construction of masculine Anglo-Saxon bravery. In case they did not get the message, a 'disclaimer' on a flyer reads more like a serving suggestion,

> Macho Men, Curryholics, Stag Parties, Initiations, Dares, Show-offs, Jilted Lovers! The habanero pepper is 100 times hotter than the jalapeño pepper [. . .] be careful if you are trying to stitch up a macho friend, attending a stag party or using them as part of an initiation ceremony.

It is, of course, an analogous waspish culture of hazing rituals and hunger for a 'bit of spice' that bell hooks had in her sights when she penned 'Eating the Other', a pointed critique of cross-cultural consumption; in particular, the exoticization and sexual exploitation of young black women by frat boys (hooks 1992). Certainly, any analysis of consumption and commodification of culture in cities needs to be acutely aware of the power-plays that both hooks and Buettner foreground.

Beyond Eating the Other

As noxious as testosterone-fuelled chilli-sauce-based hazing rituals sound, 'initiation' remains an interesting word to hear in relationship to chilli peppers.

As discussed previously with reference to Becker's 'Outsiders', becoming accustomed to a sensation entails learning the appropriate meaning to give to it, and how to experience it. As experimental psychologists have noted with regards to chilli, 'likers are not insensitive to the irritation that it produces'. The fact is, however, that they 'come to like the same burning sensation that deters animals and humans that dislike chilli' (Rozin and Schiller 1980). It might be said that the 'hedonic shift' from rejection to liking occurs, not least, the social rewards of having given the appropriate meaning to the sensation. As Becker (1963) outlined so clearly in his study of marijuana users, these rewards spring from the recognition that others have also experienced the same sensation as you, ascribed the same meaning to it, and count you as one of them by virtue of that shared experience. Elements of this were certainly in evidence in the conspicuous 'sharing' of experiences at the 'Festival of Heat'. And in the specific case of Ilhaan and Mo with which this chapter opened, there was certainly sense in which the naga pepper helped repair their relationship, serving as a catalyst for mutual recognition of each other's humanity.

Conclusion: Tropical Fruit, Temperate Multiculture

The various botanicals, fruits, flavours and sensations that fill the everyday life of the city are rarely recognized for the crucial bit-parts that they play in the complex assemblages of the new century's urban multicultures. Condemnation of food hall cosmopolitanism, it seems, is far easier for critical thinkers to grapple with. But there *are* indisputable transformations afoot in the gustatory repertoires of those living in Britain, the social significance of which cannot be reduced to mere power games. Part of the unquestionable popularity of these 'new' flavours lies in the growing numbers of those, settling or settled, with an inherited taste for such sensations. The consumption pattern, however, also reflects an ongoing change at the level of the body of those who had no prior, or obviously inherited, experience of such sensations. A change to the sensations that the body surrounds itself with, a change to what is considered 'sensible' and 'insensible', is necessarily a change to the 'sensory order' of the culture that lives through that body (Classen 1990; Geurts 2002; Howes 2006; Vannini, Waskul and Gottschalk 2011).

In a contemporary context, where centuries of global interchange make a nonsense of assimilation, acculturation or synchronicity talk, we might refer to such changes as part of a process of 'transculturation' (Ortiz 1995; Berg 2010; Rhys-Taylor 2013): a process of intermingling between both the sensoria and the *sensibilities* emerging out of discrete yet already tangled biographies and cultural histories. Like the development of globally inflected local argot, the result is a globally embedded local culinary culture that destabilizes ethnicity, related forms of taxonomy and hierarchy, creating bridges between distinct cultural milieus.

Of course, everywhere in contemporary cities we see ethnic identities being narrativized, reified, and essentialized through the meanings ascribed to particular sensations, and food sensations especially. Even when contact occurs across difference, a destructive form of 'eating the other' often follows. However, not all cross-cultural interactions are inherently problematic or reproductive of asymmetrical power relations. Some interactions may even include the potential for the 'transcultural' production of forms of multiculture in which the dangers of cultural difference, and contact across it, fade. In many of the city's everyday contexts, the ubiquity of difference in fact renders it simply 'part of the wall paper' (Wise 2010). Like the emergence of twenty-first-century London's multicultural inner-city argot, east London's olfactory atmosphere, which drifts through the streets and estates from midday onwards, testifies to the multiplicity of influences under which each resident lives: a heady mix of chilli, starchy clouds of rice, wisps of fish, warm spice, coffee, grilled meats, chutneys, fried potatoes, beer, tobacco and weed. This atmosphere and its residents relationship to it, however, is neither an artefact of 'assimilation' nor 'integration'. Rather, it is one of transcultural sensory processes giving way to a quiet cosmo-political process. For those focussing on the irreconcilable aspects of heritage culture, inevitably, when people go home at the end of the day the mosaic model of the multicultural city still remains intact. However, if we consider culture to comprise not merely of association with outwardly similar individuals, language or forms of self-identification, and take seriously the ways in which commonality is 'sensed' – including in relationships with corner shop owners – then the drift towards local forms of multiculture across today's cities becomes more apparent. What people say about their own lives, the stories that they tell themselves and others, and who they associate with, will always be important to understanding multiculture. However, it is at the level of non-discursive, or the sensuous, that we get a taste of the broader range of processes that are shaping the culture of contemporary cities.

3

Halal Katsu Wraps

Nine o'clock on a Monday morning, and Petticoat Lane market is slowly waking in the argent winter sun. Just to the west of the market, beyond the boundary between the old East End and the financial quarter are a growing cluster of colossal obelisks sheathed in tinted glass and metal. High up on the thirty-fifth floor of one of these hives of high finance is Charlie, a broker. In between answering his morning emails from Geneva and Tokyo, he sips a coffee he picked up from the truck outside and glances out of his window, absentmindedly observing matchstick men tiredly assembling the spindly frames of the street market a quarter of a mile to his east.

At ground level, a cohort of vagrants-turned-market-porters fight with cracked paving slabs to drag the heavy steel skeletons of Petticoat Lane's market stalls into place. Halfway along the market, a metallic green van chugs in between the assembling clothes stalls to its regular pitch. The driver cranks the handbrake and turns the engine off. The Tikka Express is here, and is, as always, the first to arrive at the market's food court. As the morning wears on, a small souq of tents, gazebos and food trailers assemble around the Tikka Express. Gas and electricity lines are connected, frozen food unpacked, salad garnishes are chopped and the deep fryers heat up. By half past ten, wisps of steam and charcoal smoke drift around the constellation of plastic tables and chairs, catching the sun as it burns through the remainder of the morning's thin canopy.

At half past eleven Charlie glances out of his window again, down at the assorted stalls of the market's food court. His belly rumbles and he resolves to head out for an early lunch. Over the next half hour he ties up loose ends, gathers his coat, gloves and scarf, as well as a couple of colleagues. Together they jostle into a chrome-lined lift and are carried to the ground. It is a ten-minute walk from the gargantuan foot of their workplace to the food court. A shortcut takes them through the service exit of a plaza of health food and sandwich bars. A step over the administrative border between The City and her impoverished neighbour. Finally, a stroll past the dilapidated modernist dreams of 1960s social housing before arriving at the old East End market.

By the time they reach the food court at quarter past twelve, the space is coloured by the cumin and cardamom carried on the puffy steam clouds of the Tikka Express. A little further into the food court the lunchers meet the thick carbonic meaty smell of jerk chicken. Saliva glands twitch and prickle as they move through the vinegar fog of the neighbouring fish and chip shop. Towards the middle they pass through a melange of the sweet, sizzling fragrant peanut from the Malay satay stall and the anise and cloves of the dim-sum tent.

Each stall is already developing a small queue but the stall Charlie and his colleagues are making a beeline for – the chicken katsu wrap stall – has the longest. Ten people already. As Charlie joins the line of security staff, administrators and other city workers, the smell of deep fried breadcrumbs tips his belly into a succession of gurgling fits. Approaching the service counter the scents of chopped cucumber, jalapeño and lettuce make the hunger twinges almost unbearable.

'Hi! How are you? What can I get for you today?' asks Irene, also known as Tomo, the stall's co-owner and 'customer service manager'. Short syllables define her speech, which, while retaining a distinct Asian accent, is heavily inflected by the chirrupy English of the Thames estuary. Charlie leans towards her to be heard over the sound of the diesel electricity generators.

'Two katsu wraps and er . . .' Charlie turns to his colleague behind him in the queue. 'What are you er . . . Seth! What are you having?'

His colleague looks up from his smart phone. 'Katsu curry. Sauce on the side. Thanks.'

'And a katsu curry, um . . . and er . . . sauce on the side,' says Charlie to Irene.

'You got it.' Irene turns to her workforce, a production line of four Kurdish men. 'TWO KATSU WRAP! ONE CURRY. SAUCE ON THE SIDE!'

She turns back to the hungry trio. 'You paying together?'

'I'll get these,' says Charlie.

'That's thirteen pound fifty please. I'll give you each a free drink too, hey?' She says before dropping three bottles of a Turkish branded mineral water into a bag.

Charlie has been visiting the food court of Petticoat Lane on a near weekly basis, normally Mondays or Fridays, for the last five years. Up until that point he tended to lunch in a range of restaurants, cafes and pubs throughout the City of London. These lunches were a mixture of modern Italian, English and French cuisine. Sushi, curry and Thai food, too 'pungent' for daytimes, punctuated his evenings. Then in 2008, in the immediate aftermath of the financial crisis, both Charlie's taxi and lunch fund were cut by his employer. Unfortunately for the City's cab drivers and restaurateurs, the same was true for a significant number of insurers, bankers and brokers who started using more public transport, searching for cheaper lunches and cutting out treats.

The tremors radiating from the crisis in the City wrecked a great many livelihoods at local, national and international scales. The food court of Petticoat Lane, which had hitherto served the City's less affluent workers, subsequently blossomed, drawing city workers toward the affordable east. The small patch of road that for at least a decade was home to just three regular food stalls – the Tikka Express and the Thai food vans, as well as a chip shop – grew to over ten vendors in less than a year, with Irene's Japanese food stand being one of the first new arrivals, followed quickly by a Jamaican cuisine specialist, a falafel stall, a dim-sum tent, a Cantonese style takeaway and a regular rotation of others. On any given day today there are up to ten regular food vendors in the market. What started as somewhere catering to a select few, less-affluent-than-average Londoners, is now used by a remarkable cross section of underemployed locals, white collar workers, tourists and new street-food enthusiasts arriving from the nearby hubs of the East End's culture industry.

As routine as it appears, Charlie's visit to Irene's stall offers an invaluable insight into the shifting terrain of the city's social structure and cultural texture. In the first instance, the food court's success tells a story about the ways in which the area's culinary culture shifted amidst the localized fallout of the global financial crisis. Its current success, however, is also illustrative of *at least* two more epochal culinary trends; the diversification of tastes (more dinners) and the growth of eating out (more diners). While both of these trends have been the subject of important discussion over recent decades (Mennell 1996; Warde 1997, 2000a, 2000b; Burnett 2004), regionally bound accounts of local culinary culture have often fallen victim of 'methodological nationalism' (Beck and Sznaider 2006). This chapter argues that it is impossible to discuss the nuances and implications of either more diners, or more dinners, in contemporary London, without considering the ways in which the socio-economic structure and the cultural practices that uphold it, are inflected by the transnational 'primal histories' of modernity. As we shall see, in the case of Charlie's lunch, these are histories that connect the Asian inflections of twenty-first-century London life to intercontinental colonial exchanges and cultural revolutions in the gastronomic life of nineteenth-century Tokyo. Far from being an historical footnote, such is the nature of global modernity, that these moments inform and reflect the ongoing production of transnational urban cultures more than ever.

More Diners

Over recent decades market researchers, policy wonks and academics alike (Warde 2000b: 32–37; YouGov 2012; DEFRA 2012, 2013) have noted a general increase in the number of Londoners eating out every decade except for the last. One survey suggests Londoners eat away from home, in public, on average around 2.77 times per fortnight, with a large increase in those eating out every day (YouGov 2012). Yet as historians of regional food have intimated, eating in public (Mennell 1996: 154–155), and eating in the street especially (Burnett in Jacobs and Scholliers 2003: 33), has been far from the norm for the city's upper and middle classes who, for centuries, dined solely in private with family and guests. For a reputable person – a wealthy banker or a broker perhaps – eating from a vendor on the street would, for significant parts of the city's history, have been practically unheard of. This is not least because, at the other end of the social spectrum – against which the city's wealthier residents have always defined themselves – eating away from home has always been more commonplace. Centuries of agricultural workers have taken at least one meal away from home to see them through the day (Burnett 2004: 21–34), and even when the primary mode of production transferred to cities, the toiling classes tended to eat in public. In London they did this either at a 'cookhouse' (Mennell 1996: 135–137), to which they took their own food, not having the facilities to cook for themselves, or otherwise they dined on the offerings made by one of the City's famous costermongers. We know from the accounts of Henry Mayhew, for instance, that prior to the arrival of its contemporary food court, nineteenth-century Petticoat Lane Market was populated by costermongers offering biscuits and cheese, oysters, fried fish, meat and onions, lemonade, ginger beer and watercress to its daily users (Mayhew 1861: 38).

Changes in the socio-economic distribution of 'non-residential eating' start in the nineteenth century, as cities developed new suburban residential zones. The growth in commuting that ensued resulted in a range of spaces for new suburbanites to dine away from home. The most numerous amongst these early eateries were repurposed seventeenth-century teashops and coffee houses – *cafés* – offering light meals to lower-middle class commuters of both genders (Burnett 2004: 116–117). Such spaces, and the flavours that filled them, were integral to new suburban culture of the middle classes. Towards the end of the nineteenth century, lower-middle class suburbanites were followed by the city's wealthiest classes, who also had become commuters and often needed to eat away from home. While the eighteenth century gave birth to private dining clubs for the wealthy (Mennell 1996: 151), the late nineteenth century saw the arrival of the first purpose-built chop-houses and grill rooms, offering up various cutlets of meat with vegetables and potato. Importantly, these were heavily influenced by modes of informal public dining in the United States (Burnett 2004: 145). It is also worth noting here that (and you will see why) the American trend towards informal public dining was also shaping the culinary culture of Tokyo (Cwiertka 2006: 7–13).

While the first proper restaurants were exclusive affairs, eating lunch away from home became even more commonplace, and to an extent more uniform, in the mid twentieth century. Employee canteens were, for example, made mandatory for large war-time employers lest the nation's labouring women go without a solid meal (Coombs 2013: 1857). The Civic Restaurant or British Restaurant, of which there were over 700 in London by the end of the Second World War also served a similar purpose, enabling poorer war-time Brits the opportunity to communally imbibe something beyond their limited domestic rations (Duffett, Drouard and Zweiniger-Bargielowska 2012: 142–145). As rations were eventually phased out and the austerity of war gradually faded, women's desire to stay in the workplace, reductions in family size and increases in earnings left both youths and their parents with more money, and time, to spend outside of the home. Mirroring the burgeoning shift away from a mass industry towards transnational services, both civic restaurants and industrial employee canteens were usurped by the promulgation of small eateries, often international franchises, throughout the city. Rancid 'milk bars', much bemoaned by Richard Hoggart (1998) were substituted with the luminosity of the country's first Wimpy on London's Coventry Street in 1954 (Oddy 2003: 194). Kentucky Fried Chicken arrived in swinging Finchley in 1968 (Anon. 2013, see also Chapter 5), and in 1974 McDonald's took root in south-east London's Woolwich (Royle 2000: 13). All of which were, of course, followed by further franchise extensions.

If young people were orientating their tastes towards their transatlantic peers to the west, their parents were turning their noses south and east. In a shift heavily mediated by food writers such as Elizabeth David and television presenters like Fanny Craddock, chefs and domestic cooks of the later twentieth century were busy adapting flavours of southern and eastern Europe into tools to be used as part of a competitive scramble for distinction amidst the mudded middles classes of post-war Britain. As such paté, dried pasta, olives, cheeses, wines, salamis and tinned tomatoes formed the bedrock for a whole new generation of middle income venues, such as London's Spaghetti Houses (Mars 1983: 144–146).

Despite differences pertaining to the city's socio-economic strata, the general trend towards increases in leisurely eating out was a defining trait of Londoners habits in the twentieth century. The picture changes, however, with the new millennium. At a national level, according to government agencies (DEFRA 2013: iv) every year since 2001 has witnessed a steady decrease in eating out. This decrease has been correlated with a state-encouraged reduction in the consumption of snacks and confectionery (DEFRA 2013: 10). Less clear in the statistics, but no less centrally induced, is also a middle-class return to the domestic kitchen in the wake of rises in the cost of living and the mass media promotion of home cooking.

In London the statistical sag in 'eating out' appears to be partially offset by an ongoing growth in eating out at the poles of the city's socio-economic strata. At one end is the growth of people dining out on food aid; with a median income decrease amongst the poorest of twelve per cent over five years, and an increase in the cost of the average food basket by another twelve per cent over the same period (DEFRA 2012: 11, 25), the city that emerged in the wake of the 2008 financial crisis relegated the poorest people in London to the culinary analogue of the nineteenth century. While other social classes were able to trade-down in their purchases, for the poorest there was nowhere left to trade-down to but the discarded surplus rejected by the rest of the city: the food other people would not eat. Reports (commissioned but not published by the UK government), echo many anecdotal testimonies to the fact that increasing numbers of those who eat out in the city today, likely do so because they have no home to cook in (Lambie-Mumford et al. 2014: 13; Dowler and Lambie-Mumford 2014). Or if they have a roof over their heads, then it is at the expense of food to cook under it. Amidst the austerity-induced food insecurity experienced by a growing number in London, it is, it seems, soup kitchens and food banks that are seeing the biggest growth in 'eating out'.

The other sector undergoing considerable growth in the crisis-ridden early decades of the new millennium is, perhaps predictably, a correlate of the increased demand amongst the city's poor. That is, despite early cuts to expense budgets, the dining that caters to the city's more affluent professionals has, since 2008, boomed (Lanchester 2011). The surface manifestations of this boom are an assortment of new culinary experiences, from the Duck and Waffle restaurant at the top of the City's newest obelisk, Heron Point, through Soho's Burger and Lobster to the delicate botanical dishes, complete with twigs and leaves, served at Fitzrovia's Doubouse.

Amongst the most popular of these new ways to eat is dining *alfresco*. The general prestige ascribed to alfresco dining in the UK can be initially related to the aforementioned mass commodification of southern Mediterranean and Gallic cultural practices in twentieth-century Britain. Over the last decade Francophilic farmers' markets have become a familiar symbolic repost to the 'placeless' mass-produced urban dining experiences of the seventies and eighties (Holloway and Kneafsey 2000). The period between 2008 and 2015 in particular saw an explosion of mid-range 'street-food' venues across London, offering an assortment of novel, hybrid and purportedly authentically regional, cuisines. Appealing as business prospects to a swathe of young entrepreneurs, not least for the relatively low entry costs, clusters of street food vendors are now such a common part of the city that they have corporate agencies hiring them out to different locations nearly every day of the week. As is the case with the farmers' market, this is often as an attempt to import a sense of place from elsewhere into somewhere that has sensory signifiers of place substituted by the granite stone and chrome plazas of New London. Examples can be found scattered across the serialized monotony that unites Canary Wharf, Kings Cross, South Bank, Spitalfields and Leadenhall.

Particularly popular with socio-economic classes otherwise inclined to dine out yet also feeling the need to 'trade-down', the pop-up street-food market, mobile food trailer or gazebo have become integral to a 'revolution', hyped by a torrent of television shows demonstrating both where and how to appreciate the global city's new culinary marvels. As part of an old East

End market offering affordable yet tasty food to the city's underemployed classes, or as part of a new alfresco revolution amidst the city's professional classes, the boom in activity around the city's open air food courts can be related to a number of broader trends beyond the hype of a 'street food revolution'.

More Dinners

Aside from the growth in the sheer proportion of diners, what is perhaps most remarkable amidst this epochal shift in Londoners' dining habits is, as outlined above, the range of different cuisines, styles and qualities of food on offer. This diversity has only increased in recent years. While of obvious sociological interest, the diversity of tastes – as discussed briefly in Chapter 2 with reference to chilli – has posed significant challenges to the last century's social scientific assumptions about the relationship between taste, culture and society. In particular, increases in gastronomic diversity would seem to thwart the contention that culture and the social structure it upholds are mimetically transmitted across generations through taste (Douglas 2002; Bourdieu and Nice 1984; Douglas and Nicod 1974).

That is not to say that there are no socio-cultural explanations of this trend towards gustatory diversification. Looking at one of the more patent explanations of these gastronomic discontinuities Panikos Panayi (2008) notes the last century's increases in global mobility. Whether fuelled by tourism, conflict, inequality or the city's demands for migrants, the movement of people inevitably has a correlated impact on the intergenerational transmission of local taste; both of the port of departure, and arrival. Panayi points to the diffusion of Italian, Indian and Chinese restaurants through the fabric of twentieth-century British high streets as illustrations. Perhaps a better indicator of 'mass' dining habits than London's twenty-first-century high streets, are the food halls of its malls and markets. As we shall see, foregrounding the patent 'internationalization' of the city's new food courts involves bracketing out the multitude of sensoria and sensibilities that do not 'cross-over' into the high street or mall as well as explaining how and why some do. It also risks overlooking historical transformations to the city's culinary culture that have been wrought by sojourners in a far more implicit manner for millennia. Beyond this historical oversight, the internationalization thesis also overlooks a complex bundle of social factors, economic forces and historical trends identified by sociologists as underpinning the heterogeneity of the late modern menu. Stephen Mennell (1996: 327–329) for instance, locates the 'increasing variety and diminishing contrasts' of culinary tastes in England within an epochal process of 'socio-genetic' change driven by the decreases in centralized authority and declining deference to hegemonic ideals, mirrored the nineteenth-century destabilization of class distinctions and political affiliations. As he writes, 'Just as London Society widened in the later nineteenth century with the differentiation of overlapping social circles

[. . .] so later emerged a pluralism in the world of eating. Just as people of ambiguous social backgrounds gained an entrée, so did entrées of questionable origin' (Mennell 1996: 328).

Alongside the decentralization of culinary authority, we might also want to consider the agency of what some have identified as a reflexive (Giddens 1991; Beck, Giddens and Lash 1994), insatiably omnivorous post-modern consumers and producers, devoid of clear social attachments and prone to flit between hitherto 'culturally specific' tastes (Fischler 2002; Chan and Goldthorpe 2007). Certainly, market researchers have noted increasingly fickle shifts in the domestic shopper's culinary rhythms: tagine one night, fish and chips the next, followed by jalfrezi, cous cous, quiche, pizza, jamon and maybe, on Sunday, a traditional roast. The collapse of erstwhile structures of value and taste might well be evidenced by the expansive everyday appetites of even the city's mass of low income consumers. The post-modern turn has, however, found a more ostentatious manifestation in a number of high profile and often exclusive restaurants. Self-consciously eschewing the boundaries of the last century's ethnicized cuisine of particular note are the deconstructed Franco-Anglais cuisine of Heston Blumenthal, and Jamie Oliver's short-lived Anglicized pizza shop, 'cumberland sausage with English mustard' on pizza.

Another, slightly different version of the culinary variegation story noted by Alan Warde (1997: 16–18) sees the driving force less in fickle consumers than in revolutions in production techniques. Of particular import, it seems – in contrast to the mass-market food of the mid-twentieth century – has been the production-led 'post-industrial' atrophy of mass culture (Bell 2008). Characterized as a turn towards an informational economy with concomitant flexible production chains and on-demand delivery, the post-industrial thesis credits an assemblage of technological, political and economic apparatus with the production of balkanized social networks of consumers with specific and ever-diverging tastes.

Both the post-modern and post-industrial explanations of culinary diversity point towards a correlation between the weakening of cultural attachments and the blurring of erstwhile social distinctions; as does, in a way, Mennell's 'socio-genetic' argument. That all having been said, there also seems to be traction in an argument that sees the increasing diversity of cuisine in today's cities related, less to a kaleidoscope of consumer identities, than to the retrenchment of horizontal class structures. Certainly old gut feelings for the boundaries of class endure, as we will see in Chapters 5 and 6, discussions of fried chicken and jellied eels. In a move that partly synthesizes some of the explanations offered above, a recent return to questions of class in British sociology correlates variegated culinary practices with cultural omnivorousness, and omnivorousness with expressions of middle class identity (Bennett et al. 2009: 188).

Far from disproving any one of these theses, Petticoat Lane's thriving food court offers ample empirical evidence for each account of culinary variegation. They could all, in fact, be qualified by a meditation on the crispy chicken fillets swaddled in flat bread that Charlie clutches in his hands. The combination of houmous, jalapeño and a wrap around a chicken fillet offered by Irene and her Kurdish business partner, is, after all, a definitively post-modern 'hybrid' dish. It is also, if their in-queue testimonies are to be believed, consumed by a socio-economic assortment of culinary omnivores. For some of them it seems conspicuous omnivorousness might be readily converted into capital, by way of a display of cultural mobility and distinction. But for others it also seems that omnivorousness is simply a product of striving to survive in proximity with difference.

Most of the food vended at the market is conspicuously post-Fordist in that it caters not to a mass of generic omnivores, but – by way of decentralized specialized production – to a selection of balkanized social niches and identities. Consider, for instance, that in the case of the katsu wrap, as with most other things sold at this particular food court, the meat is – although mass produced – halal and is strictly policed by local halal inspectors. The reason, Irene states, is so that it can be served to the some of the several hundred Muslims who come to pray in the nearby mosque every Friday and who, in recent years have come to expect most meat in the area to be halal. It is also worth mentioning that the meal is offered in a wrap because, as Irene notes, when she first started offering dishes with a choice of rice or noodles, the City types – archetypal 'reflexive consumers' – rejected the carbohydrate tonnage of white rice or noodles that she used to serve it with. Responding to a perceived need to locate an alternative, Irene's business partner, Mashun (who had previously run a kebab shop) knew just the thing.

If we consider that the stand, and certainly others beside it, was established to sell primarily Japanese-style fare to Londoners, there is also evidence that the city's culinary diversity is related to internationalization and the durability of ethnic identities. As discussed in Chapter 2, many cross-over cuisines arrive in new cities first as resources for the homesick, a way to remake identity, culture and associations, by way of familiar flavours, textures, sounds and smells. Consider for instance that Irene set up her stand with the traditions and inspiration of her mother, for whom – as for many modern Japanese women – home-cooked food was an important cultural anchor, even more so given her family's moves between Japan, Singapore and England.

Post-modern, post-Fordist, post-crisis, there a number of intersecting culinary trends within which to locate the success of Irene's stand. Yet, I want to argue, none of these regionally bound sociological frameworks has the acuity to explain the exceptional length of queue waiting for this particular stand, nor the particular popularity of a number of analogous dishes in the area. To explain this, we have to zoom in, draw our nose a little closer, increasing the resolution from broad structural shifts, towards the sensory qualities of, and meanings ascribed to, foodstuffs themselves.

Zooming in to the sensory qualities of a foodstuff does not mean that we need to approach it unhistorically or asocially. On the contrary, drawing closer is most valuable when we are able also to pan back out to a wider

story of global change. In the case of a conspicuously cosmopolitan city like
London, or any port city for that matter, it is imperative to understand not
just the historical production of tastes within a given region (Mennell 1996:
15), but also translocal histories of specific flavours, and embodied tastes
for them. As Sidney Mintz (Mintz 1986) demonstrated in his eloquent
meditations on sugar, the guts of a city like London's have long been
grounded in the intertwining of multiple processes, encompassing globally
disparate locations. Of lesser impact than sugar, but equally illustrative, a
taste for chicken katsu curry emerges out of analogous intertwining of
modernity's primal histories. Adding to post-modern, post-Fordist and post-
crisis, we might want to understand Charlie's lunch time stroll as distinctly
post-colonial, afforded by way of fraught bi-lateral contact between the
sensoria of the hemispheric west and east. It is this contact, as we shall see,
that primes the appetites of twenty-first century city's transnational culture.

East–West

As discussed, the second half of the twentieth century saw Chinese, Indian,
Italian and Middle Eastern cuisine expand rapidly from nineteenth-century
docksides to the high street as a new part of new 'international' urban
lifestyles. In comparison to some counterparts on the late modern city's
menu, including Thai food, which arrived in 1967, Japanese cuisine, initially
in the form of *sushi*, was introduced to Londoners relatively late, in 1974,
with the opening of the Ajimura restaurant in Soho (Grove and Grove
2008). The length of time it took to arrive is related not least to the fact
that a taste *for* the food (less mobile than the taste *of* the food) had to
travel across two oceans and a broad-bellied continent (the US). Arriving
tentatively on the United States Pacific coast in 1914, *sushi* and *sashimi*
osmosed from the port of San Francisco and Los Angeles' Little Tokyo
by way of the marketable novelty that the modern Japanese 'sushi bar'
found in the mid-twentieth century (Smith and Kraig 2013: 389). The
cuisine might have moved eastward quicker were it not for the obvious
interruption of Japanese–American relations in the twentieth century. By
the late 1960s, however, with the memory of war increasingly foggy, sushi
bars were springing up across Los Angeles (Issenberg 2007). Unsurprisingly,
a number of entrepreneurs saw the success of the raw fish and rice
dishes amongst the business men and celebrities on the West Coast of the US
and started businesses in New York. In a twist on Lévi Strauss' raw/
cooked:civilized/savage schema, *sushi* and *sashimi* were becoming the
hallmark of civilized and elegant dining. By the 1970s increased air travel
had turned London's new yuppies towards the tastes of Manhattan, where
they discovered sushi and sashimi. Thus, at the end of a trans-Pacific–
Atlantic chain of mimesis was the Ajimura restaurant; catering less to the
diaspora, as LA's Little Tokyo or even London's first Chinatown had, than
to local elites.

As the new high-status food, 1980s London saw the neon pinks and oranges of *nigiri* and *sashimi* arrive across the buffets of the City. For most people outside the Square Mile and West London, Japanese food remained exotic enough only to be seen on television, memorably, when Michael Palin, visited Yokohama's sushi restaurants in the BBC's landmark celebrity travelogue show *Around the World in 80 Days* (Mills and Valance 1989). Televisual encounters with sushi remained the norm for most of the city until the 1990s, at which point Japanese food arrived into the everyday consciousness of Londoners from several directions. This is the decade that saw the much-hyped arrival of Japanese food by way of Beverly Hills in the form of the Robert de Niro co-owned Nobu, a restaurant that makes the trans-Pacific origins of the cuisine explicit with a unique blend of Peruvian and Japanese flavours. But perhaps more significantly, it is also the decade that hosted the first of London's 'conveyor belt' sushi restaurants; the first moment in the real 'massification' of what had hitherto been an exclusive cuisine. The production line in miniature started with Moshi Moshi, a bizarre restaurant suspended above the platforms in Liverpool Street Station, just around the corner from where Irene's stand is today. The popularity of the format, however, extended quickly to a string of British-owned high-street chains. Utilizing the bright candy colouring of raw fish and the growing popularity of manga cartoons and comics, Japanese food was being presented to Londoners as fun, metropolitan and youthful – the culinary equivalent of Tokyo's Harijuku district. Large chains of sandwich shops also started selling plastic boxes of *nigari*, complete with soy sauce and pickled ginger, as did all major national supermarket chains.

The rapid profusion of Japanese food through the city is an interesting enough phenomenon. It starts with the making and marking of late modern elite culture on either side of the post-war Atlantic. In the middle part of the story is the emergence of new mass culture through the standardized production of Japanese food. This story's final chapter, however, lies in the turn away from solely sushi towards an assortment of noodles, bento boxes, ramen soups, okonomiyaki, (savoury pancakes) and, in particular, the dish that Irene, along with fifteen businesses in a 500-metre radius, sells a variation of: a bread-crumbed chicken fillet, a sweet curry sauce and, traditionally, rice. The particular 'cross-over' potential of this morsel, can only be understood by moving our attention to processes that started in another century on another hemisphere.

West–East

The chicken katsu – essentially a flattened, spikily bread-crumbed, fried chicken fillet – is a derivation of a dish better known in Japan as tonkatsu, or pork cutlet. It is not, however, an ancient artefact of Japanese culture. As remarkable it seems, given the carnivorous menus of many Japanese restaurants – especially those overseas – prior to the nineteenth century it was relatively uncommon to eat meat anywhere on the Japanese archipelago. The pre-modern Japanese meat prohibition is well recorded and its origins debated. For the main part, the prohibition is attributed to a combination of ancient animist belief systems and the introduction of Buddhist influences in 675AD. Certainly, at the latter date the 'Buddhist doctrine of mercy for all living beings' was given a legal status by Emperor Temmu (Ohnuki-Tierney 1995: 232). Five creatures in particular were proscribed: cattle, who work the fields; dogs, 'who give bark in the night'; fowl, 'who announce the dawn'; horses, 'who serve the march'; and monkeys, who 'are of the same kind as humans' (Ishige 2007: 100). However, starting with the arrival of a lost Portuguese trading ship in the mid sixteenth century, traders and craftsmen amongst the indigenous elites of Sakai, started strategically importing and reworking a wide range of European customs and practices (Lidin 2002: 149–152). Among the most infamous imports of the *'Nanban'* or 'southern barbarian' period, were hand-held guns and new boat designs (Cooper 1971). Alongside the new metal working techniques, however, were also a range of new culinary practices, not least the Portuguese penchant for frying things in batter. The technique that became tempura in Japan was also gifted to the British around the same time and later mutated into fish and chips (Walton 2000; Page 2002). It was also, Akira Shimizu argues, in the immediate wake of these first European encounters, that cooked meat vendors started appearing more prominently in some locations (Shimizu 2010: 87). In particular, the euphemistically named 'mountain whale' (boar) was hunted, sold and occasionally consumed as 'medicine' in the shadows of sixteenth-century Japan (Shimizu 2010: 92).

The restriction was tightened up, however, in the early seventeenth century following shogun Tokugawa's 'Laws of Compassion' (Shimizu 2010: 97). By this point, commitments to mercy aside, the avoidance of domesticated meats had also become an important structural component in the constitution of Japanese identity against the barbarous carnivores elsewhere in Asia and increasingly Europe, with whom regional economic competition was growing (Ohnuki-Tierney 1995: 232). The resultant diet comprised of regional variations of radishes, onions, pumpkins, citrus fruit, turnips and leafy vegetables as well, in some locations, as fish. Fish incidentally, included whales, which Shimizu argues, partly explains the use of a cetacean euphemism for boar meat. Domesticated chickens, while prized, were certainly not eaten. The only part of today's popular chicken katsu dish that was 'traditionally' eaten in Japan was short-grained rice, which was, and remains, the most important component of the Japanese diet, providing 60–70 per cent of the required daily carbohydrates (Ehara 2010). Like meat avoidance, the rice also played a symbolic role as a marker of local culture as distinct from the longer grains of rice used in Korean and Chinese cuisines (Ohnuki-Tierney 1995).

Following an early flurry of encounters with European tastes, practices and technologies during the Nanban period, concerns amidst elites around external influences gave way to two centuries of growing seclusion, and consolidation of local, and Nanban culinary practices. By the nineteenth century, however, Japan was once again forcibly opened to trade by the military muscle of the United States. With its own imperial ambitions piqued by Western imperialism, Japan's elite classes started, once again, to pursue the habits and customs that Europe and the United States lauded as pillars of its success.

Typifying the radical reorientation of fashion and culture in the late nineteenth century, Japan's Emperor Meiji, after whom the era is named, is purported to have regularly dined on beef and mutton, as well as preferring a Western-style tailcoat to the traditional clothes hitherto favoured by emperors. Above all else, such accoutrements were seen as integral to the strengthening of the nation and, by embracing them at the top, the emperor hoped that carnivorous consumption would spread further. These changes were reflected at the very highest diplomatic level, where it was not uncommon to see six-course European-style meals being served (Cwiertka 2006: 13–17). The westward turn is also recorded in the more everyday life of Japanese cities, with the middle classes pursuing western tastes with perhaps even more vigour than their superiors. As Tomoko Tamari details, Tokyo's urbanites acquired a new aesthetic disposition and taste, primarily by way of the didactic efforts of institutions such as the department store. Mimicking the grand retail palaces of nineteenth-century Paris and London, department stores such as Mitsukoshi and Matsuya were 'places of spectacle, new sensations, illusions and a montage of styles and dreams' in which the owners staged exhibitions of the simultaneously 'advanced' and 'exotic' western tastes (Tamari 2006: 100–101).

Importantly, for this story, alongside clothes and accessories, the major department stores also opened up their own canteen-style restaurants, imitating the aforementioned trend for public dining emanating from the United States. With waitresses in western uniforms and western-style crockery and cutlery, the menu also contained translations of popular western dishes. Amongst the ham sandwiches and confectionery (Cwiertka 2006: 51–53), are two dishes – curry rice and bread-crumbed meat cutlets – that would together go on to greater things in the form of *katsu-karē*.

Of course, the rice was already familiar to Japanese consumers. So too might have been the curry sauce, the origins of which are purported to lie in the navy's efforts to make rations taste better. This practice itself, however, had come directly from the renewed contact with the British merchant navy and P&O cruises who themselves used an Anglicized blend of curry spices in their own kitchens (Collingham 2010: 250). On this point, it serves to highlight the fact that the powdered style of curry sauce poured over rice and served with pork and chicken cutlets in early twentieth-century Japan, was – by way of the British colonization of India and subsequent trade with Japan – the very same blend of flavours and textures that the British themselves were acquiring a taste for. It is the same powder-based curry sauce that at least three generations of British home cooks had stirred up for their families before more 'authentically Indian' ready-made sauces appeared in jars. The mild powder-based curry sauce is *still* traditionally served with chips in the south-east of Britain.

It is little wonder then that, as twenty-first-century Londoners have discovered a broader range of Japanese dishes beyond the sushi that first drew them in, they have found something so familiar and comforting amidst hitherto exotic menus. In both contemporary Japan and Britain, the powder-based curry blend developed in the Raj, primarily for colonizers' own tastes, is lauded as a national dish, and thus synchronizes the two cities' cultures. The practice of dining out on small cutlets of meat is also the result of interrelated US-inspired moves toward public dining. In both locations, Tokyo and London, a taste for this culinary staple arises out of trans-oceanic voyages of sensoria. Of course, as discussed in the case of the chilli pepper, the meaning given to these sensoria differs depending on the context of its encounter. The point is, that because of the journey that these sensoria have taken, there are so many sensibilities that would give meaning to it in the first place. This, above all else, is what might finally explain the exceptional length of the queue coalescing at Irene or 'Tomo's' chicken katsu stand.

Conclusion: Global Histories and Futures

While the Tikka Express van packs up and goes, at the end of the day it takes Irene and Mahsun an extra hour to dismantle their gazebo, sweep up the lettuce, cool down the fryers and spray down the pavement. Once arrived at their separate homes, an exhausted Mahsun tucks into a KFC, while Irene opts for a chicken curry from a local Indian takeaway. Tomorrow they will be back again, commuting an hour from Essex, setting up the tent, warming up the fryers, chopping the lettuces, stirring the curry sauce, unpacking the bulk packs of flatbread. But it will be worth it. For while other stalls might struggle – and certainly some come and go – their 'street food' seems to have found fertile soil in the sensuous furrows carved up by previous centuries' culinary comings and goings.

As the locus of everyday practice, the existent sociology of food and taste offer crucial insights into the various processes of change that are shaping the social topography of today's cities. Different angles of approach offer differing explanations for both the size and pattern of the city's gustatory practices. 'Tomo's Japanese Food' is uniquely situated as to exemplify a number of these explanations, offering distinction for the omnivorous cosmopolite, holy food for secular carbophobes and Muslims alike, providing Charlie the opportunity to trade-down to an alfresco lunch, while being cheap and filling enough for the area's historically poorer residents. However, none of these explanations fully elucidates the ongoing success of the dish. Nor do they explain the varying success of the ever-shifting buffet of lunches offered in the city's food courts. To understand this requires breaking the food court down to its constitutive parts, and cuisines to their constitutive ingredients.

Ingredients themselves do not, however, command that individuals have a specific taste for them. The varying success of the sensations that comprise these meals lies in sensibilities through which those sensations are given meaning. Sensibilities and tastes are acquired, often over life times, and even generations. Accordingly, a full account of the twenty-first century city's culture, its sensoria and sensibilities, needs to approach the construction of specific tastes, and culinary practices, over temporal periods that are longer than any individuals' life time. Beyond that, we also have to understand particular tastes as being afforded by processes that also transcend any given territory or culture and which are, as the Cuban anthropologist Ortiz argues, transcultural (Ortiz 1995). Not just transcultural in the sense of the occasionally conspicuous exotic hybrid mixology of the city's food court. Rather transcultural in a deep historical sense, in a way that the planetary scope of modernity's primal histories leave distinct resonances between seemingly disparate cultures.

That these connections are historical, however, is of no less import for understanding the city's future, nor that of planetary globalization. In fact they give us a very strong sense of the networks of association, particularly an intensified East–West set of connections, out of which new global configurations are emerging. An attention to such histories seems particularly apposite given rhetoric about Chinese, Singaporean and Malaysian conglomerates buying up London's properties (Johnstone 2012, 2013a, 2013b). With such developments taking place against the backdrop of political and economic crisis in the global North, there is a tendency to fall back on very simplistic understandings of globalization, albeit in an inverted form. Fear, in the West, about the newfound globalizing power of the East, in fact, draws on many of the tropes of erstwhile centre and periphery models of globalization, particularly the idea that the West might have to adapt to another hemisphere's culture, while capital is simply sucked from it. We know, however, from critiques of this model of globalization that this is not what happened when the West was at its hegemonic prime: that globalization of technology, culture, capital and ideas all move around the world in different patterns and speeds; that they mix and mingle with local forms and that they are adapted, adopted and mutated according to the geography, history, culture and other contingencies of each location they land in (Appadurai 1986, 1996, 2009; Pieterse 2009, 2011). More importantly, they have done so for a long time, with cultural practices in particular, intermingling even when political powers and economies were fiercely competing. Against the backdrop of tectonic shifts in global power, it is worth recalling that, while our shared planetary future is creating new types of inequality, our future emerges out of interconnected pasts that we in Tokyo, in London, and everywhere else, would all do well to recognize. The fortune of our global future, how we will live together, lies, in part, in a better understanding of the intertwined histories from which 'we' have emerged. As shallow as food hall cosmopolitanism might seem, a closer consideration of our lunch can be a good start.

4

From Horses to Cane Rats: Meat, Moral Panics and Race

Nineteen forty-seven was one of those really hot British summers (today, still one of the seven hottest on record) (Webb and Meaden 2000: 298–315). In Hackney the local papers were full of reports on the soaring petrol prices triggered by instability in the Middle East (Anon 1947a) and angry reportage about the death of British soldiers at the hands of Jewish militants in Palestine (Drew 1947). Long columns also detailed the ins and outs of the British Empire's impending demise with Indian independence, as well as the struggles of local farmers to compete with the imports that started arriving during the War (Anon 1947b). It was against the background of these late summer stories that the leader of the fascist organization 'The British League of Ex-Servicemen' saw opportunities in the ebullient bodies that coagulated daily at what he referred to as 'Yidd-ley Road' market, otherwise known as Ridley Road (Macklin 2007: 42). Accordingly on one of the market's busiest days – a Sunday in late August – he erected a platform in a clearing at the foot of the market, surrounded by grocers, bakeries and kosher butchers, all of which were 'controversially' open on the Christian Sabbath. Strategically located in an enervating mixture of smell, heat and noise, he orated a narrative aimed at converting his audience's experience of the market place into one of disgust, fear and hatred for its 'alien horrors': 'We will fight it to the death. Never will you impose your Oriental, Mongolian, Asiatic creed of Communism upon us . . . That is the answer of the British people . . . Buy British!' (Hamm 1947: 8, 17).

This speech, the pamphlet that accompanied it, and the clashes with militant antifascists it precipitated, snowballed into weekly bouts of what the Gazette referred to as 'Open-Air Politics' (Anon 1947c) As much as this was open-air politics, 'The Battle of Ridley Road,' as it was later coined (Anon 1947d), was politics of the open air itself. It was a struggle over the meanings ascribed to the smells, flavours, rhythms and textures of London's atmosphere.

In many respects, the tirades could also be located in a centuries-long tussle involving Jewish groups in London over their presence in public space, and especially their trading on Sundays. But there is no ignoring of the extent to which they were triggered by a moment of acute national crisis: post-war austerity, the end of Empire and emergence of new conflict in the Middle East. It was precisely against the backdrop of public chatter about Israel, Palestine, Empire, rations and food imports that Hamm saw his moment, and his ideal location, in the immigrants' market place. In choosing this particular location, Hamm was effectively able to articulate a set of sensoria, sensibilities and practices that were (in)appropriate to being British. He did this, first and foremost, by associating the flavours, smells and textures of the market in which he stood, with racist discourses of cultural and biological degeneration. Rendered as vectors of contagion, the multicultural sensoria were construed as threats to the realization of his racial utopia.

By this point, Hamm's deployment of scientific racism was nothing particularly new. The discourses of scientific racism had, for centuries already, provided resources for Europeans abroad to hierarchically evaluate and arrange colonial subjects according to their skin tones and bone structures (Dubow 1995). The practice also developed at pace 'at home' in the nineteenth century, with physiognomy a major preoccupation of an emergent European criminology as well as urban reformers (Forrest 1974; Gidley 1997; Twine 2002). Importantly, as recent historical work has revealed, scientific racism did not operate through vision alone (Corbin 1988: 209–210; Smith 2006; Obasogie 2013). While grounded in the supposed rationality of the eye, racism was also a strategy that altered the ways in which Europeans perceived and interpreted the textures, aromas and flavours associated with the lives of both the colony and inner-city. That is, beyond shaping the way in which 'white Europeans' consciously thought and talked about 'others,' the narratives of biological racism burrowed deep into bodies to colonize the non-conscious formula through which the ambience of everyday live was interpreted. Racism existed then, not only in conscious thought but, as Iris Marion Young puts it, 'at the level of routine habits ... and in unconsciously motivated reactions and symbolic associations' (Marion Young 1990: 204). Once established in habit, folkish stories about the sensible differences between migrant groups, especially in terms of what they ate, how they ate it and when they ate it, served to reflect, resurface and intensify the association between 'senses' of difference and biological hierarchies of race.

Taking mid twentieth-century oratory about multicultural metropolitan market place as a starting point, this chapter considers the ways in which twenty-first century discourses around food, in particular those propagated through the daily print media, resurface and intensify racialized processes of exclusion that continue to beset the cosmopolitan city. Importantly, this chapter is developed *against* an emergent strand of thinking that sees the senses as an 'affective' or 'non-representational' sphere of 'gut feelings', distinct from and irreducible to, the spoken word, language and discourse (Thrift 2008; Anderson and Harrison 2010; Pile 2010). Rather, as we will discuss over the next few pages, the narratives through which urbanites give meaning to the sensory city and the discourses they draw on, play an important part in shoring up an insidious, gut-felt sense of 'them' and 'us'.

Perhaps unsurprisingly, a great deal of the most obviously divisive 'issues' within London's culinary culture revolve around meat. Unsurprisingly because, as Marshall Sahlins' notes, 'the line' we draw 'between flesh and meat', like the lines drawn 'between edible meat and inedible offal', are amongst the most culturally contingent, yet deeply held, taxonomies that humans operate with and thus a likely source of disagreement (Sahlins 1976: 174). In a global city then, where disparate cultures meet, it is perhaps predictable that there would be some contestation as to where those lines ought to be commonly drawn. In recent years, however, meat has increasingly been placed at the fleshy heart of a series of intense 'moral panics' curated, propagated and crucially *amplified* through the news media. Whether it is about horse meat labelled as beef, the growing preponderance of halal meat in the city's restaurants, the ubiquity of fried chicken in takeaways (see Chapter 5) or the alleged availability of illegal African 'bush-meat' in an East End market, gut-felt commentaries about 'meat problems' are not particularly hard to come by.

While contestation over the line drawn between meat and flesh is probably as old as humanity – if not older – what is particularly significant about the way in which these issues are played out in the city today, are the ways in which, these debates have become a vehicle for the endurance of raciology and racist forms of social stratification. This chapter, then, aims takes on two of these meaty panics together to focus on their centrality to the endurance of everyday forms of racist malice and prejudice.

Bush-meat

In the decades following Hamm's, and later Oswald Mosley's, xenophobic incursions into Ridley Road, much of the area's Jewish community moved away from the market. For the main part, the diaspora moved either further into the more middle-class suburbs of North London, or otherwise to New York. So too Ridley Road's traders, some of whom stayed on in the area and reorganized to accommodate the palates of Caribbean and South Asian migrant labour. While the migrant population using the market changed, the far-right interest in the market and its wares endured deep into the tail end of the twentieth century. This was particularly pronounced in the late seventies and early eighties following a string of 'moral panics' about the introduction of crack cocaine and Jamaican 'Yardy' gangs into and around the market.

Significantly, given our focus on the relationship between text and the senses, these were panics that were primarily amplified and circulated by the print-media (Keith 1993: 41). As Cohen famously says of 'moral panics', the tabloid stories provided an index with which to 'identify' signifiers of the new threat, as well as amplifying the extent and severity of that threat (Cohen 2011: 76–77). Alongside the new tropical fruits and vegetables that adorned Ridley Road's grocers, the ganja smoke and sub-sonic dub that filled the dance floors of the nearby Four Aces club were identified, through representations of Ridley Road in the tabloid press, as new vectors of contagion (Summers 1988). Relatively innocent in and of themselves these primary signifiers were, by way of carefully constructed narratives, coupled to a chain of loaded secondary signifiers – the colony, the shanty town, the rebel, the savage – that rendered particular fruits, vegetables and vibrating waves of air, primary threats to the everyday life of the city.

With the increasingly Caribbean market place successfully defended (again) by local anti-fascists, the area's diversity continued into the final years of the twentieth century. First, in the late seventies, Ridley Road market fed Cold War refugees arriving from Turkey and Vietnam. A few years later, as the century turned, it became a favoured destination for Nigerian and Ghanian migrants. Diversifying at the same time as mainstream middle-class tastes were themselves diversifying, by the new millennium the market formed an exciting and 'edgy' backdrop for the new gentrifiers encroaching further east through London. Accordingly, the various dislocated diaspora searching for the taste of home at Ridley Road were starting to rub shoulders with petit-bourgeois omnivores scouring the market for its novel ingredients.

As omnivorous and liberal as they seemed, however, the area's new cosmopolitans have still depended on the identification of sensorial and culinary limits to define their identity amidst the area's multiculture. Throughout the last decade, those limits have been repeatedly identified and articulated with reference to the meat sold at Ridley Road market. The following account of the street market is offered by Ellis, a well-educated community worker from the home-counties, working, and at that point also living, near Ridley Road. The conversation takes place in a community centre, following my mentioning that I had been nosing around local street markets.

'So... Ridley Road Market.'

'Yeah, I cycle past it in the mornings. The centre of the bush-meat trade in Europe, isn't it?'

'What do you mean – bush-meat?'

'You know? Monkey meat ... Imported ... They get strips of monkey meat, pile it up, cover it in rum and set light to it. The hair all singes and the insides of it are left rare. It's like a delicacy.'

'Where did you hear this?'

'That's what they were saying here.' (Referring to the community centre we were sitting in).

I laugh. 'Doesn't sound like it would be particularly nice.'

Ellis's eyebrows rise with incredulity before tilting back down in concern. 'It's how AIDS gets spread, mate. You seriously like the market, do you?' His frown turns into a scowl and he starts shaking his head at me. 'It's minging, isn't it? In the morning I've seen them dragging carcasses of the meat across the ground before anyone gets there. It's dirty, mate. Filthy.'

Stories about bush-meat at Ridley Road first came to public awareness through a spate of national journalistic interest between 2001 and 2006. During this period, stories about the abject imports sold at Ridley Road Market seemed to find a renewed valance amidst wider discourse about crises in Britain's 'multicultural experiment' following the 'race riots' in the north of Britain, and '9/11'. Among the most sensational, emotive and lurid, were stories such as *Daily Mail* journalist Sue Reid's, who claimed to have followed 'suitcases dripping with blood' from the West African jungle to the 'urban jungle' of Ridley Road (Reid 2004). Slightly less salacious accounts of the presence of illegal meat at the market were offered by the likes of Angus Stickler in a 2004 BBC radio documentary:

> Ridley Road Market in Dalston, Hackney. It's reminiscent in some ways of the markets of Cameroon . . . [S]tores cater for the tastes of the local community. Boxes of yams piled high, imported from Ghana, racks of brown, dried fish, plantains. You can buy virtually anything here – and until recently that included the flesh of gorilla.
>
> [. . .] Yes, we found a quantity of antelope, monkey and gorilla, which were confirmed [. . .] from the DNA. Most of it was stored in a tatty freezer out the back, which I wouldn't have used for keeping dog food in.

Indeed a small number of traders at the market *were* prosecuted for trading illegally imported meat from Africa. And to be sure, 2001 saw the entrapment and arrest of a trader at the market for selling tantalus monkey meat to an undercover investigator posing as an African prince. However, it is also important to note that *by far* the majority of the illegal African meat consumed in London – and that which keeps the health inspectors busy – is banal 'micro livestock': the finely grained fillet-steak-like flesh of grass cutters (a large rodent species), or otherwise antelopes. More important than the species and even the quality of the meat to prosecutors (if not journalists) is the fact that it is illegally imported, and as such is subject to neither formal safety checks nor taxation. To the papers and their readers, however, the purported species of the meat in question was everything.

Following another BBC documentary, 2012 again saw another flurry of print-media interest in the market (Lynn 2012; Robinson 2012). While the journalists' articles were often very good at identifying and describing the distinguishing sensoria of the market – its cassava, exotic fruit and music – the headline and central focus of the stories this time was that the West African diaspora using the market were trading in a species of rodent; a rat, but also – as before – *possibly* monkeys, (Browne 2002; Reid 2004; Goldhill 2014; Malone 2014). The latter, it was repeated in every article, were sequestered from both reporter and inspector (Malone 2014), but the reader was assured that they were there nonetheless.

Notably, the vast majority of these stories, while opening with impressionistic portraits of recognizable landscapes of urban multiculture, quickly deliver their gruesome punchlines in a tone that communicates and elicits disgust. Such revulsion would be familiar to the majority of readers, with the very idea of both 'rat' and 'monkey' meat testing the embodied limits of a normative cultural tolerance. Which is to say, that there are very specific historical, cultural and social contingencies that inflect what is often a post-hoc rationalization of a deep-seated disgust for these particular forms of meat.

Before exploring the subterranean tributaries that this disgust swells from, it would it be improper not to consider first the rationales offered by the stories' narrators for their squeamishness. Ellis is perhaps most explicit when he states, 'it's how AIDS gets spread mate'. Sue Reid's piece for the *Daily Mail* (Reid 2004), later cut and pasted into Malone's reportage, adds several flourishes:

> Humans are believed to contract the virus by exposure to the blood and body fluids of wild apes. . . . So it follows that the virus is almost certainly present in the illegal bush-meat being sold in Britain. No one knows what the long term effect of the virus is on human health, but the potential danger is here. Now (Malone 2014).

In both Reid's and Ellis' responses, the deeply emotional tenor of the narrative is rationalized with reference to the objectivity of science's extra-somatic sensory devices – in particular, the zoonotic contagions revealed through microscopy. The 2014 spate of media interest in the meats sold at Ridley Road was even more explicit, rationalizing the journalists' disgust with reference to 'science', emerging as it did in the wake of a West Africa Ebola outbreak. Contact with diseased jungle fauna, either by humans or other animals that were subsequently eaten by humans was, at the time, widely thought a possible source of the outbreak of the illness amongst humans. Accordingly, the *Daily Mail* paired the usual kaleidoscopic photographic portrayals of Ridley Road's 'colourful' customers, vegetables, fruits and fabrics, with electron micrographs of the offending microbes in question. As the reader scrolled down (by now the *Mail* is primarily a digital publication) through photos of Ridley Road and electron micrographs of the disease, they reached embedded videos of people writhing on stretchers in Liberia (Malone 2014). The message was clear: the street market in East London was a serious threat to the biological health of the city's populace. It is worth noting at this point that when the disease did arrive in the UK it was not accidentally through meat but through the government's deliberate extraction of an infected aid worker.

Occasionally, especially in broadsheets (Browne 2002; Goldhill 2014) and National Geographic (Clarke-Howard 2011; Boyes 2012), the anti-bush-meat narratives departed from an anthropocentric concern with zoonotic contagions to focus on the endangered nature of the species being consumed. Therein the author's barely concealed disgust is rationalized primarily through the practice's contravention of trans-species ethics and ecological morality. There is, however, something slightly disingenuous about the deferral to the objective gazes of both medicine and ecology in an effort to rationalize the author's disgust. Not least, this disingenuousness is clear when considering the fact that consuming rodent meat has never been an accepted practice in modern European or North American life. Likewise with primate meat. Even the US author, Calvin W. Schwabe, whose remarkable encyclopaedia, *Unmentionable Cuisine*, contains recipes for 'skewered turtle meat,' 'extramadurian cat stew' and *hachi no sanagai* or 'wasp pupae,' finds recipes for primate meat too 'unmentionable' to mention (Schwabe 1979). As unremarkable as this omission sounds, the abjection of monkey meat in particular, is nonetheless worth some further consideration, as this squeamishness, especially amidst Europeans, has a clear provenance, and one that relates to the construction and identification of non-European 'savages'.

Cannibals and Bush-meat

In a famous essay, William Arens suggested that the cannibal, who was depicted regularly in the travelogues of sixteenth-century European and American travellers (alongside giants, mermaids and tree people) were primarily a 'useful' exaggeration (Arens 1980). Useful because, regardless of the extent of actual cannibalistic practices (which Arens argues were negligible at best), the stories secured funding for further colonial expeditions and missionary activities. They were also useful stories for the manner in which they transferred attention from the brutality of the colonial explorers onto the colonized. Rehashed accounts of cannibalism 'observed' by sixteenth- and seventeenth-century explorers also allowed the growing audiences of both literary fiction and fact to 'sense' vicariously the simultaneously geographical and moral boundaries of their 'superior race'. In many ways, the imputation of alimentary practices, such as cannibalism, trumped even physiognomy as a means of identifying 'savagery'. This was, as Giorgio Agamben (2004) notes, even the case for the godfather of modern taxonomy, Carl Linnaeus who saw little observable physiological difference within the genus *homo*, save for small differences in hair distribution and tooth patterns. Accordingly he defined *Homo sapiens* (knowing man), not by physical traits as he did *all* other creatures, but by having a specific ability: being able 'to recognise himself as human,' and to sense other humans as human (Agamben 2004: 24). Fitting neatly outside these criteria, cannibalism provided an off-the-peg practice for writers, explorers and scientists of all sorts, to instantly place all of those accused, irrespective of physiognomy, as originating and existing somewhere outside of humanity. Likewise, for Sue Reid, her disgust for the primate eater, dealer and hunter arises from their perceived lack of ability to sense, with their eyes and taste buds, the distorted humanity of their quarry: '[. . .] the ape often adopts a pleading expression and holds out its paw to the killers [. . .] Tragically for the animal – and perhaps for all mankind – the bush-meat hunters of Africa take no notice at all' (Reid 2004). Importantly in this instance, the disgust Reid is trying to communicate has little to do with the objective threat posed by zoonotic contagions. Rather, the feeling of disgust that Reid apparently feels in her stomach and then communicates, accompanies the anthropomorphic elevation of the ape to the human, and the relegation of primate meat dealers and hunters to a sub-species. That is, it emanates from the folkish sensibility through which European 'humanity' traces its limits through 'others' ways of sensing, or ways of not sensing as the case may be, 'humanity'.

There is a strong parallel here with the way in which Marshall Sahlins explains the North American taboo around eating canine and equine meat: 'Dogs [...] participate in American society in the capacity of subjects' (Sahlins 1976: 175). As such, those that do not recognize the humanity of these creatures, (for example, in a North America beset by oil crisis, wherein horse meat was tabled as an alternative to beef), are regularly figured as inhumane savages, precisely for their inability to see the distorted humanity of their dinner. Many Western meat taboos then are, as Sahlins' argues, 'a sustained metaphor on cannibalism' (Sahlins 1976: 174). It is in these ways that an analogy between Arens' 'cannibal' stories and the alleged primate meat eaters of Ridley Road Market might be strongest: regardless of what it is really found in the crevices, storerooms and freezers of the market, the bush-meat story serves to construct an entire community as beyond the limits of civility, because it suggests a whole community is unable to 'sense' the relative humanity of a specific animal group.

To stretch the analogy between 'the man-eating myth' (1980) and the alleged primate pedlars a little further, however, we might also ask how precisely are the barbarous expeditions funded, yet obfuscated through accusatory stories about inhumane 'goings on' at Ridley Road? Firstly, as with most accounts of inhumane practices emanating from twenty-first century West Africa, the bush-meat narratives conveniently frame out the extent to which mining and forestry concessions, driven by hunger for advanced electronics, luxury chocolates, rubber tyres and exotic wooden furniture, are related to the trade in bush-meat. Forestry and mining concessions in particular, expose the tropical forests' innards to displaced families of hunters starved of the status, cash and calories. Scaling up the traditional hunting or rearing of micro-livestock satisfies all of those deficits. Moreover, it is the infrastructures required by logging and mining that 'allow hunters in and meat out' giving them access to 'a huge market of urban consumers' (Peterson and Ammann 2003: 120–212). Tell-tale signs of the relationship between the extraction of West Africa's raw materials and the bush-meat trade surfaced in 2014, when newspapers reported European, Australian and American mining concerns shutting down in the wake of the Ebola outbreak (Miller 2014; Koneh 2014). It was, in fact, at the US rubber company Firestone's million-acre forestry concession in Liberia, that the wife of one of the company's executives became the first local victim of the disease (Reaves et al. 2014). Yet at no point did any of the mainstream coverage of the Ebola pandemic question the relationship between the extraction of Africa's resources by transnational corporations and the trade in potentially dangerous meat. Instead, it homed in on the most spectacular aspects of the disease and its transmission, namely indigenous funerary rituals and gustatory practices.

A little closer to home, stories about abject meat also both obscure and feed into various forms of far more prosaic habitat 'capitalization'. Between 2001 and 2006, stories about the meat sold at Ridley Road coincided with a host of other stories about the area including exaggerated reports of illegal gambling and drug dealing (Hackney Council 2006), and reports of people trafficking and ritual child abuse (BBC News 2005). Along with tales of suitcases dripping with blood arriving from the heart of darkness, these stories fuelled intense anxiety within a local government ostensibly concerned with delivering 'community cohesion'. Significantly for Ridley Road and its users, the stories also erupted at the peak of a municipal budgetary deficit, and a decision to address that deficit through the 'potential disposal opportunities ... of land [around the market] for residential development' (Hackney Council 2007; Open Dalston 2008a, 2009). The decision to overhaul as much of the area as possible was lubricated by the fact of the upcoming 2012 Olympics, and the belief that the market and its environs, as they stood, might not be best suited for attracting the 'right type' of international investment in the borough. A series of events soon followed, all seemingly intended to make life harder for the market's customer and traders. First, in 2007, a set of double yellow lines were painted along the length of the market. This left any traders who had not paid the sizeable fee to park nearby at risk of fines as they parked vehicles to unload their produce. In the next year, the market's electricity was also cut off for six months, apparently in response to the alleged siphoning of electricity by a handful of traders. Dependent as they were on electricity, it was butchers that were among the first to go out of business. Not long after the meat had been removed, 'Hackney bean-counters' went 'bananas' stepping up attempts to repeatedly fine market traders for negligible weights and measures 'offences' (Open Dalston 2008b). While local groups of urban conservationists and a loose traders' association put up resistance to these measures, they were met with a defensive stance from the borough's mayor who characterized the market's defenders as 'the "keep Hackney crap" brigade' (Open Dalston 2008c). Despite the claims of his detractors, the borough's mayor was not necessarily revealing his own explicitly 'racist', or 'snobbish' perception of the market. Rather, it seems he was channeling the view of Ridley Road derived from the property market and developers interested in the area. Or rather, he was channeling the view of a market grounded in omnivorous cosmopolites' hunger for property in the city's 'edgy' or 'fringe' neighbourhoods, which nonetheless falls within the limits of their own sensory repertoires. From this influential perspective, Ridley Road Market and its users, or at least the meats and fruits filling their bags, were a significant obstacle to profitable development in the area.

Of course, diseased meat, be it bovine, swine, avian or primate, presents various scales of threat to a populations' physical well-being. It is because of this 'objective risk' posed by meat that the regulation of the meat trade, in the UK at least, is amongst the most universally consented to forms of bio-political intervention. But as we know, stories about Ridley Road's illicit meat trade have never been stories about objective physiological threats. Instead they have been panicky narratives that, by drawing on the historically and culturally contingent sensibilities shared between journalists and their readers, spread with little argument or discussion. Far from a story pertaining to some dry risk, every flurry of Ridley Road meat myths has a whiff of racialized moral panic about it.

Horse Meat

During the first weeks of November 2012 representatives from the Food Safety Authority of Ireland walked into an assortment of supermarkets and walked back out with bags bulging with processed meats and ready meals. In previous years the same inspectors had revealed the murky provenance of the proteins pumped into chicken breasts and traced the dubious origins of smoked fish (FSAI 2003). Somewhat remarkably – given previous decades of bovine (BSE) bio-drama – 2012 was the first year that processed beef products would be put under these particular inspectors' microscopes. Thus nineteen different salamis, an assortment of thirty-one different cottage pies, ravioli, lasagne and cannelloni, along with twenty-seven different varieties of burger, were sent to a lab to determine the precise species of protein in these products (Reilly 2013). Perhaps unsurprisingly, nearly half of the salami were found to contain an unlabelled mix of porcine and bovine DNA. But salami never really claimed to be anything other than salami. In contrast cottage pies, lasagne and ravioli were all generally understood to be, or were labelled as, beef products. Over two thirds of them, however, along with nine out of ten burgers, contained porcine DNA.

The whole testing exercise might have gone relatively unreported were it not for the fact that, as the chief executive of the FSAI Alan Reilly notes, in addition to the porcine contamination, over a third of the burgers also tested positive for equine DNA (Reilly 2013). While most contained only traces of horse, the blue and white striped box of Tesco everyday value burgers, one of the most widely consumed value burgers in Ireland and Britain, contained nearly one third horse meat. Follow-up analysis on a wider range of supermarket produce revealed many more products, from many more retailers, and their suppliers testing positive for horse meat.

On the fourteenth of January the Irish authorities informed their British counterparts about their findings and their implications for UK retail, enmeshed, as it is, with the food systems across the Irish Sea. On the fifteenth the authorities formally informed the initial retailers that were affected: Tesco, Iceland, Aldi, Lidl and Dunnes. And on the sixteenth the news media were informed of the facts as they stood. That the news broke at this precise time was particularly irksome for supermarkets and meat suppliers. The lull after the Government's Christmas recess had left Westminster and Fleet Street yet to resume their usual dance across the front pages. As Hall et al. (1978) and Stanley Cohen (2011) inadvertently reveal in their studies of moral panics, the holidays present particularly fertile ground for widespread, media-driven, public anxiety. The heat of summer can be an additional catalyst, but it is not always necessary. Following the FSAI press release in mid-January, the story hit the headlines immediately and stayed there for weeks. '99% Horse in Findus Lasagne!' exclaimed *The Sun* (Hawkes 2013). 'Scale of Horse Meat Scandal "Breath Taking"' remarked the flabbergasted *Telegraph* (Hope et al. 2013). Never outdone in terms of sensationalism, the *Daily Star* found a new angle on the story every day for weeks. Highlights included 'Queen Eats Horse' (Walker 2013) and, taking a eurosceptic's off-the-cuff remarks about Italian meat-processing as scientific fact, 'Now There's Donkey Meat in UK Salami' (Lemanski 2013). The story held its place in the imaginations, conversations and guts of newspaper audiences for a whole month, before a celebrity murder swept it off the front pages.

As Gabriel Scally (2013) notes, 'there's nothing new about the adulteration of food [. . .] Indeed, what is held to be the very first piece of public health legislation passed by the Westminster parliament was the 1757 'Act for the due making of Bread; and to regulate the Price and Assize thereof; and to punish Persons who shall adulterate Meal, Flour, or Bread.' And to be sure, the British public have been subjected to their fair share of meat-related scandals over the last thirty years, from salmonella panics through mad cow disease to celebrity chef Jamie Oliver's public attack on the ambiguous offal used in school children's meals. In recent years, however, potential panics, such as the widespread presence of the harmful *campylobacter* in British poultry (see Chapter 5), have fallen victim to meat scandal fatigue and failed to really take off. The contamination of ready meals alone then, might not have been sufficient news story to capture the headlines by itself. For a food scandal to really burn, it required ignition, accelerant and fuel. The ignition obviously in this case seemingly came from the sheer fact that it was horse meat, rather than the usual mix of bovine and porcine offal, that was being used as a cutting agent in the nation's TV dinners. This is doubtless the element that caught the public's interest, and served as the face of the scandal. In most cases, however, equine meat, which has never been as anthropomorphized, and therefore as taboo, in the West as either canine or primate meat, was merely the hook that pulled the reader into other areas of interest. And it was these other areas of interest, often resting in deep seams of resentment, that gave the scandal its slow burning longevity.

In fact, across the broadsheets and in some of the tabloids, eating horse meat itself was rarely, if ever, actually presented as taboo. Rather, when the meat was discussed it was regularly described as being a more viable, and healthy alternative to mass produced bovine meat (Duffin 2013; Mackenzie 2013; Stone 2013; Newman 2014). Papers of all reading ages, alongside lifestyle magazines such as London's *Time Out*, sent intrepid reporters out to survey and sample horse meat in the outlets where it was suddenly being made explicitly available (Mackenzie 2013; Stone 2013; Duggins 2013). Which is to say that for many, the main ingredient in 'horse-meat-gate', and one that occupied the relatively less sensational narratives (Bennett 2013) was not the horse meat *per se* but the other aspects of society that it revealed. For some (particularly those that might have read the liberal left papers like *The Guardian*), the real problem lay in the remarkable centralization of ownership in the meat industry that the story revealed. Adulteration by just one major processor, the APB group, which owned many of the processors involved, affected nearly every supermarket chain in the UK and Ireland, from budget stores Aldi and Lidl to higher-end outlets such as Waitrose. Even small independent restaurants and retailers pulled their beef products, seemingly supplied by the same producers as major supermarkets. Another related fact revealed in the reportage was that, while *ownership* was centralized, the adulterated meat had not come from the centralized disassembly lines of the previous century's meat packing industry. Rather, as both left- and right-leaning broadsheets were keen to highlight (although not in so many words), the scandal was the inevitable result of agro-industry flexible specialization (Kim and Curry 1993). As details unearthed in the articles reveal, the adulteration was related to suppliers in Spain, the Netherlands and Poland, and processing plants in Ireland and England. A second source of contamination, resulting in 100 per cent horse meat lasagne, was identified as originating in a large French-based supplier, Comigel, which sold meat products to Belgium, Germany, Switzerland, the UK and Ireland. In an effort to shift the blame, the French company pointed out that they had subcontracted a factory in Luxembourg, who themselves had bought meat it claimed was labelled 'beef', from another multinational, Spanghero. Spanghero bought the dubious meat from a Cypriot company called Daarp, owned by a Dutch national, who himself had bought it from Romania. In Romania, authorities later confirmed, the meat had been sold legally as horse. Daarp, not coincidentally, is an anagram of paard – the Dutch word for horse. The complexity of the supply chains revealed by the meat scandal was, for some on the left of British politics, a genuine concern. Speaking through *The Guardian*, New Labour's erstwhile policy advisors highlighted the austerity-driven cuts to food regulation that allowed nefarious associations to develop along the chain of flexible specialization. This, alongside the obsessive pursuit of profit through outsourcing production to cheaper labour markets, was taken as symptomatic of neoliberalism desperately in need of state intervention (Taylor and Meikle 2013; Bennett 2013).

In contrast, as Abbots and Coles (2013) note, the general tenor in right-leaning broadsheets such as the *Daily Telegraph* was to blame the dodgy supply chain on the demands of irrational and uneducated consumers for cheap meat (Abbots and Coles 2013). Therein editorials effectively asked, sneeringly, 'what do people expect to get for a £1 box of burgers?' If the sneering broadsheets saw a profitable opportunity in heating up Britain's simmering class antipathy, the tabloid press made little effort to blame their readers who were far more likely to have been consumers of the cheap processed meals. In fact at least two of the red-topped tabloids went so far as to partly excuse their reader's alimentary sins with reference to the popularity of equine protein amongst the plucky working classes during the Second World War (McGuinness 2013; Reilly 2013).

The third theme in 'horse-meat-gate', and the one that *really* kept the story burning across the front pages of the tabloids – and therefore within the imaginations of the newspaper reading majority – was related to a specific aspect of agro-industrial specialization detailed above. Not, however, the fact that the adulteration had seemingly been carried out by a hilariously brazen Dutch fraudster. Rather the element of the story that was placed front and centre in tabloid accounts was that it was trade with Europe's margins, specifically Romania, that enabled the adulteration. In this respect, it is no coincidence that the horse meat scandal engulfed the public imagination in quite the rapacious manner it did, when it did. Emerging exactly one year prior to impending removal of restrictions on the movement of workers from Bulgaria and Romania into the UK, the tabloid press had, since at least the previous November, been running speculative comment pieces on what would happen in a year's time when restrictions on economic migration to the UK would be dropped. Utilizing a familiar set of sloshy metaphors *The Sun* and the *Daily Mail* spoke of 'tidal waves' and 'floods' of Eastern Europeans 'swamping' labour markets (Francis 2012; Craven and Arbuthnott 2013; Webb 2013). This, however, was merely the most recent flurries of factually dubious stories featuring Romanians that had passed through headlines in recent years.

As discussed earlier with reference to the National Front's incursions into Ridley Road Market, in the mid-to-late twentieth century the majority of racist vehemence was directed at the migrant labour imported from Britain's erstwhile colonies. In this way, labouring migrants from India, Pakistan, Bangladesh and the Caribbean provided a sort of limit figure against which to define the essence of a normative British identity. In recent years, as inter-EU migration increased and visas for non-EU nationals dried up (Small and Solomos 2006; McDowell 2009), the prime source of both migrant labour, and limit figures of a particular vision of British identity, emerged from within Europe itself. These limits were partly defined legislatively, through the designation of quasi-Europeans status, to those on the geographic and cultural margins of the continent (Fox, Moroşanu and Szilassy 2012). The limits of an exclusive British identity were also mediated by press stories that identified and amplified the appearance of criminality, dilatoriness and cunning amidst Europe's new prospects. Romanians, it seemed, were particularly singled out. As Fox, Moroşanu and Szilassy (2012) note one particular story featuring abject meat, was particularly effective in achieving this. In 2003, *The Sun* ran a story entitled 'Swan Bake' that reported that Eastern European migrants had been capturing, killing and cooking swans. Although *The Sun* was later pushed to disclaim that it had 'confused conjecture with fact' (Ponsford 2003), the story re-emerged with the same headline in 2008, at the very moment that the first Romanian workers were granted limited rights to work in the UK. This time the story appeared in the *Daily Mail* and described an abandoned 'encampment of tents' on London's as-then-unbuilt Olympic park. Among the empty tents, fishermen reported finding evidence of a butchered swan alongside 'a Romanian bible and cooking equipment'. 'These swans belong to the Queen. . . . It's a disgrace.' remarked the unnamed angler who found the carcasses (*Daily Mail* 2008). Again in 2010 (Malone 2010) and in March 2014 (Russell 2014) the stories about the swans-eaters reappeared, with consistent descriptions of the temporary dwellings found nearby. The reference to impermanent homes ensured a short-cut to association with the ready-made stigma of the Roma, while the remains of Cygnus *regalis* offered patent evidence of these migrants' unsuitability to living in the UK. As Fox, Moroşanu and Szilassy (2012) argue, like Ridley Road's Jews half a century before, Romanians' 'putatively shared whiteness does not exempt them from the effects of racism'. Indeed, highlighting abject gustatory practices, be they real or mythical, served to impute essential and irreconcilable cultural differences to Romanians, racializing them in the process.

Thus, when it was revealed that a French meat processor, based in Luxembourg, had bought meat from a company, registered in Cyprus and owned by a Dutch man, who himself had bought the meat from Romania, only one part of that chain really interested the tabloids: the bit that suggests that the adulterated meat might actually stem from Romania itself. Immediately, the *Daily Mail* followed fingers pointing eastward. Their website, which was and remains the most viewed news website on the internet (BBC News 2012), featured a hurried audio-visual depiction of 'Horse-Meat Central', the 'desolate abattoir' set against the backdrop of a cold, drizzly Transylvanian (read 'blood drinking') winter. The *Daily Mirror* were hot on the tails of the *Mail* (Collins 2013a, 2013b), tying the meat in the abattoir to reports of Romanian 'gangs' herding horses for slaughter. So too were the BBC (Thorpe 2013), who generally avoided speculation while, nevertheless, foregrounding the eerie landscape and soundscapes of the horse-meat abattoir. Then there was *The Sun* (Parker 2013), whose piece on the abattoir started with the sentence 'Grim beast slaughterhouse built with EU cash'. The conflation of the horse-meat scandal with both myths about Romanian savagery and 'Little England's' distrust of European bureaucracy were, however, evidently not quite enough to fully titillate the tabloid's readers. Thus the editors took the extra step of taking the scandal and attaching all the stigma and anxiety accrued under the previous century's most intense moral panic with the headline, 'Romanian Livestock AIDs Fear'. The AIDS reference was to an equine virus – harmless to humans – that *might* get into the food chain were it unregulated.

Again, even in the tabloids, what every paper, news outlet and blogger claimed at some point to be a 'taboo', was not actually horse meat at all. While the broadsheet taboo lay in agro-industrial flexible specialization and the irresponsible consumers, the taboo in the tabloids emerged from the fact that the meat was sourced from a geographical and cultural location that had no place in Europe, let alone Britain. The issue was not necessarily the European acceptance of horse meat *per se*, but rather the essential criminality and deviousness of Europe's margins that allowed for adulteration.

While 'horse-meat-gate' was relevant to understanding patterns of social formation within London, it was, at many levels, a national scandal; national in the sense that the meat products were nationally distributed, but more so because of the way it played into the efforts of populist media, vernacular culture and government, to define 'British' values and ways of making sense (Cameron 2014). In some respects, metropolitan Londoners' omnivorousness shone through the whole scandal, with local artisan butchers and independent suppliers of horse meat reporting significant growth (Newman 2014; Smith-Dawkins 2014). That is not to say that metropolitan multiculture always triumphs over the ossification of ethnically exclusive identities. In the same period, London's Metropolitan Police reported a fourfold increase of attacks on migrants from Bulgaria and Romania. This growth fails to correlate with the – less than expected – new migration from those countries (Datoo 2014; Easton 2014).

Discourse and the Senses

As the last century's anthropologists noted, eating – and eating meat in particular – are amongst the most visceral ways through which culture has traditionally been delineated, experienced and reproduced (Douglas and Nicod 1974; Caplan 1992; Lévi-Strauss et al. 1992; Lévi-Strauss 1997; Douglas 2002). Despite the 'post-traditional' appearance of the late modern metropolis, the lines drawn between meat and flesh continue to inflect processes of social inclusion and exclusion. As the chapter has detailed, these processes are articulated through heartfelt gut feelings. Which is to say that, while city dwellers might rationalize their relationships to their neighbours' sensory life worlds, these relationships are partly grounded in unspeakable yet discursively informed, webs of sensuous affinities and repulsion. For all the apparent rationality of the technocratic global city, London's social forms still have strong, and highly arbitrary, cultural aspects. These aspects are not, however, necessarily spoken, written or 'imagined'. Rather, they are 'sensed'. The sensory aspects of these social processes do not, however, mean that the 'discursive' is absent from the construction of sensibilities. On the contrary, as the case studies in this chapter aim to outline, meat-based narratives reproduce and interact with the embodied senses of culture, modulating forms of both association and estrangement in the process.

Smoke without Fire

Focussing on the social and symbolic construction of mythologies that hide behind meat-based moral panics in no way implies that there is nothing 'real' at the core of these conspicuously public issues. As Stan Cohen noted in the preface to his final edition of *Folk Devils and Moral Panics*, 'calling something a "moral panic" does not imply that this something does not exist or happened at all and that reaction is based on fantasy, hysteria, delusion and illusion, or being duped by the powerful' (Cohen 2011: xviii).

Equine meat is eaten across the European continent. And as a major exporter of meat to the UK, if contamination with horse meat is allowed to happen, it would likely be somewhere in Europe. Lethal contagions *could* conceivably arrive by way of the transnational trade in illegal meat. Both the horse meat scandal and the 'problem' of bush-meat are real issues, objective facts amenable to a degree of quantification, measurement and risk calculation. They are also issues that ought to be discussed. That there is something 'real' at the core of the issue does not stop the coverage of these issues having a whiff of 'moral panic' about them. The 'moral' element of the 'panic' arises from the extent to which the threat perceived by journalists, editors and their publics is a risk to the maintenance of a culturally contingent moral code. Which is to say, in both the bush-meat and horse meat scandals, the 'objective risk' is clearly framed by an assortment of culturally received ideas as to what a risk is, who poses a risk to whom, and which risks are worth paying attention to (Douglas 1994). The 'panic' aspect of the episodes is evident in media efforts to swerve analytical depth in favour of gross exaggeration of salacious details which, in turn, muddy the waters of any serious reflection on the issue. Even when focussed on objective 'facts', in presenting these alongside particular chains of images and associations, media-driven 'moral panics' about meat do less for public health, than they do to fortify the broader social hierarchies of the city.

Conclusion: The Expedience of Meaty Panics

In his infamous account of moral panics around youth subculture, Stan Cohen famously noted that '[Societies] appear to be subject, every now and then, to periods of moral panic' (Cohen 2011: 9). Cohen offered little sense, however, as to when, how or why panics occur when they do. Around a decade later Stuart Hall (Hall et al. 1978) and his colleagues started to answer those questions when they related a late twentieth-century 'moral panic' around 'mugging' to a colossal crisis in the hegemonic consensus holding British society together. At that time it was a crisis in the economy, in government and in national cultural identity. At each level of the crisis, specific social classes and their proxies in 'race' were constructed as the problems to be dealt with. As the authors of this landmark study detailed, highlighting these 'dangers' and 'dealing' with them punitively helped to shore up a fractious hegemony and conserve social order at a time of great upheaval. In some respects, the same could be said of the invective Jeffery Hamm and his followers in the mid-forties directed at 'Yidd-ley Road'. The British Empire was falling apart, aristocracy was crumbling, the cost of middle-class living was increasing while the working classes were agitating. There was a crisis in the hegemonic order of society, which, at a very visceral level, identifying and ostracizing outsiders sought to repair.

As was the case in the moral panics of previous centuries, each of the flare-ups outlined above also takes place against a backdrop of protracted crises in the hegemonic order of British society: from the soul searching that followed the trio of millennial bombings in New York, Madrid and London, through wars in Afghanistan and Iraq, to unprecedented financial crises and the tectonic shifts of global power bases. Against such a backdrop, mass-media-lead moral panics about abject outsiders can play an important role for anybody with a vested interest in the status quo. In such moments, moral panics can serve two important functions: first, the legitimating of punitive forms of state 'justice' through which particular forms of order can be asserted, and second, shoring up a vernacular 'sense' of 'national identity'. Herein, the media play a crucial role. It was, after all, the mass production of print media that first made possible the imagining of national identities (Anderson 1991: 33). The types of stories outlined above, however, extend far beyond conjuring an 'image' of a national community and its outsiders. The stories selected here make stomachs churn, skins prickle and faces wince. In this way, moral panics around food especially, have a considerable power in conjuring an exclusive sense of communities.

Today's talk of 'them' and 'us' is no longer couched in the language of racial science. Nevertheless, mass media discourses about essential culinary differences burrow down into the non-conscious praxis of everyday life, filling it with potential vectors of cultural danger and contagion. In many respects, the disgust and moral outrage at others' abject practices is analogous to the ways in which the nineteenth-century discourses around culture and physiognomy made the idea of distinct races, and their cultures, fully 'sensible' (Smith 2006; Obasogie 2013). While racist science may have lost many of its adherents, and racist talk lost many of its most fluent speakers, the ways in which racism and xenophobia are articulated through gut feelings, clearly endures. Fuelled by textual narratives coupling real and imagined sensations to historically contingent meanings – and despite all efforts to develop colour-blindness – racism is alive and well within all the other senses.

5

The 'Fried Chicken Problem'

By 6.30pm on Brick Lane in early December, it has already been dark for nearly three hours. The evening's activities are all well underway. At the very northern end of the street new media workers, students, designers, yoga teachers and artists have been gathering – for at least an hour and a half – behind the dark, condensation-slicked windows of hookah lounges and cocktail bars. Midway along the street, lairy business parties – at least two pints down – are pulled, staggering, by touts, off the street into one of its famous curry houses. At the southern end of the lane, where the 'the cultural quarter' meets the poverty of the old East End, the last three hours have seen a steady stream of locals ducking into the warmth of *Al-Badar Fried Chicken*, one of Tower Hamlets' two-hundred-and-something fried chicken takeaways (Foster Intelligence 2013).

The tiles on the floor of the takeaway are a lightly speckled, matt grey-blue. Twelve inches by twelve inches. Slightly larger beige tiles line the walls, interspersed every eight or so with a three-quarter-length mirror.

Under the blue-green glare of a neon strip light, a twenty-something Londoner – black, black jacket, black jeans and black baseball cap – checks himself in one of the mirrors. He is examining either his beard line, an ingrowing hair, or a spot on his neck.

His friend leans on the chest-height polished-steel counter, chatting to the cashier before turning to the mirror guy, making eye contact in the reflection.

'Bruv! You got any change? I've only got . . .' He checks through the change in his palm. 'Two forty. I'll sort you out later.'

The mirror guy briefly meets his friend's gaze in the reflection, before returning to an examination of his beard line. 'Yeah, yeah.' He takes a step back and straightens his baseball cap out, pouting at himself. 'How much d'you need?' he asks, over his shoulder, throwing his hand into jangly jacket pockets.

The takeaway is two shop units knocked through, with a long steel service counter spanning its length. At any one moment there are up to five cashiers-cum-chefs serving customers. Today there are three. At the other end of the customer counter from where I sit is a small boy, no older than twelve, his t-shirt draping over skinny shoulders. It's cold outside but he lives nearby.

The cashier serving the boy is Arif, a middle aged Bengali man with a greying beard. Paternalistically, he recites the order he has just packaged up for the boy. 'Two number fours, one number two, a portion of hot wings, chana and a rice. Three cokes, one Mirinda.'

The boy nods, smiling.

'That's fourteen ninety-five.'

The boy hands Arif a twenty, and takes his change before being handed two steaming carrier bags over the counter.

The boy nods deferentially. He turns and walks away. As he approaches the exit, the door swings inward. A blast of chilled air comes in from the outside, followed by a family. The boy makes to stand aside but then decides to hurriedly squeeze past as the family shuffle in. Father, son, daughter and mother. They are laughing and talking between each other in Mandarin. The cashier greets them.

'Good evening.'

'Hello,' smiles the father. His young daughter, no older than four, cranes her neck back to take in the menu above the cashier's head: twelve illuminated photographs showcasing the various combinations of chicken breast, thighs, wings and chips. Hands in her puffy pastel-pink jacket pockets, she starts jumping up and down excitedly.

Back at the other end of the counter, the two young men are shouldering their way out of the shop's second door, orange and yellow boxes in their hands. No sooner have they left than they are replaced by two more young men, late teenage, second-generation Bengalis from a nearby housing estate. They are talking loudly in Benglish and giggling about an incident that had just occurred outside.

'Did you see him?'

'[. . .] He's always like [. . .]'

'Yeah but you can't . . .' One of the two looks up and meets the cashier eye to eye, and greets him by the universal name of all the area's takeaway staff, 'Bigman!' (also known as Boss or Bossman).

The cashier nods as the two swing into the two plastic bucket chairs either side of a small Formica table. Quilted coats inflating around them as they hunch into their bucket seats, their public exchange dissolves into a private huddle. After less than a minute, and without having placed an order, the cashier brings them over two paper plates, steaming and sagging under the large chunks of fried chicken and mountains of spindly fries.

'Ahhh! Bigman! Bigman!' Recognition, respect and thanks from the more vocal of the two men.

The Chinese family have placed their order and have sat down to await its preparation.

At the slightest break in the evening's relentless rhythm, the three cashier-chefs turn to each other and chat briefly, laughing about something.

Three minutes, twelve meals served. The door swings open again.

London's first fried chicken takeaway and restaurant, Kentucky Fried Chicken, opened in Finchley in 1968. Alongside the early burger chains that arrived in the upmarket retail resorts of 1960s Britain, takeaway fried chicken was, for a long time, an exceptional treat. To say that the city has since acquired a taste for fried chicken is something of an understatement. The popularity of fried chicken across Britain first started accelerating in the late 1980s, wherein the red and white signage of KFC was part of the increasing presence of globalized American brands in British high streets, shopping centres and new out-of-town retail parks. KFC is still a significant presence in the city's ready-to-go poultry-scape, with just under 200 across the metropolitan area of Greater London.

While initial growth in the eighties and the nineties was driven by one major global brand, the more recent growth in annual consumption (in urban areas) of around 4.5 per cent a year, has been driven by a diverse assortment of independent entrepreneurs (Meltzer 2011; DEFRA 2014). The majority of takeaways in today's city are in fact independent operators or otherwise one of a number of competing smaller franchises – *Perfect Fried Chicken*, *Morley's* and *Chicken Cottage*. However, rather than operating in the prime retail units of the city's main high streets, as the original KFCs did, many of these newer outlets cluster in the city's poorer neighbourhoods and boroughs: Hounslow, Hackney, Tottenham, Barking and Stratford, Mile End's 'chicken mile', Lewisham's New Cross Road or Whitechapel Road, which, not counting the four on neighbouring Brick Lane, boasts at least seven outlets: *Whitechapel Fried Chicken*, *Kentucky Fried Chicken*, *Perfect Fried Chicken*, *Perfect Fried Chicken Plus*, *Royal Perfect Fried Chicken*, *Holy Fried Chicken*, *HFC* (*Halal Fried Chicken*) and *Ponchokhan*. This distribution is understandable, if only for the fact that the fried chicken takeaway offers, by far, one of the highest doses of calories for the least money in the city. Fried chicken is, in this respect, an archetypal Bourdieusian 'taste of necessity' (Bourdieu and Nice 1984: 177).

With such a density of outlets, the fried poultry connoisseur, ostensibly at least, has plenty to choose from. For all their differences (and more of these later), most outlets also share certain key characteristics. At a distance these similarities present themselves in the glossy confederate red, white and blue of the shop's plastic signage, the flickering pale green glare of strip lighting and the flaming orange, yellow and red of the steamy cardboard packaging clutched by their customers. Moving closer other similarities appear: a distinct odour, primarily that of crisping batter and herbs, carried on clouds of oil vapour; the cacophonous banter shared between patrons and the cashier. Closer still, the gustatory signatures emerge: salty, crispy, spiced batter, steamy, gullet-filling white flesh, tsunami's of syrupy coke and fistfuls of sharp, fried potato chips, spiked with sweet, vinegary ketchup, chilli sauce and/or mayonnaise. All these sensations, are integral to the 'sensory orders' of urban culture in which fried chicken plays such an evidently important part (Classen 1990; Geurts 2002; Howes 2006; Vannini, Waskul and Gottschalk 2011). Yet, as well established as the sensory signatures of the fried chicken takeaway are on London's high streets and corners, a taste for them is equalled, if not exceeded, by distaste. In fact distaste is perhaps too less of a word to describe the deep corporeal anxiety and disgust that, for some, is elicited by the sensoria of the fried chicken takeaway:

> You smell it before you see it. The sickly sweet and salty tang of deep-fried cheap chicken chunklets, emerging from a grease-stained box. You'll probably spy the packaging later, squashed under a bus stop, on your way home. Frequently it'll lie next to the remnants of that fried chicken, bathing, reconstituted by a drunken human stomach, in a pile of beer-based vomit (Tobin 2014).

Importantly, unlike many of the visceral gut reactions to specific sensoria – a life-long loathing of licorice or cardamon for instance – remarkably few of the *many* critical commentaries on fried chicken (Tobin 2014; Cloake 2015; Tweedie 2015) present their disgust as simply arbitrary. On the contrary, as was the case with the meat panics in the previous chapter, the gut-felt revulsion for fried chicken is readily justified with reference to a specific 'problem' with fried chicken. Much like the multi-faceted meaty 'moral panics' of the previous chapter there is, however, far more than simply one 'problem' pertaining to fried chicken. In fact, in the case of fried chicken, there are a truly remarkable number of discourses coalescing around the dish. The next part of this chapter comprises a movement through the assorted 'problems' accreting around the fried chicken takeaway (animal welfare, nutrition, deviant urban subcultures), dissecting the 'discursive or non-discursive practices' that bring various claims 'into the play of true and false' (Foucault in Rabinow and Rose 2003: 18). As you will see, picking through the bones of 'the fried chicken problem' reveals a great deal more than the construction of one-dimensional culinary folk-devil. Rather, it unearths the confluence of normative ideas about taste, identity and culture translated into visceral relationships with specific urban cultures and the neighbourhoods associated with them. In anatomizing the construction of this urban 'problem' the chapter provides a broader view of the role of 'sensibilties' and 'sensoria' within the processes of 'regeneration' sweeping across inner-London.

In the penultimate section of the chapter, we will also consider the sociologically significant roles performed by the fried chicken takeaway that are otherwise framed out in its problematization. As the chapter concludes, amongst all the other ingredients filling the pages of this book, the sensoria of the fried chicken shop are objects *par excellence* for understanding the contestations over the city's 'sense-scape' (Degen 2008) that are shaping the future of the city's culture and its communities.

The Problem of Industrial Agriculture

The saturation of the city with fried chicken takeaways is, without a doubt, a phenomenon specific to British urban areas. It has not occurred with anywhere near the same degree of intensity for instance in Paris, Berlin, Barcelona, Nicosia or Gothenberg, nor the other non-British European cities to which KFC expanded. Compared with the UK, even the US – from whence the dish *apparently* originates – has a sparsity of fried chicken takeaways. Moreover, while they are a regular feature in secondary and tertiary British cities, the relative density of fried chicken outlets is in fact, specific to London. It is, then, a conspicuously local issue. The viability of London's fried chicken outlets is, however, entirely related to a far more global trend: namely, the half-century long ascent of chicken from a smallholder's occasional meal, to a thrice weekly protein hit for any and every individual on earth, that can afford the astonishingly cheap avian carcass.

Domesticated chickens have been familiar to humans for millennia (Xiang et al. 2014). For most of that time, however, they were only ever raised in small numbers; kept around the farm to clean up any spilled grain and provide occasional eggs, but not worth farming in and of themselves. Not least this was because, despite domestication, they remained inefficient at converting grain into meat – three units of grain were required for every unit of meat produced (Boyd and Watts 1997; Boyd 2001). Moreover, as grain feeders, their profitability was tethered to the notoriously volatile price of grain. As such, they were generally too risky for the big farmer. Halfway into the twentieth century, however, the place of chicken within global food systems started to rapidly change. The changes start with the considerable investment the United States poured into agricultural research following crises in grain farming, urban migrations and the war-time demand for rationalized food production (Striffler 2007). The mid-century investment led to advances in automation, shelter, medicine and nutrition across a range of species and crops. Of the many outcomes of this investment was, in the 1920s, the egg that hatched the first 'broiler' hen. Fast to mature, easy to fatten, from the 1940s onwards the broiler's unique qualities have been refined time and time again. Where, in the 1920s, a single chicken used to take five months of intense feeding to raise to an edible size, at present it can take as little as five to six *weeks* to raise a chicken. At the same time, the amount of grain required to make the same amount of meat has halved (Striffler 2007: 43–52; Elfic 2008).

With the winds of mid-century advertising in its sails, perhaps unsurprisingly, the advances in North American production were matched by growth in consumption. In post-war Britain, the lifting of rations on chicken feed and the importation of America's intensive practices and breeding stock saw consumption leap from around one million chickens per annum before the war, to over two hundred million birds a year by 1967 (Godley and Williams 2007). More recently, consumption of chicken at home – leaving aside the last decades' explosive growth in takeaways – has increased again from 125g per person per week in 1974, to 213g per person per week in 2012 (DEFRA 2014).

The growing trend for poultry consumption is reflected worldwide, where, buoyed by a turn away from pork and beef in China, poultry is now set to overtake all other meats in 2017 as the world's primary source of meat (Leonard 2011). The vast majority of the hens that make up this mass will be broilers, whose ancestors hatched in the aforementioned mid-century intensification of American farming (Kim and Curry 1993; Goodman and Watts 1997: 140–141). More tellingly of the industry's centralized nature, 90 per cent of the chickens consumed on any given day in the UK are in fact descended from assiduously bred 'primary stock' of one of two companies (DEFRA 2006; Emmett 2013). Rationalized, centralized and mass produced, chicken is *the* modern, industrial meat.

It is in light of the intensive rationalization of its production that we find the first of the 'problems' pertaining to fried chicken: because of the extent to which its production exemplifies the massification of meat, poultry production has become something of a totemic issue for a coalition of individuals and institutions pitted against industrialized agriculture and the food cultures it has afforded. Although generally overlapping in their concerns, within the coalition's assorted narratives are also a number of distinct sub-discourses. Of particular note, given our concerns, is a distinctly 'animal-centred' sub-discourse that takes as its key 'problem' agro-industry's tendency to ignore the sentience of animals. Not exactly a new argument, early modern discussion of animal sentience and the ethics of meat production emerged in the work of Jeremy Bentham (Duncan 2006). Twenty-first-century iterations of this discourse, however, can be traced back to Ruth Harrison's 1964 classic *Animal Machines* (Harrison 1964), in which the author railed precisely against the newly rationalized poultry industry.

The 'problem', then, of poultry sentience is as old as the poultry industry itself. Nonetheless, in recent years the discourse and its associated activism have seen a resurgence grounded in a raft of empirical studies that have made animal consciousness, and thus animals' proximity to humanity, properly visible (Williams 2004; Dawkins 2006; Duncan 2006; Spencer et al. 2006; Boissy et al. 2007; Norwood and Lusk 2011; Proctor, Carder and Cornish 2013). While the studies themselves have been as (in)accessible as most academic outputs, general discussion of animal ethics have percolated into popular consciousness through a number of outlets in the mainstream press and television. Notably these include a series of articles by *The Guardian*'s George Monbiot (Monbiot 2014, 2015), an entire television series about factory farming chickens by Hugh Fearnley-Whittingstall (Fearnley-Whittingstall 2003; Channel 4 2008) and 2014's best-selling airport book, *Farmageddon* (Lymbery 2014). Central to each iteration of the anti-factory-farming/pro-chicken discourse is the presentation of specific facts: that factory-farmed chickens live unnaturally short lives at a highly accelerated rate; that they are 'cooped up', partitioned from others and often without daylight; that they have their eyes blinkered, their beaks mechanically mutilated and their bodies regularly flushed with antibiotics. A chicken's lot in life, the message suggests, would be significantly improved were we not to expect a fried chicken meal to cost less than a loaf of bread. Such stories are not ineffectual. Rather, vivid and emotive stories such as these about factory farming deliberately engage the senses so as to lodge the message in the audience's viscera. As such, while the smell of fried chicken might not be intrinsically revolting, those receptive to such stories might have a gag-reflex primed for their next encounter with the aura of a fried chicken takeaway.

The Problem of Dirty Chicken

Also reaching a degree of public prominence in 2014 was a far more anthropocentric set of problems regarding the agro-industrial production of poultry. These erupted into public consciousness when *The Guardian* (again) published a viral-friendly five-minute video exposé of industrial chicken farming practices (Lawrence, Wasley and Ciorniciuc 2014). The aforementioned intensive farming techniques – required to ensure chickens remained cheap and abundant – played a central role in this exposé. However, before the short documentary got to the familiar, grainy, waist-height secret-filming of animal brutality, it confronted the viewer with a less familiar image: a slowly rotating electron microscopy slide featuring a single bacterial cell. As a result of intensive farming, the viewer is told, this toxic bacterium (campylobacter) coats over two-thirds of shop-bought British chicken carcasses (Lawrence, Wasley and Ciorniciuc 2014). Utilizing an assemblage of scientific imaging techniques, academic discourse and affective media practices, the journalists had – as they had with animal sentience – given visibility to an otherwise imperceptible problem (Loon in Adam, Beck and Van Loon 2000: 275–276). As with the 'animal-centred' condemnation of factory farming above, what became known as the '*campylobacter* scare' shone a further light on perilously intensive industrial agricultural and a lack of sufficient oversight. In this instance, however, the problem was introduced and concluded, in terms of an explicitly anthropocentric 'risk to humans' health'. Perhaps more acutely potent than the already-established discourses pertaining to animal welfare, the story effectuated short-term changes in behaviour, briefly reducing chicken sales by seven per cent.

The mainstream critiques of intensive farming offered in *Farmageddon*, or as part of the '*campylobacter* scare', generally fell a long way short of urging a halt to meat consumption. Rather, they had the more pragmatic – and markedly more profitable – aims of elaborating norms for acceptably 'happy' meat. Through mobilizing an assortment of indignation, empathy and shame, the narratives aim, not to wipe chicken off the menu, but instead to put organic and free-range chicken on the centre plate. As part of the crowning of a new poultry hierarchy, intensively farmed cheap chicken is simultaneously relabelled as a biological risk, but also as morally repugnant and, as such, both a physical and moral danger to society. In fact we might say, leaning on Mary Douglas (2002), that the structure of these stories about chicken serves to construct what we might refer to as 'dirty chicken', a form of meat that has no place in normative notions of propriety and which, as such, ought to be repelled by right-minded bodies. Indeed, the headline of *The Guardian*'s initial revelation of *campylobacter*'s ubiquity was 'The *dirty* secrets of Britain's poultry industry' (Lawrence, Wasley and Ciorniciuc 2014, emphasis added).

Yet, despite the clear public concerns regarding the poultry industry, the everyday crusade around chicken has barely touched the home-cooked roast or quick evening stir-fry. And while there was a drop in general sales of chicken during the *campylobacter* scare, chicken consumption continues to grow. Even at the time of the *campylobacter* scare, in contrast to BSE or foot and mouth scares, the official advice was – and remains – to carry on buying industrial meat. The key advice offered was simply to avoid washing it (Food Standards Agency 2014; Hicks 2014; Smithers 2014). Instances of food poisoning were being caused, it was argued, only when laudably risk-conscious consumers placed their dirty meat under a running tap, inadvertently spraying the toxic residues of industrialized slaughter over their kitchens. Cheap chicken was not, then, irredeemably 'dirty' chicken. It could be cleaned, ironically, by not cleaning it. For some, as we will see, dirty chicken only really becomes resolutely dirty, when it is fried and served from an inner-city takeaway.

> Ha, dirty chicken is slang . . . maybe it's only slang in London, I don't know. It's how we describe takeaway fried chicken that really shouldn't be classified as food. Just think of KFC if it were 1,000 times worse (Kdragonwon 2013).

> The new 'Il Grillo' restaurant is a lovely addition to the area which I just don't think another dirty chicken shop (or whatever it would be) could ever be (Sockmonkey 2012).

> I've succumbed to the dirty chicken shop on a drunken night out and it's not a good thing (Rayner 2013).

It is entirely plausible, even likely, that in the mind's-eye of the speakers quoted above, the *dirty-ness* of chicken is derived from the abject treatment of animals and/or the equally abject bacteria that industrialized poultry spawns. Campaigns about intensive farming and meat scandals are a common feature of popular media in Britain and are firmly lodged in public consciousness. And nowhere is the likely ill treatment and general riskiness of chicken more obvious than when contemplating the economics of producing eight undernourished poultry wings for two pounds.

In the takeaway shop, however, it seems that there is a range of additional factors, beyond the 'un-ethical' and 'risky' features of the raw meat, compounding its dirtiness so as to determine the dish's popular nickname. Not least of the additional factors over-determining the dirtiness of fried chicken is, of course, the fact that this meat is cooked in what has become popularly known as the least healthy way possible: deep frying (Swinburn and Egger 2002; Soriguer et al. 2003; Guallar-Castillón et al. 2007; Schlosser 2012; Moss 2013). As opposed to the apparently acute risk revealed through visualization of bacteria, the dangers of frying seem to lie in the more chronic risks lazily associated with fried foods. Lazily because, despite ongoing disputes as to the actual causal relationship, bi-variate correlations between chronic obesity and the consumption of high-energy takeaway food form the back bone of formal nutritional discourses in the UK (Fraser and Edwards 2010). With the cooking method even referenced in the name of the dish, it is impossible that the majority of those that would use the term 'dirty chicken' are unaware of this determinant of fried chicken's 'dirtiness'. For some individuals the fried nature of the dish, doubtless, goes a long way to explaining the visceral revulsion they feel around the oily odours of its preparation.

Beyond shaping the ways individuals make sense of the dish, the 'obesity angle' also has the most notable impact on the ways in which state apparatus seem to 'make sense' of the hot-food takeaway; while the last three decades have seen the British government devolve a number of its erstwhile duties to private service providers, the state has begrudgingly retained part of its twentieth-century responsibility for the surveillance and maintenance of a physically healthy population. This has assured that, even if they are not fit to be mobilized for war (Foucault 1999), a sufficient number are able to get out of bed and to compete for work. Which is to say that, for the government, in the wake of studies correlating hot-food takeaway consumption with obesity, the problem of fried chicken is approached as a problem of working days lost and tax-payer funded healthcare spending (National Obesity Observatory 2010). That is not to say that animal welfare and agro-industry are not raised as issues in Parliament (Animal Welfare Act 2006; Treaty of Lisbon 2007: Article 13 Title II). But it is to say that these issues pale in significance when compared with the thought, talk and effort that goes into measuring and mitigating the growth of the nation's waistlines.

Despite recent discussion of a 'sugar tax' and 'takeaway taxes', for the main part, central government's efforts have shied away from restricting availability of 'unhealthy' food. Instead they have worked both with the NHS, and incentivized partnerships with the private sector, to endow the public with better knowledge with which to navigate the 'obesotgenic environment' (Swinburn, Egger and Raza 1999). Alongside public sector programs, the bio-pedagogues of the 'obesity epidemic' (Wright and Harwood 2012) have included arts agencies, private nutritionists, television presenters, behaviour change consultants, community groups and fast food producers (Powell and Gard 2014).

Amongst the other unlikely ranks of professionals, newly tasked with policing the spatial production of the nation's girth were its municipal planning departments. Starting in 2005, local planning departments have gradually honed a number of techniques with which to try and curb the continuing growth of takeaway outlets in British cities. For instance, in the British planning system the city recognizes two types of hot food outlet, the 'A3 use class' and the 'A5 use class'. A3 usage signals to interested parties that the ventilation systems, required separately by health and safety law, have been installed at a sufficient height and location so as the odours of cooking do not bother neighbours. Ostensibly, A5 premises are subject to the same requirements, with the additional proviso that the majority of the customers should eat their food off-premises. More recently, however, a number of London's inner-city councils have developed supplementary planning guidance that specifically restricts the presence of A5 class buildings around 'sensitive areas'. As outlined in the guidance, 'sensitive areas' refers primarily to secondary schools, whose pupils were revealed, through statistical correlation, to be suffering from ill-health, seemingly from the fast food sold cheaply around the school gates (Bagwell 2011; Ross and Consultancy 2013; Burgoine et al. 2014). The legislation has since been used on a number of occasions to thwart efforts to open hot food takeaways around one of these 'sensitive areas'.

The aforementioned correlation between fried chicken clusters and poverty, however, has consequences for the ubiquitous and achingly naive 'hot food takeaways = morbidity' hypotheses upon which the aforementioned interventions are based. Not least of these consequences is the fact that there are necessarily many intervening variables – coextensive with the deprivation of which cheap chicken is a part – that might be injurious to young people's heath. These include overcrowding, noise pollution, long parental working hours, housing insecurity, heightened stress levels and educational difficulties. That is, of course, without even considering the assortment of other injurious food and drinks stuffs available to those on a low income. Moreover, in such contexts, there may be a number of factors – manual work, sporty lifestyles, periodic fasting – that go a long way to mitigating the specific impact of hot food takeaways on to the general population.

Concerned with assumptions that increasingly inform urban policy, a recent systematic review of studies of proximity to hot food takeaways and childhood morbidity 'did not find strong evidence at this time to justify policies related to regulating the food environments around schools' (Williams et al. 2014). Yet it is also clear that, evidence-based or not, the exclusion of fried chicken takeaways has a degree of popular support. Moreover, with such public support, the policing of fried chicken shops also serves a wide range of additional uses to London's inner-city boroughs, far beyond 'protecting the health of young people'.

The Problem of Poverty's Odour

The additional uses to which restrictions on hot food takeaways can be put become clear when viewing local authorities' discussions of fried chicken takeaways in strategic planning documents, or surveying their more vocal residents' contributions to public planning consultations. Evidently, to local and national government, of additional significance to the actual health problems associated with fried chicken are a range of perceived economic, social and cultural 'impacts' that fried chicken takeaways have on the urban environment. Consider, for instance, the excerpts below, extracted from reports published by the London Borough of Hackney:

> Compared to other retail uses, an over-concentration or clustering of HFTs [hot food takeaways] are likely to have a detrimental impact on amenity and on the retail character and function of a shopping centre. Such harmful impacts relate to increased incidence of litter, smells, crime and anti-social behaviour, noise and general disturbance, parking and traffic problems. Where concentrations occur in our town centres, they can pose a serious threat to the local economic vitality and viability (Hesketh 2014).

> For years, fried chicken shops and burger bars, pound shops and cheap clothing stores have dominated the main shopping area along Kingsland High Street, especially the part close to Kingsland (formerly Dalston Cross) Shopping Centre. [...] In 2009, Italian *Vogue* described Dalston as the trendiest, coolest neighbourhood in London and the young and fashionable of East London [...] are changing the shop scene of Kingsland High Street from a 'traditional' lively Victorian high street to something more eclectic and dynamic (Hackney Council 2015).

> Yes to more places to eat & drink but only small sole traders or places like puji puji, organic/free trade, café Otto etc. Enough fried chicken/junk food restaurants (Laura Williams in Hackney Council 2009).

Precisely because of their clear entanglement within the ecologies of deprived neighbourhoods, the fried chicken takeaway is routinely credited with sustaining a wide range of behaviour negatively associated with working class inner-city 'culture'.

Alongside pound shops, betting shops and loan operators, chicken shops are clearly equated – by an assortment of influential urban actors – with a distinct (im)moral quality; a 'seediness' that signals the increasingly degraded quality of inner-city lives (Tweedie 2015). Payday loan operators and betting shops, however, are a high-street nuisance mentioned not nearly so often as the fried chicken takeaway. This, it would seem, is in part because a sensory encounter with them is never as literally visceral as an encounter with a hot-food takeaway. That is, pawnbrokers and bookies do not speak directly to the literal sense of taste. As Deborah Lupton summarizes, across society, it is 'distinctions of taste' that are amongst the most 'frequently employed as ways of denigrating other social classes' (Lupton 1996).

Contrary to an etymological understanding of 'distaste' or disgust, however, it is not the literal 'taste' of fried chicken that agitates London's inner-city councils and residents. Rather, it is the smell. As Constance Classen (1992: 134) notes, perhaps even more so than taste, 'the odour of the other' also 'serves as a scapegoat for certain antipathies toward the other for whom [. . .] an animosity [is felt] for unrelated reasons.' And, doubtless, the smell of the fried chicken takeaway is powerful. The cooking process involves the evaporation of a wide range of intense volatiles which are carried on hot plumes and pumped out of ventilation units. And, by virtue of the 'open air' of cities – the flow of bodies, vehicles and breezes through its streets – the smell spreads. For some, the odour is a seductive wink inviting them in for a lunch-time snack. For a many more, however, the smell provides a vector for a reservoir of negative feelings – nurtured through family, community, media and state – for London's working class cultures.

Olfactory class antagonisms are, of course, nothing new. As George Orwell noted in the mid twentieth century, 'the real secret of class distinctions in the West [. . .] is summed up in four frightful words [. . .]. The lower classes smell.' (Orwell 1958). From Henry Mayhew's accounts of the wretched stench of herring emanating from the homes of the poor of London (Mayhew 1861: 64), through the bacon-like reek of Orwell's Wigan Pier, to the anxiety around the smell of chips recorded in Charles and Kerr's *Women, Food and Families* (Charles and Kerr 1988: 192), particular food smells have long been associated with the less affluent communities and neighbourhoods. But as these examples suggest, the relationship between olfactory markers and working-class cultures is more than one of neutral association. Rather, by way of association with social classes constructed as morally and culturally abject, the smells of fried chicken, like herring or fish and chips before it, are also viscerally reviled.

Perhaps this is unsurprising. The body's disgust mechanism indisputably exists, in the first instance, to enable us to identify, by way of association, things that might be injurious to it (Ridley 2004; Kelly 2011). And certainly there are elements of all the historically reviled foods listed above (except perhaps herring – so nutritious) that have been revealed to be potentially injurious. However, from erstwhile medieval moralities to miasma theories of biological risk and Protestant puritanism, it has never simply been the mere biological body that is protected through the disgust mechanism. Rather, the disgust response – 'revulsion [. . .] nausea [. . .] gaping facial expression [. . .] retching' (Kelly 2011) – has also consistently served to police the boundaries of the specific forms of culture, morality and sociality that live through the body (Rhys-Taylor 2013b). In this respect, disgust does far more than police against toxic miasma. Rather, disgust works in conjunction with specific forms of knowledge and ideology to coordinate the formation of specific subjectivities and dispositions (Kelly 2011: 6).

Orwell's point, then, was not that it is the working classes alone that smell. The point was that the stratification of British society was upheld, partly, by the manner in which wealthier socio-economic classes ascribed an intrinsic and immoral wretchedness to the 'stench' of the working classes. To paraphrase Julia Kristeva, abject smells are the primers of class culture (Kristeva 1982). Despite the waning of these earlier markers of olfactory distinction, the pertinence of smell in British social structures clearly continues. Indeed, quietly identifying and denigrating 'bad smells' remains a central mechanism through which the power differentials of London's socio-economic class structure are expressed and spatialized. This becomes all the more clear when considering the efforts of inner London's poorer boroughs to bate the elite sharks of transnational finance circling the city's margins by tweaking the area's 'sense-scape' (Degen 2008).

Race (Over There)

Increasingly, the fried chicken takeaway offers both London's urban technocrats and its majoritarian public a shorthand reference to a problematic inner-city working-class culture. As we will see, inextricable from that set of associations, are the ways in which the polyglot working-class culture of Britain's major cities is approached as a 'problem' of race and ethnicity. This, however, is far from the first time in the history of fried chicken that the dish has become entangled in an assemblage of disgust, oppression and racialized social stratification. Rather, as the next few paragraphs' brief trip across the Atlantic demonstrate, fried chicken has, for at least a century, been one of the most potent symbols of race, racism and anti-racism in the United States.

Arriving in the Americas by way of either Scottish settlers of the Apalachians (Mariani 2013: 305–306), English 'tidewater settlers' of Virginia (Fischer 1989: 351; Randolph 2004) or West African slaves (Opie 2013: 11, 18), fried chicken is intimately associated with the unique culture of North America's southern states. Regardless of who introduced the fried bird to the continent, what *is* clear is that for much of its early history it was probably African women and their descendants that would have been cooking and adapting the dish (McWilliams 2012: 88–89). It was certainly women descended from slaves that are first recorded as pioneering fried chicken as a purchasable, mobile meal. It is, in fact, one particular woman, in Gordonstown, Virginia, who is credited with first vending fried chicken – in the days before dining cars – to passengers through the open windows of trains (Woodson 1990: 119). Once dining cars were introduced, fried chicken, easy to transport and eat on the go, was also purportedly a favoured meal for black Americans otherwise banned from the dining car (Mitchell 2009: 18).

These early entrepreneurial efforts are no doubt part of what tethered fried chicken to African-American culture. Such practices, however, evolved in tandem with a compendium of myths and accusations that circulated Jim Crow south about black Americans' inherent propensity to steal poultry from their white masters. Lynchings were, in fact, routinely justified by their perpetrators following allegations of chicken theft (Smith and Walton 1899: 32; Ginzburg 1962: 93; Harrison and Perry 2001: 32). Perhaps most significantly, fried chicken itself featured prominently in D. W. Griffith's seminal 'white power' film, *Birth of a Nation* (Griffith 1915). There, in a carefully staged shot, the camera pans over a city hall full of black Americans, laughing, with their bare feet lounging on the desks. Finally, the camera comes to rest on a one particular man who is standing and laughing while chewing on a drumstick of fried chicken clutched in his fist. Above all the other ugly tropes deployed in Griffith's film, a black man eating chicken with his hands in a place of work offered a particularly effective shortcut to his intended viewer's sense of propriety and ethnic protectiveness. The unpropitious consumption of fried chicken was integral to how race was constructed to be, more than a visibly self-evident category, felt in the pit of the stomach.

In the 1920s the racist stereotype was set in concrete by a chain of US restaurants operating under the name 'Coon Chicken Inn' (Williams-Forson 2006: 66), wherein customers entered the restaurant through the gaping mouth of a cartoon minstrel. With its road-side restaurants, Coon Chicken Inn spread fried chicken – and associated racist stereotypes signified by fried chicken – from sea to shining sea. Coon Chicken Inn did not, however, survive the groundswell of sentiment that led to the civil rights movement. Accordingly, it was instead under the banner of a bearded southern colonel that, by the 1950s, fried chicken franchises finally reached over six hundred roadside restaurants across the country (Jakle and Sculle 1999: 220). It was at this point that the dish was first exported overseas to London.

If the racist connotations of fried chicken did not fully translate over to the arrival of KFC in London, they nevertheless endured in the US, albeit in the absence of 'Coon Chicken Inn'. Responding to both the stereotypes associated with, and the increasing appropriation of black-American culture by new international brands, a number of middle-class black writers and cooks sought to reclaim fried chicken as part of the African-American repertoire of 'soul food': meals originally associated with Sunday prayer but reworked into a secular refuge against the era's abundant racism (Callahan 1969; Jackson 1978; Wallach 2015: 85–86). Such positive assertions of ownership inevitably walked a tightrope between reworking identity *against* white representations of black culture, and, as the Nation of Islam put it, tying black Americans to their slave past (Witt 1999: 102–126; Rouse and Hoskins 2004).

Despite the continued all-round growth of chicken consumption throughout *all* sectors of the US in the 1980s and the 1990s, fried chicken is still intimately associated with the ways in which race is not simply seen, but also smelled and tasted in America today. And as such, it is subject to the panoply of meanings ascribed to race, and deeply entwined within the heated racial politics of the continent. Eating fried chicken in public has, as a consequence, become something of a touchstone in renewed debates about black American identity. In recent years several figureheads of contemporary black American culture have spoken explicitly and poignantly about the anxiety they feel eating fried chicken, especially around white people (Chappelle 2012; Anderson 2015). At the same time, activist and scholar Cornell West refers to eating fried chicken as practice of resistance, refusing 'to curtail [his] life because of a fear of the white gaze'. Unsurprisingly, then, when in 2009 Mohammad Jabbar changed the name of his Brooklyn restaurant to 'Obama Fried Chicken' – a moment of naive enthusiasm for the newly elected President – he became the burning hot focus of public attention (Fahim 2009).

The Problem of Race (Over Here)

In the US, the abjection of fried chicken pertains to the specific histories of slavery, segregation and enduring racism that, while being forged out of transatlantic traffic, are also specific to the ways in which racial categories are constructed, seen, smelled and ascribed meaning on that side of the Atlantic. While it is true that fried chicken in the UK is ostensibly a North American import, it is not clear that its racial connotations and related abjection have been imported quite so straightforwardly.

That is not to say that xenophobia has no role in the discourses mobilized against the assorted fried chicken franchises lining London's high streets. Anti-Americanism, for instance, once had a firm hold over the ways in which many Britons saw the world beyond their western shores (Rubin and Rubin 2004). Yet, if it was routinely portrayed as the lesser nation in the century before, by the second half of the twentieth century the United States was routinely, if begrudgingly, refigured as Europe's saviour. Any anti-Americanism that endured into the second half of the twentieth century has largely been shrugged off by scholars as petty jealousy that emerged as part of the Second World War: 'Oversexed, overpaid and over here' (O'Connor and Griffiths 2007). But it is also true that, entangled within early twentieth-century British anxieties about the 'vulgarity', 'flashiness and 'degeneracy' of American culture, were the residual ideas pertaining to the simultaneously cultural and biological dangers of the 'melting pot'. Consider post-war anxiety around teddy boys in zoot suits, tapping their feet to the blues-meets-gospel of rock 'n' roll (Hebdige 1979; Hoggart 1998). Or likewise, consider the moral panics about the purported arrival of subcultural practices such as 'mugging' from the 'new world' into British inner-cities (Hall et al. 1978). Or more recently, the moral panic that has surrounded London's purported 'gang' culture (Alexander 2000). In each instance, the problem of imported American culture, is also – if only implicitly – a problematization of black American culture.

Conversely, however, in a cultural context removed from the North American realities of race, the dish's associations with black American culture have also helped market fried chicken to mainstream consumers. An early millennial advertising campaign for Kentucky Fried Chicken, for instance, featured five or six young white adult men, and one overtly sexualised black woman pouting in a bikini between bites of 'tender strips of meat'. Over a northern soul soundtrack, the print on the screen explained to viewers, 'No need for knives and forks . . . [remember Birth of a Nation] Got chicken, Got soul!' (Gill and Scott 2003; Gill, Brown and Fox 2003).

Making the racial significance of fried chicken all but explicit is likely a lucrative tactic. From the early days of rock 'n' roll and zoot suits, to today's footwear, fashions, slang and popular music, fragments of black-American culture have regularly found fertile soil in the assorted lives of young Britons (Seeley 1967; Schou 1992; Horn 2009). This is true across the board of British youth. However, as we will discuss in the final stages of this chapter, the codes and symbols of urban cultures from across the Atlantic have found a particular importance in the lives of those who have grown up in inner-city contexts transformed by post-colonial migration. And herein lies the final, and perhaps definitive, aspect of the problematization of fried chicken in the UK; not that it is an American import, or that it is a black American import, but rather that it nourishes the culture of twenty-first century Britain's most abject of social groups: low income *multicultural* inner-city youth.

Explicit anxieties about the ethnic mix of inner-city London can be traced back to at least the early nineteenth century, wherein the racial features of London's East End were first problematized by eugenicists and philanthropists as a potential obstacle to national prosperity and wealth. Therein the likes of Charles Booth and Beatrice Webb mapped degrees of poverty onto the Jewishness and Irishness of the East End (Gidley 1997). At the same time their peer Francis Galton advocated the sterilization of the inner-city's inhabitants, lest their biology and culture unsettle social order and jeopardize future prosperity (Galton 1883: 198–220). To this day, as Imogen Tyler reveals in her dissection of London's 2011 riots, amongst the most politically influential problematizations of the inner city are still those that are, at the very bottom, eugenic framings of a mongrel 'race' of youthful miscreants (Hall et al. 1978; Tyler 2013: 188–189). Take, for instance, the infamous remarks made by historian David Starkey following the riots that spread across London's high streets in 2011. For Starkey, one of the most prominent of the UK's historians, the roots of the disorder that swept through British cities following the police killing of a young man, could be traced back to fact that the working class of the inner city had 'become black', at least in terms of 'culture' if '[. . .] not skin colour' (Newsnight 2011). That is, he was arguing that the reason inner-city youth were rioting was because they had adopted the culture of a 'people' that he quite openly saw, and referred to as, inherently degenerate. His comments were far from outrightly condemned. Rather, as Tyler argues, the abjection of inner-city youth culture – with its mix of Caribbean, Arabic, African and American cadence, with its use of the aesthetic codes of black Americana – is widespread, and echoed by politicians and right-wing media commentators alike.

Not only, however, is this problematization of the racialized inner city widespread. It is also integral to the economic model on which the financial security and growth of London's economy is based. Therein the public abjection of a racialized inner-city youth culture serves three key purposes: first, it garners the hegemonic consent for the retractions of welfare (Jones 2012; Rodger 2012; Hancock and Mooney 2013; Tyler 2013; Cree, Clapton and Smith 2015). Second – as we saw in the wake of the London riots – it justifies the use of authoritarian tools to impose hegemonic forms of propriety at times of crisis (Briggs, Heap and Smithson 2012; Roberts and Hough 2013). And third, and perhaps most importantly, the abjection of the inner-city youth has served to justify the displacement of bodies for the private purposes of extracting capital from potentially lucrative land (Tyler 2013). This last point is particularly important with regards to the fried chicken shop. For, while inner-city signs of 'diversity', 'vibrancy' and 'dynamism' help marketing professionals to sell new blocks of luxury apartments to cosmopolitan omnivores, the actual sights, sounds and smells of cultures cooked up amidst poverty, are often way beyond the limits of a transnational elite's ideas of omnivorousness. Indeed, in their recent refusals of applications for hot food takeaways, London borough's have started explicitly citing 'place making', 'transforming local character' and 'quality urban design' (London Borough of Newham 2012: 92, 95; London Borough of Newham 2013). Sequestered in all of these concepts, is often an implicitly racialized understanding of what the 'good city' and 'good urban culture' looks, sounds and smells like.

What's Your Problem, Bruv?

Junior Spesh, 7up, fried legs
Make sure you gimmie mayonnaise on the left
If ya ain't got 7-up then I want Dr. Pep
Ain't got what I want then I go HF
Feelin' rich then I go KF
Gimmie Jaxor, then I want side breast
Make sure you gimmie chips forks and pep. (Pep-ahhhh!)
Junior Spesh (One fifty)
With a bite or a side-breast. (Two pounds)
How much is the breast? (I don't know)
All mayonnaise on the left. (Twenty Pence)
Chicken in a bun! (One sixty)
(Red Hot Entertainment (Ft. Jaxor, Klayze Flaymz, Ray & Terra) –
    Junior Spesh 2007)

There is certainly no denying that fried chicken is massively popular with young people living in densely populated, historically poorer and thoroughly multicultural parts of London. Of course, the price of chicken plays a part in securing this food's popularity amongst this demographic. As we have already established chicken meat is ridiculously cheap. It is tempting, then, to write off the popularity of the fried chicken takeaway, as the orthodox Bourdieusian might, as being its offer of the most calories for the least money possible. Taken by itself, however, this explanation, is unsatisfactory. Not least because clearly, the fried chicken shop has achieved a revered cultural status amongst a sea of equally cheap calories. And while independent chicken franchises also sell an assortment of additional kebabs, fish and chips or pizza, the common denominator is nearly always fried chicken (Bagwell 2011: 6). What precisely, then, might lie behind the unparalleled popularity of quick fried poultry?

Casting aside the stifling analyses of economic rationality, one of the more obvious reasons that fried chicken outsells other dishes in its socioeconomic niche is because it is very tasty. A portion of fried chicken thigh or drumstick with wings, for instance, offers a unique combination of saltiness, sweetness, heat, spice, crunch and chew. All of these qualities are also enhanced by the fattiness of the dish, which increases the crunch while spreading the heat and savoury flavours around the mouth. The dish is also highly amenable to customization, with an assortment of sauces, of various piquancy, sweetness and flavour, offered at even the most basic of fried chicken takeaways. This obvious and literal 'tastiness' clearly sits alongside price at the heart of the dishes demographic gravity. Moving beyond the raw sensory qualities of the dish we might consider the cultural value ascribed to *mise en scène* of the actual fried chicken takeaway. It is here, in the social and cultural roles of the setting of the fried chicken takeaway itself – roles otherwise framed out by a narrow economic and nutritional focus on the food – that perhaps the most significant value of the fried chicken takeaway resides.

As part of a 2015 project conducted by the Mile End Community Project, a group of young people from one of the largest social housing estates in Tower Hamlets worked with youth leaders and media technicians to produce a series of films about the things in their lives that mattered to them. Under the label 'HoodForts' ('thoughts about their neighbourhood') the young people's aim was to produce a document explaining issues about which they felt there was widespread misunderstanding. After much debate as to which of the myriad issues bisecting their lives they would talk about – drugs, religious extremism, gangs – the young people finally landed on a topic that mattered to them all: the fried chicken takeaway (Islam 2015). In a great many respects the film, which was co-produced by, edited and starring the young people of inner-city London, offers a remarkable insight into the value of these spaces to their users.

Featuring a broad range of the area's residents, including a mixture of young people, parents and elderly Eastenders, the film revolved around a series of vox-pops, spliced with footage of sauce drizzling over portions of chicken or young men boisterously socializing in the chicken shop. Within the vox-pops, the viewer is presented with a wide range of rationales for each individual's choice of chicken for their meal. Unsurprisingly, price is mentioned several times. The young people 'aren't earning any money, so

they want to save as much as they can of what their parents give them'
(Alamin in Islam 2015), while Mohammed notes that while the cost of
everything else has gone up, you can still always afford chicken. 'It's like free
food,' concludes Aisha. Tastiness also evidently plays its part, with almost
every interviewee on film expressing the enjoyment they find in eating the
meal. The reliability of the product – a legacy of the dishes twentieth-century
Fordist refinement – is also mentioned by a pair of young women interviewed
for the film.

Most significantly, however, for a number of respondents featured in the
film, the key attraction of the fried chicken takeaway had less to do with the
dish itself. Rather, it lay almost entirely in the social setting of the takeaway.
According to Aisha, 'it's more than just a chicken shop, it's some people's
second home'. More than a home, it is a village square. That is to say, the
atmosphere of the chicken shop convenes a unique assemblage of
associations, affinities, romances and occasionally conflict. As one of the
young people in the video notes, 'PFC [Perfect Fried Chicken] is a very
warm place, it's safe, especially in wintertime when it gets dark very early
[. . .] you go there with your mates [. . .] you go there as long as you want
and you won't get kicked out[. . .] it's a friendly atmosphere, like your local.'

Therein it is not just the taste of chicken that draws people in, but also
the white light, the literal warmth and the more abstract 'social heat' (Chau
2008; Steinmüller 2011) that the takeaway affords. As Mahdi notes, 'Very
rarely does anyone go to PFC by themselves, it's always two members at
least . . .'. Significantly, the relationships incubated by the fried chicken
takeaway are far from mono-ethnic. Rather, they develop across ethnicity
and in some places, gender, class and generation, both through explicit ties
between individuals, and the tacit affinities developed through sharing 'food,
time and space' (Jones et al. 2015). 'At PFC,' Samad concludes, 'I feel part of
a society' (Islam 2015).

Making a similar observation, another interviewee, Iftekahn, compares the
role of the independent fried chicken takeaway to that of the 'Englishman's
pub'. This is a particularly insightful and instructive analogy in more ways
than one. Both the pub and the fried chicken takeaway are, for instance, social
spaces, wherein both the economy and sociality is sustained by acts of
consumption that are nonetheless increasingly framed as 'bad for you'. Yet
there are crucial differences between how these institutions are perceived
by the city's most powerful agents. For instance, where alcohol is widely
recognized as being addictive and associated with anti-social behaviour, the
'atmosphere' of the pub is now, as a consequence of 'The Localism Act 2011',
formally recognized as nurturing important forms of association and mutual
support integral to 'healthy communities'. As a result, a number of pubs
threatened with re-development in London, starting first and famously with
the Ivy in Peckham (Miller 2013), have recently been granted protected status
as 'assets of community value'. On the other hand, as we have already
discussed, the only supplementary guidance on fried chicken shops pertains to
their prevention and closure.

In its widespread stigmatization, the chicken takeaway bears less of an empirical resemblance to the 'Englishman's pub' than it does to the 'commercial recreational' institutions studied by the second wave of Chicago School scholars – the bowling alley in William Foote Whyte's 'Cornerville' (Whyte 1993), Paul G. Cressey's Taxi Dancehall (Cressey 2008) or even Becker's jazz clubs (Becker 1963). In each instance the institutions, widely derided from the outside as degenerate, were described by the ethnographers as having their own rich symbolic systems, languages and social structures. Likewise, more than simply 'a space of association' the fried chicken takeaway has also its own distinct culture, complete with vernacular and specific practices. For instance, as the young people in the HoodForts video discuss, it is customary in East London to refer and greet the server behind the counter as 'bossman', to which he responds by calling the customer 'bossman' or 'bigman'. In fried chicken shops, aside from the relationships that develop between customers, it is also entirely common to see young people learning to barter and hustle the cashiers who, in return, play their own games of jocular give and take. Transplanting the 'emic' analytical frames of the Chicago ethnographers to the chicken shop would go a long way to revealing the variety, and the incredible complexity and meaning of the everyday rituals that play out over its disinfected tiles. Where they would arguably fall short, however, is in fully unpacking the ways in which these institutions were shaped in relation to wider social, cultural and economic processes.

British Cultural Studies, on the other hand, brims with efforts to locate youth subculture within the broader shifts in urban economy and demography. Within this tradition, an assortment of studies of inner-city subcultures (Clarke and Jefferson 1973; Hebdige 1979; Hall 1990; Cohen 1997) and their 'rituals of resistance' (Hall and Jefferson 1993) have shown the linguistic and aesthetic codes, crafted and adopted by young people, as intrinsically related to the political economy of urban life. More precisely, British cultural studies have presented youth subcultures as constructed both within, and importantly *against*, normative ideals expounded through the media, family and state apparatus of a post-colonial city. In such contexts, as Angela McRobbie notes with regards to 'the hoodie', signifiers of a marginalized black-Americana act as 'a socially cohesive force that unified young people' (McRobbie in Braddock 2011). For those second-, third- and fourth-generation descendants of London's mid-twentieth-century migrants, living through the roll-back of welfare and roll-out of surveillance, the fried chicken shop is an equally unifying resource. That is to say, it is one of several institutions, replete with its own sensoria, symbols, codes and social conventions, through which inhospitable social landscapes and unnavigable cultural mazes, become habitable and navigable.

This is not to say, however, that young people are unaware of the ways in which mainstream society positions both fried chicken shops, and their patrons as 'abject'. On the contrary, such anxieties might, in part, help explain the heightened symbolic value of the chicken shop to London's inner-city youth. As the parent of any teenager knows, young people can find it emotionally and socially risky to be seen to be interested in healthy eating (Jeffery and French 1998; French et al. 2001; Bowman et al. 2004; Maddock 2004). At the same time, explicitly 'not caring' about normative ideals – or as Howard Becker (Becker 1963) once put it, 'being hip' rather than 'square' – has long been integral to the production of subcultural identities. As Sarah Thornton recorded in her late millennial studies of the folk devils of the British 'acid house' scene, provocation, rebellion and 'mass media misunderstanding [is] often a [deliberate] goal [. . .] of youth's cultural pursuits' (Thornton 1994: 184). Similar observations could be extended to earlier studies of seventies punk (Hebdige 1979). And they can be extended forwards to the inner-city youth culture of which the chicken shop is a part. The difference between the two being that, where art-school punks used chicken bones as toggles on parker jackets as a stylistic retort to their parents' sartorial propriety, today's youth knowingly abandon boxes of half gnawed poultry limbs for the pigeons to peck at. Importantly, they do so not out of raw ignorance. Rather they do so in a repost in the face of a city whose majoritarian culture and economy shows them so little regard (Jones 2012; Tyler 2013): one of a handful of continually evolving 'resistance through rituals' (Hall and Jefferson 1993).

Flat Whites and Nouveau Fried Chicken

Fried chicken takeaways are so well established a symbol of everything that makes a neighbourhood undesirable to property investors, that one wily internet entrepreneur recently developed a method of using the takeaways as part of an algorithm for assessing a neighbourhood's potential for profitable gentrification. Using a simple ratio of artisan coffee shops to fried chicken shops, the web designer and his 'data scientists' identified areas that had enough fried chicken shops to *suppress* the *potential* value of the land, but enough coffee shops so as to seduce a wealthier socio-economic class into colonizing the space, and growing the profits of early investors. In this respect, the threat posed to the fried chicken takeaways and their users, is entirely analogous to the threat that Sharon Zukin saw facing the residents of New York's Bryant Park in the 1980s: the threat of 'pacification by cappuccino' (Zukin 1998). Only, in London's case it is the colonization of space by way of the flat white (a lighter less frothy coffee that arrived in London courtesy of gap-year Australian baristas). Despite these superficial differences, the analogy with Zukin's New York in fact runs very deep. Consider, for instance, Zukin's more recent research on demographic transformations in Brooklyn and Harlem (Zukin 2009, 2014; Zukin, Lindeman and Hurson 2015). Therein we learn of the accelerating demise of everyday multicultural culinary spaces in which the city's distinct cultures had hitherto been anchored. Facing the greatest threat of gentrification are, in fact, some the city's oldest fried chicken and 'soul food' joints. They are not, however, simply being displaced by new artisan coffee shops. Rather, in an irony painful to Harlem and Brooklyn's erstwhile residents, some are in fact being displaced by a new breed of 'nouveau soul-food' restaurants. In such locations, the old food of the inner city is elaborately de- and reconstructed so as to market it to new intra-city tourists, albeit at a greatly increased cost.

Similarly in inner-city London; as of 2014, alongside the rash of new, white-tiled coffee shops a number of 'reconstructed' fried chicken restaurants have emerged – *Ma Clucker, Mother Plucker, Dirty Chicken, The Bird, Butchies, Lucky Fried Chicken* and *Chicken Box* – each in areas undergoing some of the most rapid demographic 'upscaling': Peckham, Shoreditch, Dalston and Brixton. Opting for low-lighting, table service and often foregrounding their 'grade A quality' 'organic' and/or 'free range' chicken, the new outlets ask up to and over ten times the price for a chicken wing than their more 'popular' predecessors. Utterly unaffordable to any of the erstwhile chicken shop's regular patrons, these new eateries represent a wholesale, and often entirely explicit, appropriation of inner-city culture.

Of course, such outlets are unlikely to be subject to the type of supplementary planning guidance that restricts them from opening up in 'sensitive areas'. On the contrary, *Chicken Box* is being promoted by its local council as a preferred alternative for young people on their way home from school, despite it still selling fried chicken (like KFC it uses a high pressure frier, an ostensibly healthier cooking method). Nor, at the same time, are existing poultry-based social hubs – *Chicken Cottage, Cottage Chicken, Chicken Run, Royal Fried Chicken* – likely to be credited with English Heritage's hallowed 'asset of community value status', as pubs in several of these gentrifying neighbourhoods have been.

If curating the habitus of high net-worth resident remains as central to the municipal planning of London as it is today, then ultimately restrictions on inner-city hot food takeaways are less necessary than they were in an era of 'mixed tenure'. All that is required to rid an area of the abject malodorous chicken shops, and the social life that they sustain, is to squeeze out the customers that sustain those shops, and to hike up the rents of premises they occupied. And starting in 2010, the coalition government and its successor have developed a raft of policies (bedroom tax, housing benefit caps, cuts to housing associations and many measures proposed in the 2016 Housing Bill) that help property developers and owners to that effect (Hodkinson and Robbins 2013). Looking simply at the rapid decline in the number of inner-city school pupils eligible for free school meals, an oft-cited indicator of an urban area's relative income, a drop from 47 per cent to 35 per cent in five years in Tower Hamlets, and from 37 per cent to 32 per cent in Hackney (Department for Education 2015), significant demographic changes are underway in London's inner-city boroughs. Importantly, fewer children dependent on free meals also likely equates to fewer children visiting fried chicken shops, which itself reduces the viability of takeaways and feeds the further transformation of the inner city.

Conclusion: Picking Through the Bones

Totemic artefacts of an apparently 'degenerate' urban 'underclass' have often served as rallying points for an array of policies garnered towards re-colonizing the inner city. To be sure, the panic around fried chicken fits this model. It is also true, however, that there are an assortment of less obviously 'cultural' discourses constructing the 'problem' of fried chicken; discourses pertaining to industrialized slaughter, animal welfare, zoonotic contagion and health care bills. All of these compete for space in the media and as such there is no singularly identifiable discourse that sits behind the construction of the fried chicken problem. However, as reflected in the oratory of London's mayoral candidates (Nsubuga 2015), national politicians (Wintour 2013) and the pen work of municipal officials, the confluence of these issues ensures that public probity finds particular traction in the inner-city fried chicken takeaway. Above all other urban institutions it is, as such, the fried chicken takeaway that is most routinely trotted out as both cause and symptom of society's ills, and an obstacle to an ideal urbanism.

None of the problems with fried chicken outlined here are simply 'social constructions'. The dish is not especially disposed to the sustenance of a long and illness-free life (if routinely consumed in the absence of a balanced diet and physical exercise). And evidently, the life of a chicken destined for the orange and yellow cardboard carton is especially dire. A portion of fried chicken three times a week does little to improve that chicken's life. And to be sure, the subculture of London's fried chicken outlets is embroiled within social forms that challenge normative ideas of community, identity and nation. However, it is also clear that the fried chicken takeaway is an invaluable resource – calorifically, symbolically and socially – for London's young people. All the more so in a city that has seen sixty million pounds worth of cuts to youth services between 2012 and 2014. Sitting at the intersection of key debates about the future of inner-city London's demography, the city's health, its food systems and negotiations over its post-colonial identity, there is perhaps no dish better suited for understanding the pivotal role of gut feelings with regards to urban atmospheres. There is, as we have seen, a great deal more at stake in a gut feeling, than merely individual expressions of distaste. Cumulatively, gut feelings are at the very core of the spatial injustices currently unfolding in the city.

6

Eels and Eastenders

It's ten-thirty on a damp and dark Friday morning in early November. I walk south down a gloomy road dividing the City of London from the old East End. A blanket of drizzle slicks the gentle slope dropping down toward the Thames. Moving away from the City, glass towers give way to three-storey Victorian blocks. Ground floor retail units hosting sushi restaurants and bespoke tailors are transposed for array of importers, exporters and wholesalers: hair extensions, printed fabrics, desk fans, rice cookers and bongs. The wholesalers are all open bar one late starter. The rusty eyelids of its roller shutters lift lazily, revealing a row of faceless mannequins, lounging in colourful 'no-brand' hoodies. Each window casts a fuzzy Rothko on the rain-slicked pavement. An elderly couple in hooded anoraks assemble the metal frame of their fruit and vegetable stall on a corner. Turning south again, down a deserted street, back towards the Thames, there is a piscine tinge to the air – a hint of the river beyond. I move past a car park stuffed with Porsches, Mercedes, Lotuses, Bentleys; these are the only ones that park inside the city's congestion charge zone. Looking up through the fine rain, I see the candescence of the lonely white food trailer at the end of the road ahead of me.

Located on the same three by six feet pitch since 1919, Tubby Isaac's has been open, between ten in the morning and eleven in the evening, year round, at least six days a week, for ninety years. From behind the counter of the seafood stall, Tubby Isaac's vendors have sold a shifting range of cockles, whelks, crabs and eels to an assortment of customers. Such is the connection between the lightly salted and fishy flavours sold at Tubby's and the mythologies of its locale that, in the popular imagination, the foods vended by the stand are taken to be the 'authentic essences' of the London's 'East End'.

Arriving a little earlier than normal, I am glad to see that Paul, the stall's owner for the last three decades, has already set up for the day. He has been getting a little later recently. There is even a customer at the stall. I reach the stand as Paul spikes metal price labels into the lemons sitting affront the trays of cockles and whelks. Paul's customer is in her early forties, wearing jeans and trainers and a thick red anorak. Her hair is tied in a ponytail, and her breath is visible in the damp air as she exhales between mouthfuls of eel jelly, which she lifts into her mouth using, not a spoon, but a small 'crab flavoured' stick of reconstituted white fish.

'Alright,' I say, lifting my chin towards Paul, and nodding at the customer.

'Oh, hello, mate,' Paul says, eyebrows tilting up as he wipes his hands with a white cloth.

The woman at the stand turns very slightly towards me, eyes still fixed forward and down.

'Alright, darling,' she says, before returning a crab stick into a bowl of jelly.

'How's it going?' I ask Paul, raising my voice above the traffic at the junction to the south of us.

Paul smiles a desperate smile, failing to move muscles beyond his mouth.

'Brilliant. Put it this way. You're the second person that's come here all day.'

'It's only ten thirty. It could pick up.'

'Nah. I mean, it's been dead all week. And last week.'

'Any special reason today do you reckon?' I ask. This is a common exchange, and the answers are familiar. A shrug and a long pause, before Paul wipes the stainless steel counter.

'Well, yeah. I don't know mate. I just don't know.' There's a mix of despair and resignation in his voice. 'Things are changing around here a lot, aren't they?'

'I guess so,' I reply. 'I mean, it is up there.' I indicate with my chin northwards toward the glass-curtained rare-granite paved streets I came from. 'But what's changing down here?'

'It's just like up there, isn't it? People like you, you love sushi and all that. Don't get me wrong. I do too. But none of you are coming down here.'

I nod in concurrence. 'They might if they knew you were here.'

'I don't know,' replies Paul, doubtfully. 'You know I tried serving at one of those music festivals once and I don't think we even broke even. Younger generations just aren't interested [. . .] And this new junction doesn't help,' Paul continues, 'you know it used to be six lanes going that way?'

I nod.

'Cars could pull up on the main road. Taxis'd just pull off the main road and stop here. These two lanes now, and the congestion charge cameras here.' His eyes lift to the tower of CCTV cameras above his stand, monitoring traffic in and out of the City. 'No one stops.' Another pause. 'Price of eels has been going through the roof as well. The wholesaler can't do anything about that. Plus he's also started selling retail, which doesn't do my business any good.'

Paul's customer, who had been quietly listening while slurping up mouthfuls of eel jelly breaks her silence. Raising her head she looks at Paul, a glint of admonishment in her eyes, before turning towards me. 'I tell you why there's no one left round here.'

'Go on,' I say. Paul inhales deeply through his teeth. He seems to know what is coming.

'All the Bengalis and Pakis getting the housing. Well, now it's the Poles, Ukrainians, Russians. I know why it's so quiet here, believe you me, love.'

'It's changed a lot, hey?' I ask, faux naivety shining through.

'Believe you me. Listen – I was born here. So's my mum. I've been coming here since I was two. First solid food I had was jellied eels. We're a dying breed. No one English. No one eating English food. Simple as that.'

She finishes her last mouthful, and slaps the empty bowl into Paul's hand. She relishes the emphatic exit. 'See you next week,' she says to Paul.

'Yeah, see ya,' he replies.

'See ya, darl'.'

'No doubt,' I reply.

In a great number of respects, the morning's exchange was, if not typical, then common among the many exchanges I had round the seafood stand in my years visiting it. The background was cold and damp, the mood melancholic, and the discussion was nostalgic. Within the exchange, which often took place over a bowl of eels or cockles soaked in vinegar, the stall's owner, Paul, outlined the numerous barriers he sees between potential customers and his tubs of traditional seafood. These ranged from global financial crises, health and safety inspectors, road layouts, the Labour government, the subsequent coalition government, petrol prices, rail fares, the arrival of new socio-economic classes into the End End, and the movement of old Eastenders further out into the more affordable and spacious Thames Estuary. All of these factors clearly had a degree of impact on the viability of Tubby Isaac's as a business. Their impact has been amplified, however, by the fact that in the midst of these tumultuous changes the stand itself has stood resolutely still – literally – in a wheel clamp for at least twenty years.

Amongst all the factors Paul outlines as threats to his business, the relocation of old East End families to the home counties, appears to be amongst the most significant. Once a staple of the community's culinary rhythms, a taste for cockles, eels and mussels soaked in vinegar or smeared in seafood sauce, barely exists in the immediate environs of the stand. Restaurateurs setting up shop in new East End, such as those behind Curtain Road's Hoxton Pony or Worship Street's Whistling Shop, tried to pay homage to the old city, placing jellied eels on their debut menus of reconstructed

English food. Such dishes, however, rarely stay on menu beyond the opening fortnight. For a number of reasons (Rhys-Taylor 2013b), East End seafood has become too over-determinedly abject, even for the city's new omnivores.

In the minds of many of Paul's long-term customers the recent revaluation and appropriation of historic inner-city neighbourhoods is not, however, perceived as the most significant threat to their local culture. Far more significant in *their* narratives about the relationship between locality, taste and culture, are the last few decades of migration from Europe's extremities and the fringes of an erstwhile Empire. The narrative offered by Paul's customer typifies this explanation. It is a narrative of 'cradle to grave' craving for seafood, transmitted intergenerationally through the blood and culture of an 'island race', interrupted by the city's new global connections. You might be able to 'sense' why she considers this account to be valid, by taking a stroll through some of the streets running off from the seafood stand: within two hundred metres of Tubby Isaac's there are two Thai food stands, one kebab van, one pub selling Thai food, a falafel stall, a barbecue rib stall, a van selling Caribbean cuisine, two fried Dixie-style chicken takeaways, a Brazilian cafe, a Japanese noodle bar, two sushi restaurants, a 'greasy spoon' cafe, a Japanese food tent (katsu curry and wraps), three Japanese canteens, a pizza joint and a tapas bar. Against this streetscape and alongside a deluge of anti-immigrant sentiment in the popular press, the coastal flavours vended by the lonely seafood stand easily lend themselves to the narrativization of an embittered island race.

As Alan Warde points out, 'cuisines of origin are particularly important emotional and symbolic markers' (Martens and Warde 1998: 113). They are also often important geographical markers, with specific flavours generated by environmental factors – *terroir* – connecting cultures to specific senses of place. And as such, 'cuisines of origin' are often integral to the rituals that bind discrete communities of people together, and are intertwined with mythologies of geographically specific cultures. More than simple *symbols* of culture, 'flavours of origin' comprise a key part in the ways in which cultural communities are 'sensed' and experienced (Howes and Classen 2013: 84). As we know from the acutely distinct food regions of most European nations, local communities and their cultures have historically had distinctly sub-national regional flavours. It was only in the nineteenth and twentieth centuries, as Eric Hobsbawm famously detailed with regards to dress and music, that *some* of these flavours were elevated to the status of props within explicitly *national* myths (Hobsbawm and Ranger 2012). As such, 'gastronationalism' is integral to the ways in which the extent and boundaries of the European nation states we know today were articulated (DeSoucey 2010). Coastal seafood was initially a very potent cuisine for these purposes, in the sense that it tangibly connected national identity to the cultural practices of capital city, its coast, symbolizing both the nation's territorial limits, and its maritime ambitions.

Unsurprising, then, that Tubby's customers understand the demise of their favourite snack as less to do with the shifting socio-economic composition of the inner city, than with migration and the import of other nationally distinct culinary practices. Such narratives find a modicum of validation in popular scholarly accounts of Britain's gastronomic evolution. Panikos Panayi's culinary histories of modern Britain are, for instance, notable for their numeration of the flavours added to British palates by Chinese, Italian, Eastern European and Indian migrants over the last century (Panayi 2008, 2012). Importantly, for Panayi, all these developments are understood against the background of centuries of previously unadulterated 'British cuisines'. That is, up to the nineteenth century local tastes are perceived to have endured through generations of geographically bound communities. Panayi, in fact, even uses 'jellied eels,' as an example of a pre-global, quintessentially ethnic British 'cuisines of origin' (Panayi 2008: 8). Such histories stand in predictably stark distinction to the increasingly globally inflected culinary conjunctures of the twentieth and twenty-first century city (Bell and Valentine 1997; Ritzer 2004; Issenberg 2007; Mukherjee 2014).

However, to suggest that competition and negotiation between culinary cultures living on the banks of the Thames is new to the twenty-first century serves only, as Phil Cohen writes, 'to underwrite the invented tradition of Englishness itself, to accept at face value its own myths of origin and destiny' (Cohen 1998: 4). This is no small point. In a great many respects, Panayi's division of food into 'British and Foreign Food' (Panayi 2008: 1) is only possible through the obfuscation of what Luce Giard refers to as the 'minuscule cross roads of histories' present in just about 'every alimentary custom' (Certeau, Giard and Mayol 1998: 171). Today we are certainly used to recognizing culinary cross roads in a conspicuous range of new post-modern culinary 'mash-ups' of the twenty-first century city: Chicago's udon noodle hot-dogs, Glasgow's haggis pakora, London's katsu chicken wrap. However, it is not just twenty-first century post-modern 'fusion foods' that harbour transcultural cross roads (Miles 1993). Rather, such meeting points are discernible in the production of the tastes *of*, and the taste *for*, many of the 'authentic' 'national' cuisines against which the 'global' palates of the twenty-first century are symbolically pitted.

The rest of this chapter is dedicated to unearthing the historical cross roads and intercultural exchanges that lie behind the custom of snuffling a bowl of jellied eels in the cold damp air of a London street. In doing so, the culinary culture 'local' to an old city's ports will be revealed to be, and to have always been, inflected by the contributions of immigrants to the city. This is not to say that eating bowls of cold jellied eels, cockles, whelks and mussels doused in malt vinegar is not, or was not, distinctive of a local culture. It is to say, however, that beneath the seemingly linear intergenerational transmission of this culture, are also myriad intercultural negotiations, disruptions and synergies that reveal the pragmatic amenability to difference that used to underwrite the culture of London's East End. In tracing these disjunctures, the chapter suggests that the use of London's local seafood in the narrativization of a historically fixed identity and community – the white working-class backbone of the nation – represents the reduction of an inherently transcultural social milieu by a nationalist narrative intent on forgetting all but its own fictions.

The Prehistoric Thames

In previous eons' oscillations between ice ages, tropical and temperate periods, each successive glacial melt and re-freeze left significant deposits of molluscs, crustaceans and marine fauna embedded in the banks of the Thames (Preece 1999). Dating from millions of years ago, the hauls dragged up over the last century and a half by archeological shell collectors were not, however, the same species as found in the river and its estuary today. Instead of the species of cockles, whelks, eels and oysters associated with the Thames today, discoveries included an assortment of gigantic tropical oysters, long deceased arctic whelks and colossal prehistoric prawns. Varying according to the shifting climate, these were found alongside the fossils of elephants, wolverines, mammoths, hippopotami and lions, all of which at one time strolled along the banks of London's fluvial artery (Bridgland et al. 2004). The contemporary colonization of the Thames estuary, English Channel and North Sea basin with *Ostrea edulis* (the edible oyster), *Ceratoderma edule* (the edible cockle), *Buccinum undatum* (common whelks) and the European Eel (*Anguilla anguilla*) began more recently at the end of the Pleistocene era: tens of thousands of years ago, as opposed to tens of millions.

After an extensive and deeply hostile glacial period, during which most of Britain, Scandinavia and the seas between them, were under an ice sheet, a period of warming led to significant glacial melt and rapid sea level rises which swept floods southward from Scandinavia. After carving its way through the landscape so as to partition the British Isles from mainland Europe, the waters of the North Sea then swirled with the run off from the Thames, the Rhine and the Elbe to create one of Europe's most fertile marine environments. As the water settled, the seabed grew thick with what roughly resembled today's assemblages of molluscs and maritime fauna (Bailey et al. 2008; Morigi, Schreve and White 2011).

For *most* of northern Europe, these resources were a key source of protein as human settlers followed the glacial retreat north. In a paleontological sense – and in the absence of hippopotamus steak – the collection of fauna sold by Tubby Isaac's are as close as you can get to the essential flavours *of* the contemporary Thames. This does not, however, imply that a taste *for* these morsels is equally ancient. On the contrary historical evidence suggests that a local taste for these morsels has a more recent, and crucially, a more cosmopolitan history.

When in Rome: Acculturation, Adaptation and Innovation

In 1995, about a five-minute walk due north from Tubby Isaac's seafood stand, archaeologists were conducting a mandatory survey prior to the implementation of a large regeneration project around Spitalfields Market in East London. Of particular interest was the dig being conducted at Spital Square, a site of stubborn poverty since the market gardens were hurriedly built over with slum dwellings for workers with the onset of the Industrial Revolution. Over the course of their excavation, the archaeologists unearthed many artefacts relating to the area's shifting role throughout the life of the city. Especially notable, for its rarity and immaculate preservation, was a sarcophagus belonging to a high-status female in her early twenties, dated to around three centuries after the Romans' first arrival. As with many discoveries of ostensibly wealthy individuals, the body was identified as proto-royalty. More recently the 'princess' was identified, through isotope analysis, as having either come from Rome, or having eaten a lot of Roman imports (Montgomery et al. 2010). Particularly interesting given our maritime attention is that the sarcophagus of this Romano-British hybrid noblewoman was decorated on the outside with a border of perfectly imprinted scallop shells. As a guide at the Museum of London (where the sarcophagus is now interned) points out, at one level, the shells are 'just very pretty [. . .] decorative'. Alongside other evidence – in particular pre-Roman iron-age bone analysis – such patterns, however, take on a deeper significance. Not least, the reverence to the sea alluded to by the sarcophagus' decorative lining, ought to be considered alongside the conspicuous lack of *any* evidence suggesting the consumption of any fish or seafood in south-east Britain prior to the Romans' arrival in AD 43, despite its abundance and its widespread consumption in other coastal areas of Europe at that time. Comparing the archaeological traces of Iron Age settlement in south-east Britain to analogous coastal regions in Scandinavia or even North America, for instance, there is a conspicuous absence of mountainous middens of mollusc shells that characterize the late Iron Age and pre-Classical era. What is more, through isotope analysis of pre-Roman Londoners' bones, scholars have discerned a complete lack of atomic traces of the sea (Barrett, Locker and Roberts 2004; Dobney and Ervynck 2007; Locker 2007). With such an abundant source of protein at their door, and in light of other known instances of sacred water (Dobney and Ervynck 2007: 404), a prohibition around eating fruits of the Thames estuary in Iron Age Britain seems highly likely.

The local prohibition, however, wanes not long before the Spitalfields Princess' burial. Across London, and in the same strata of earth as the sacred scallop-lined sarcophagus was found, are also the first traces of meals containing fish bones, mollusc shells and amphorae holding the Romans' beloved salt-fish sauces (Locker 2007: 143). As the commingling of sacred shells and fish bones in the earth suggest, within two hundred years of their occupation, the Mediterraneans' infamous taste for all things brackish had become widespread across the capital. The exact process through which locals 'acculturated' to their occupiers' alimentary regime is as murky as the Thames, and the archaeological evidence too scant to even speculate. What is clear, however, is that those living in proximity to these new battalions of administrators, whether in Rome or not, would increasingly do as the Romans did. In perhaps one of the earliest demonstrations of the relationship between social formation and 'taste' within the British Isles, revered sea *fauna* became sea*food*.

From the export of the first batch of Colchester oysters to Rome (Pliny 1890: 468), and the import of Roman farming, fishing and consumption practices, seafood consumption in London grew in a series of leaps for nearly two millennia (Barrett, Locker and Roberts 2004). A whole millennium after the Romans' arrival, between the eleventh and thirteenth centuries, for instance, the Hanseatic league of cities – which included Lubeck, Hamburg, Stockholm, Cologne, Bruges and London – swelled considerably off the back of the 'easterling herring' dredged from the fringes of the North and Baltic seas (Camden, Moule and Lower 1870; Dollinger 1970; Pye 2015). The Norman invasion in the thirteenth century, it should also be noted, significantly incentivized the advancement of fishing practices around south-east Britain through the allocation of fishing licences, designated fishing and trading rights and the formal establishment of markets (Dyson 1977: 36). From the sixth century, as Catholicism spread across Europe, the culinary rhythms of Benedictine doctrine synchronized diets around the continent, while driving fish consumption further into the culinary rhythms of Londoners' weeks. Every Friday, under the rule of Roman Catholicism, was officially designated 'fish Friday'. Despite her finally shaking off the yoke of Papal authority, Queen Elizabeth's London also had seafood as the core fuel source – in an economic, calorific and technological sense – of an expanding empire. As well as providing fuel for a proto-industrial work force the fishing industry had, throughout the Tudor period, also been technologically and economically implicated in the advancement of navy and the emergent colonial trade in commodities and humanity (Loades 2009).

Railways, the City and the Coast

In terms of the wider availability of sea fauna, centuries of growth in the consumption of seafood and fish are dwarfed in significance by the nineteenth-century advances in steam power. Once they became viable in the late nineteenth century, coal-powered steam boats considerably increased the efficiency of fishing fleets and, with them, the viability of vast new deep-water fishing grounds (Dyson 1977: 74). However, as important as the water-borne advances of steam were, it was *above all else* rail travel that irreversibly yoked the British coast and its fauna to the nation's capital city.

It did so both in symbolic and in more obviously material ways. First, fishing towns that had railway stations connecting them to the city flourished as the favoured holiday resorts of an urban population newly endowed with occasional bouts of leisure time. From the very earliest days of rail, Londoners had set off for short trips to the wet sands and rock pools clustered around the cliffs and dunes of the isle's south-east shores (Dance 1966). As rail grew more accessible, so too did the British Isles' coast, with lines such as the Great Eastern Railway's 'cockle special' to Southend (Green 1996: 143), stopping at all stations in the impoverished east of the city before depositing its passengers to stand, sand between toes, gazing at the Empire that existed beyond the horizon.

More significantly, on the way to such trips, which no doubt intensified a taste for the sea in the actual city, colossal trains laden with mollusks and fish were passing in the opposite direction, towards London. So voluminous was the daily movement of sea-fauna across the country by rail that the main rail companies soon opened special departments to co-ordinate the unprecedented land-borne migrations of fish, molluscs and crustaceans. The scale of the transition from water to land-based transportation of seafood is summed up well in an account from the time:

> Of old, nine-tenths of the supply came by way of river, the little that came by land being conveyed from the coast, at great expense, in four-horse vans. Now the railways are day by day supplanting smacks, and in many cases steamers; for by means of its iron arms, London, whilst its millions are in slumber, grasps the produce of every sea that beats against our island coast ... Thus every night in the season the hardy fishermen of Yarmouth catch a hundred tons, principally herring, which, by means of the Eastern Counties rail, are by next morning at Billingsgate (Anon. 1854: 273–274).

Not only did the age of the steamer and railways affect the quantity and range of fish available to Londoners, but also the price; making relatively fresh seafood available to the majority of the city. As recorded in Henry Mayhew's famous surveys of the rubbish collected from various neighbourhoods of London, a preponderance of oyster shells and fish bones (Mayhew 1861: 285–287) was found across the city. In many respects, the fruits of the North Sea were comparable in economic and social importance to the crude oil extracted from the North Sea towards the end of the twentieth century.

Eels and Immigrant Entrepreneurs

The general trend for growth in the consumption of seafood in London is, therefore, diffused across two millennia. The local significance of one dish in particular, however, is related to far more specific contingencies. A plausible myth has it that the tethering of local identity and culture to jellied eels, pivots around the 'Great Fire' that swept from the city's port through the entire city in September of 1666. On the night it took hold, the conflagration roared from London's liquor laden docks and warehouses through the rest of the inner city and its east, purportedly turning the sky over the Thames estuary a smoky orange. At the same time, one hundred miles away, on the other side of the North Sea, mature *Anguilla anguilla* (European eels) were preparing to leave, *en masse*, on their moonlit autumn migration out of Dutch lakes and river estuaries into the ocean (Deelder 1954, Behrmann-Godel and Eckmann 2003; Bruijs and Durif 2009). Having swum up into European river estuaries some eight to fifteen years before, the eels were leaving *en masse* with the intention of crossing the Atlantic for retirement in the tropical waters of the Sargasso Sea. Once there, if all went to plan, they would – as their parents had – breed and die.

Dutch eel fishermen, however, had the eels destined for other futures, setting a series of traps along their sculpted coast. No more than two days later, the Dutchmen sailed up the Thames, hulls laden with squirming eels, to the smouldering ashes of a city. Inundated with starving Londoners needing sustenance, the fishermen served the public directly on their boats. The crucial supply line provided by the fishermen was recognized in the coming years by King James II who, when reopening the city's main fish market (Billingsgate), granted the Dutch eel fishermen special permission to bypass the market's notorious middle-men. Instead they were allowed to sell directly to the public off their boats; a reward for feeding the starving city in need (Tsukamoto and Kuroki 2013: 8). Accordingly, for the next three centuries the Dutchmen sold eels directly to the public, at a discount rate, off their boats. The practice lasted well into the nineteenth century (Mayhew 1861: 66), and, it would seem, was integral to establishing jellied eels (eels cooked and cooled in their own gelatinous juices) at the heart of working London's culinary repertoire.

Having been sold in the streets for many years, in the mid-nineteenth century, the first of East London's dedicated pie and eel shops is recorded as opening, and belonging to a Dutch man called John Antnik (Hunt 2002: 16–17). In the years immediately after Antnik's success, several chains of eel and pie shops started emerging, notably the Cookes, Kelly's and Manzes chains. In each instance, these new caverns of polished brass and tiles were owned by migrants to London, arriving from Holland, Ireland and, in the case of the Manzes chain, an Italian who migrated to London from the Amalfi coast.

It was in the midst of this industrial growth in eel shops, fuelled by immigrant entrepreneurs, that Itzko Brenner, a rotund twenty-six-year-old Jewish-Russian known locally as 'Tubby', acquired his small rectangular pitch at the bustling junction of Whitechapel and Aldgate High Streets on the edge of the City. Having looked carefully at the business opportunities available to him, Itzko noted the success of eel and pie bars, which numbered over a hundred in London at the turn of the century (Hawkins and Garlick 2002). Accordingly, and ignoring Jewish orthodoxy (eels are strictly non-kosher), Itzko started his own small business buying up eels, wholesale, every morning from the fishermen at nearby Billingsgate market. His barrow full, often before dawn, Tubby would wheel his produce up the steep alleys perforating the banks of the Thames towards the morning burble of Petticoat Lane market. Tubby and his eels did particularly good business, as evidenced by the fact that the coster quickly expanded to acquire his own premises for cooking and preparing the eels, as well as additional stands around London. The business would last for over nine of the decades that followed.

Nation Myths and 'the Cockney'

At the very same moment (in the nineteenth century) that families of 'ethnic entrepreneurs' were elaborating the city's cuisine, representations of the East End's 'local culture' were also becoming increasingly frequent across the pages of the national print media. Central to these appearances was the re-interpretation and reification of the ancient figure of 'the Cockney'. Nineteenth-century publications with titular references to cockneys include the poetry collection *Letters from Cockney Lands* (Ainsworth 1826), travelogues such as *Cockney Adventure* (*Or Sketches of London Life*) (Nicholson 1838), *A Cockney in Arcadia* (Spurr 1899), and *The History of Cockney Dandies* (Buzz et al. 1819). London-based newspaper 'Reynolds' contained a weekly section entitled 'Cockneyisms', while a Scottish newspaper ran a feature called 'On the Cockney', an extended travelogue introducing their readers to 'native' inhabitants of East London (Anon. 1893).

Always referring to the East End, the term had far from always carried the class and moral connotations it acquired in the late nineteenth century and retains today. In the first instance the term 'cockney' was used to refer, variously, to an assortment of spoilt and work shy young men of the city's ports (Dobson 1798: 119), urbanites ignorant of the rural way of life (Griffiths 1797: 204) or any Londoner born within sound of the Bow Bells (Dobson 1798: 119). As the writer Johnathon Green details (Green 2015), for many years, even wealthy businessmen in the city's east were known as cockneys and often revelled in the name. As the Industrial Revolution rolled on, the East End, and thus the term cockney, became synonymous with poverty. It was only, however, when the twentieth century loomed, that the term came to consistently denote a moral quality with reference to that poverty. Not, however, necessarily a negative moral quality. More precisely, the term (as reflected in the newspaper features mentioned above) came to denote a 'salt-of-the-earth, hardworking, wily, fun-loving and family-bound Brit', a native 'striver' that made the most of their limited lot in life on behalf of their nation. This specific usage, of course, is directly correlated with the fact that at the very same moment the city's ports were increasingly destinations for an assemblage of sojourners and refugees from Eastern Europe, the Mediterranean, Ireland, Asia and Africa. The cockney – as Phil

Cohen puts it, re-emerged as 'a discursive composite [. . .] the very back bone of nation and Empire [. . .] constructed by distinction from, and in opposition to, the figure of the immigrant [. . .] a corrupting presence dragging the nation down' (Cohen in Morley 2002: 199).

The irony of this negation is particularly poignant in the next stage in the biography of Tubby Isaac's. In many respects, efforts to impose a cohesive national identity over the knotted mess of histories and culture in East London came to a head in the 1930s when the East End, like much of Europe, became a hotbed of fascism. Throughout the 1930s, amidst a climate of economic uncertainty, large rallies through inner East London were coordinated regularly, with the aim of intimidating locals and 'returning' the streets to its 'indigenous' heirs (Macklin 2007: 14, 41, 69). A European war, with a likelihood of conscription for many working-class Londoners, was also on the horizon. Accordingly, despite the continual growth in his business up to this point, Tubby (Itzko Brenner), along with his wife, two sons and a large number of other local Jewish families, left East London, through Southampton, for New York.

While the original Tubby left for a new start, his nephew, Solomon, who had worked the stall with him since he was a small boy, remained in East London. Seizing the opportunity to take on the family business, over the next fifty years Solomon and his descendants expanded their range to include whelks, winkles, prawns, scampi, cockles, oysters, shrimps and crabs, as well as the old Yiddish favourites of herring and salmon. They also started selling imported green lipped mussels from New Zealand (originally a war-time import), cray fish, squid rings, scallops, and in the eighties, reconstituted shrimps, crab sticks and lobster tails. Paul, the stand's proprietor at the start of this chapter, is Solomon's nephew.

The fare sold at Tubby Isaac's may well contain the essential flavour of London. Molluscs are encased in shells born of the calcite of the Isle's coast. The herring and eels are flavoured with salt that is – season depending – quite literally of the region's earth. Yet, as the brief historical sketches in this chapter suggest, the local *taste* for these morsels (sensibility as opposed to the material sensoria) arises out of a less territorially bounded set of social, technical and economic processes. First and foremost, the taste for British seafood – and the systems for farming it – emerges directly by way of colonial occupier, to whose tastes locals acculturated. Between the eleventh and the thirteenth centuries the entire economy of London was sustained through the fish – and the silver – carried up the Thames by the Hanseatic league of north European fishermen. In the seventeenth century the connections between British and Dutch ports swelled cities on either side of the North Sea. During the nineteenth century, newly available quantities of local seafood were also delivered by way of steam to the city's masses by a new cadre of immigrant entrepreneurs from across Europe. Perhaps most importantly, the specific history of Tubby Isaac's own seafood stand testifies to the processes by which immigrants acculturated to, but also partly transformed, the East End's local culture. In light of this longer view of local culture, the very notions of 'here' and 'there' upon which 'cuisines of origin' are often seen to rest, look fragile at best. What emerges instead is a sense of the drawn out process of 'transculturation' through which the local tastes of a port city have been acquired, reproduced and transformed (Ortiz 1995; Berg 2010; Rhys-Taylor 2013a).

Presenting transcultural histories is not to remove the consumption of jellied eels of from its local specificity, nor the validity of the seafood stand's patrons' attachment their culinary home. On the contrary, what emerges through this potted history is an account of highly significant and local practices and tastes. Importantly, however, cravings for the brackish flesh of the island's near shallows are not grounded in the muddy territory of the city. Rather, the taste emerges through the city's connection to the sea; and through that, to the rest of the world.

'Ello Stranger

There is little evidence of London's historical 'amenability to difference' within the melancholic exchanges transcribed at the start of this chapter. Despite their obvious knowledge of the city's migratory histories, the way that a number of Tubby Isaac's customers narrate difference and identity can often suggest that there's a relative hostility towards 'otherness' at the core of old-time culture and social practices. Yet even within culinary rituals heavily over-coded with nationalistic meanings, transcultural processes of attachment, identification and association are still tangible; for the main part, the majority of visitors to the area during the week were one of three types: lost tourists looking for Brick Lane and Spitalfields, women visiting the area's wholesalers to buy West African-styled dresses, or builders, cleaners and office workers from the nearby City dropping in for a cheap lunch. Accordingly, alongside a trickle of 'old-timers' (over fifty years old, white, working class) the stand's weekly customers contained an assortment of Polish electricians, Nigerian carpenters and Chinese sightseers. On seven occasions over five years, as mentioned in Chapter 2, some of these visitors pre-empted their visits to the stand by bringing their own sauces, notably jars or bottles of *shito* – a West African blend of powdered shrimp, cayenne, herring, salt and onion – to pour all over the small cartons of seafood.

Most of the stand's visitors did not, however, bring condiments to their maritime meal. Instead they simply dressed their portions of cockles, eels, mussels and whelks with rich sensory memories. The diversity of the memories and meanings ascribed to the seafood are foregrounded in the account of one thirty-five-year-old visitor to the stand – a twice-weekly regular for five years. Arriving at the seafood stand during his lunch break from the trading floors of the neighbouring financial district, Raheem came to participate in the purple banter that often accompanies a bowl of mussels. Having previously seen him at the stand on a handful of occasions and even shared a joke, I take advantage of a cheerily bright morning to ask him questions about his visit.

'So when, exactly, did you first try this food?' I ask Raheem as he chews his way towards the bottom of a pot of green-lipped mussels slathered in pink sauce.

He glances up and to the side towards me and replies, after swallowing, 'What, this stuff here? Or fish in general?'

'Both. Well, no, actually, seafood like this.'

'All of my life. I've eaten this all my life.' He returns to his mussels.

'What about this stall? You sound local. Have you lived in London all your life?'

A long pause as he nonchalantly chews and swallows another mouthful.

I nudge the conversation on. 'Sorry. You don't mind?'

Shaking his head 'No no. That's fine. Iraq. I was born in Baghdad. We left. We moved to Syria first. But then I came here'

'Huh. Wow. How long have you lived here then?'

'I moved to London fifteen years ago.'

'The first gulf war?'

'After it.' He starts poking the last mussel around in the remaining coral pink seafood sauce at the bottom of his small plastic pot, staring through it. 'There's good fish in Baghdad. We've got this local dish "margous". It's like a barbecued fish.' A longer pause. Raheem stops playing with his food and rolls his eyes through his memory. 'I don't know the English translation.'

'Is it from the sea or a freshwater fish?'

'The fish? It's from the river.'

'The Tigris?' I respond, at an octave too high for normal conversation.

'Euphrates.'

I inhale through my teeth. News reports of bodies floating in the river have been an uncommon feature of evening news since the last war in Iraq started.

Another, longer, pause. Having nearly killed it, I re-start the conversation again.

'What about seafood and shellfish and stuff. Like mussels? Did you, do you get that in Baghdad?'

'Yeah, yeah.' Raheem carries on, swiping aside my insensitivity. 'I mean, I think. But we didn't. I used to have that on holiday . . . in Egypt.' Raheem puts the final mussel, now coated in seafood sauce, into his mouth, chewing it more slowly, more tensely than before; ruminating.

Bringing no seasoning or condiments to his lunch, what Raheem brought with him was emotionally bitter-sweet sensation. Such feelings might not be that uncommon as lunch-time accompaniments for the dislocated diaspora that populate cities like London. It is after all, smell and taste that are most able to conjure entire episodes from previous experience. Importantly, however, the embodied connection to elsewhere and other times is not mutually exclusive with the cultural life of London.

The extent to which a particular culinary practice conjures associations with both 'here' and 'there' is particularly clear in the case of John. At the time of interviewing him, John was eighty-six years old and, from his birth in early twentieth-century Hackney, had been a regular customer at Tubby Isaac's. John was such a regular customer – and entertainer of other customers – that for a time in his later life he also worked behind the stand. While not the most efficient stall-holder, John always drew a crowd, not least because of the ways in which his accent and general comportment epitomized what is thought to be the 'real Cockney': white, working-class, cheeky and fiercely proud of local culture. So perfected was John's performance of an old-time East Londoner that in his final decades, he found a career in acting. He even had an agent that would regularly put him in contact with directors and advertisers looking to conjure the spirit of the nations' backbone. The distance, however, between the archetypal defensive and embittered London native, and the reality of John's relationship with 'others' is revealed when he spoke about the two loves of his life: his late wife and seafood.

Speaking in his modest living room, John had two herring prepared for lunch, and a sea-bass already defrosting for his evening meal. He ate seafood, he claimed, 'six and an' 'alf times a week,' a habit he credited with his longevity and 'vitality' in his old age. As might be expected of a man born into the East End of the early twentieth century, jellied eels, cockles and whelks were part of his everyday life as a youth. Although not a staple of his diet, he recalled how as a youth such dishes were viewed as 'local' and distinct from the garlicky food emerging in North London's new cafes and bistros. The development of his real love of seafood, and its complete integration with his everyday routine, however, occurred later in life, in near perfect reverse of the gustatory journey taken first by Mr Manzes, the West Italian eel shop owner mentioned briefly before. In 1943, John was part of the Allied forces that entered Italy by way of the Amalfi Coast. Sharing a base with American forces on the coast of the Tyrrhenian Sea, John 'had the good fortune' to meet and marry 'an Italian fisherman's daughter,' who remained his wife for more than forty years. Over the period of their marriage, they spent nearly every summer in Salerno, during which John learnt to speak, pray and sing in fluent Italian. Importantly, his wife and her family of fishermen started to 'really teach' John about seafood (until a year before we met, John was still going out with his extended family for the summer on their fishing boats). A widower, and unable to travel for health reasons, John spoke of the enduringly powerful connection he felt with his late wife, and her culture, through food. In particular, he specified his preference for cooking the seafood he bought from Tubby Isaac's 'in the Italian way, a delicacy way', with 'white wine, Italian herbs and garlic'.

Significantly, this affinity for the sea informs the way in which John thought and spoke about himself, as well as the East End culture through which he lived. The following response to my questions about where he felt most at home, Italy or the UK, is particularly instructive.

'Listen, do you speak Italian?'
    'No', I reply. '*Ciao, grazie mille*. That's it.'
    'Well, in Italy there's a word, *straneri*.'
    '*Straneri*?' I ask, rolling the 'r's in a way that I consider to be an Italian accent.
    'No. *Straneri*,' he corrects me, subtly affecting an Italian accent. 'It means stranger. Listen. We are all strangers in this world, and we all bleed red blood. And we all worship God irrespective of what we call him. We're all strangers.'
    'Huh. Well, yeah,' I remark, checking that my recorder was on.
    'Would you like a glass of wine' John asks. 'I've got this lovely little Italian.' He winks.

For John, the stranger is not an exception through which sameness is constructed, but the rule, a characteristic of all human relationships whether at home or overseas. Thus, while for some the taste of seafood is integral to the ways in which they 'sense' an endangered and exclusive community, the flavour of the food, for John, is a medium for sensing his enduring belonging to an explicitly more cosmopolitan community.

The pragmatic conviviality of the seafood stand and its environs ought not to be a surprise. The ease with which people bring something new to local culture, or find some reflection of their selves in life of the inner East End is, historically speaking, not anything new. From the sixteenth-century Dutch pioneers of the eel trade, to the Manzes, Kellys and Brenners cooking up cockney culture in the nineteenth century, analogous processes have taken place. Raheem is simply among the most recent arrivals to the British Isles to have used polyvalent flavours of the sea as both doors to the atmospheres and practices of lost homes, and a sensory anchor in a new context social and cultural milieu.

Of course, there is little doubting the extent to which the planetary span of transportation and communications have intensified cross-cultural traffic. And it is indisputable that this traffic has heavily impacted the sphere of flavour and taste; untethering whatever connections culinary culture had to fixed terrains. Yet despite the anxiety about the 'novelty' of global processes, a glance at the evolution of London's culinary life over the *long durée*, through the prism of seafood, demonstrates the lengthy provenance of transcultural processes in the city.

What people eat, the flavours they are drawn to, those which they crave and the aromas that they miss, are integral to their senses of who they are. Yet, as the previous chapters have demonstrated, the routes out of which local culture grows are often far more tangled, and globe spanning, than most gut-felt understandings of 'us' and 'them' account for. Despite the transnational histories that afford these bodies' sensuous attachments, the meaning attributed to gustatory sensations is ultimately inflected by the narrative through which the culture is understood. In a twenty-first century English city, governed by a frail hegemony between neoliberal technocrats and parochial nationalists, narratives about an island nation have found a special political utility. As the recent rise of anti-immigration sentiment demonstrates, 'strangers' offer an enduring scapegoat for shoring up that hegemony. Understandably then, the experience of the seafood stand surrounded by a global food court is readily over-coded by gastro-nationalist narratives about an island race. Unfortunately, this is at the expense of recognizing the truly cosmopolitan history from which London's everyday culture has historically emerged.

Coda (Four Years On)

Eleven thirty, June sixteenth, 2013. It's a bright weekday morning and I make a familiar journey southwards, down Middlesex Street. Once upon a time, the road bisected the City and the East End, a silver griffin marking the legislative boundary. The stalls of Petticoat Lane were emptier than they had been three years before. Noticeably, an old Jewish couple who grappled everyday with the metal frame of their fruit and veg stall have not been back for two years. Rounding a corner, I see Tubby Isaac's white seafood trailer in the distance. Unusually today it has a lengthy queue of what looks like seven or eight people snaking around the pavement and dangling onto the road. Behind the queue are a swarm of camera men, journalists and production teams shuffling about. Sound booms swing around as camera lenses zoom in on a wrinkled old-timer pushing a mouthful of eel flesh around his gums. They are there because the day before, a widely read local blog – given to archiving nostalgic representations of East London's culture – had announced that today would be Tubby Isaac's last day in business.

I cut to the front of the line to greet Paul, sidling alongside the stand's most regular customer, a portly street cleaner.

I open with an upward flick of my chin and an observation. 'This is pretty grim.'

'Yeah.' Paul replies, exhaling deeply. 'It's been like this all morning. It's 'cos of that Spitalfields Life blog. And I got a bit of press last week. Everybody wants a photo with me. Smiling, obviously.'

'Vultures.' I say, with sympathy. 'Are they even buying food?'

'Not all of them. Some. And they're all, "It's such a shame? Why are you shutting down? This food's great! It's such a great tradition." Where've they been for the last twenty years? Where've they all been?' Paul looks understandably distraught.

'Sushi bars probably,' I offer. 'Do you want me to grab you a Guinness? I think the pub's open. Terry? You want one?'

'Still working, officially,' replies the street cleaner.

Over the next couple of hours we sip our beer as the seafood seller services a long line of salivating foodies, curious tourists, inquisitive-yet-squeamish local history enthusiasts, and mournful regulars. In the background, photo journalists waited like sharks for more of the elderly customers to reach the front of the queue. As each one reached the front, they swooped in to snap the archetypal image of the old-time Cockney. Nostalgic images, if not tastes, are prized collectables.

The change in the road layout drastically impacted on the viability of the seafood stand, relying so much as it did, on passing taxi drivers. So too did the decision of Tubby Isaac's nearby wholesaler to start selling retail portions of jellied eels to passing taxi drivers. Likewise, the shove and drift of old Eastenders toward the extremities of the Thames estuary had, for decades, eaten away at the city-based business' established customer base. While immigration of Bengalis, Somalis and Eastern Europeans into the East End also had an impact, the consequences of their arrival are far from straightforward. As the biography of the seafood stand shows; the local taste has endured, in part, precisely through new arrivals to the city, who have either acculturated to, synchronized with, or subtly adapted local tastes. Indeed, on some mornings, aside from me and my notebook, the only visitors to the stand were a Polish and Nigerian street cleaner.

Of perhaps greatest significance to the stand's viability, in its final years, were politicians' efforts to place transnational finance and international property markets at the heart of London's economy. It is telling, in this respect, that the final years of the seafood stand come in the aftermath of the 2008 financial crash. Tubby Isaac's was an early victim of the 'credit crunch'. This owed primarily to its reliance on the taxi drivers and the knee-jerk withdrawal of the expenses budgets of the city workers. While thriftiness led to more city workers drifting east for a cheaper lunch (see Chapter 4), few went so far as to venture the few hundred yards further required to reach East London's traditional seafood stand. Of the few City workers that had regularly used the seafood stand – most of whom were older East End barrow-boys-cum-financial traders – early retirement was also the most appealing option. As the financial quarter recovered, the re-consolidation of capital in the City, accompanied with the deliberate inflation of London's property markets, sealed the fate of the seafood stand and the social life it sustained. By 2013, a wave of towering blue-tinted glass and steel had already broken the ancient legislative boundary of Middlesex Street, sweeping past the mythical beasts that marked the boundary between the City and its east. Dwarfed by the new thirty-storey towers emerging around it, the seafood stand sat on a corner primed for development. With his lease up for renewal, Paul could not secure a new lease of the right length or cost to fit his needs. So it closed.

That is not to say that 'local heritage' played no part in the 'renaissance' of the inner city around Tubby Isaac's. Salacious narratives about the old iniquitous East End continue to draw in crowds of tourists seeking out vicarious transgression on Jack the Ripper tours. Young creatives lean beneath a pop-art painting of their local pub's old gangster owners – the Kray twins – while drinking draught ale brewed in revived local breweries. A few hundred metres up the road from the seafood stand, mid-century British memorabilia adorns the walls of hyperreal fish and chip bars. As Jane M. Jacobs (1996) detailed, an entire neighbourhood of Georgian and Victorian facades have also been protected, not far from Tubby Isaac's, as part of the regeneration project that unearthed the aforementioned Romano-British princess. However, while aspects of East London's migratory history are recorded in a small museum of migration and an assortment of plaques, little residue of the area's uniquely transcultural, and yet distinctly local, culture actually endures. While nostalgic imagery and architecture is invaluable to a specific heritage-led generation of the inner city, the actual textures, aromas, cadences and flavours of its everyday life, as well as the oceanic histories behind them, appear tragically undervalued.

7

The Senses, the City and Social Formation

*Their 'common' aura must be dissolved to make spaces for a
new city through which clearly delineated individuals can circulate
with unlimited freedom. For the nose, a city without aura is literally
a 'Nowhere'. A* u-topia.

ILLICH 2005

Digest

Over the last two centuries an assortment of sociologists, philanthropists,
novelists, historians, geographers, psycho-geographers and bloggers have
produced libraries' worth of descriptions and analysis of East London's
neighbourhoods, streets, businesses, culture and family life (Mayhew 1861;
Booth and Argyle 1902; Hobbs 1988; Jacobs 1996; Cohen 1998; Lichtenstein
and Sinclair 2000; Sinclair 2009; Engels 2012; Morrison and Miles 2012;
Samuel 2012; The Gentle Author 2012; Young and Willmott 2013). Yet,
particularly in the more social scientific of these texts, the multisensory
texture of the city has been routinely rendered, at best, as a backcloth against
which actors perform. In contrast, the preceding chapters have presented the
sensoria and sensations as key players at the front and centre of the city's
economy, social forms and its culture.

From stomach-churning mirages of alien meat, through the addictive
intensity of capsicum, the oceanic tang of eels and the comforting gloop of
Japanese curry sauce, the text sought to identify sensoria and sensations
nestled within the urban assemblage at a particular moment in time.
Developing an aromatic and delectable index of East London's material
culture has been an important part of this book. Archiving the array of
sensoria that fill the early millennial inner city, however, was never the
book's sole intention. Rather, by moving the multisensory texture to the
foreground of analysis, the preceding pages sought to reveal how less partial
our sociological understandings of class, race, multiculture, power, space,
locality and globalization might be if we look beyond the appearance of
these phenomena, and consider also their texture, aroma and flavour. Class

cultures, racism and multiculture are not simply discursive constructs nor merely visible phenomena. Rather, they are made out of specific smells, tastes, textures (sensoria), and cemented together by specific ways of making sense of these sensoria (sensibility).

Although relatively self-contained in and of themselves, taken together, the previous chapters help build up a broader picture of the variety of ways in which processes of association and estrangement in cities are inflected by sensory experiences. The first two chapters sought to explore the interaction between the senses and social formation by focussing nearly entirely on global histories of particular *sensoria* – materials with specific smells and flavours – and the bodily feelings (*sensations*) aroused by those sensoria. As well as tracking the global passage of particular material artefacts, the chapters also considered the histories of habituated ways of actually making sense – otherwise known as sensibility, through which sensoria are rendered sensations. Through detailing these plaited global histories of sensoria, sensibility and sensation, the chapters considered the ways in which these historical trajectories re-converge in twenty-first-century London. As the chapters disclosed, the sensoria and sensibilities dispersed through the colonial, and even pre-colonial, networks of earlier epochs heavily inform the local culture of the post-colonial city. In this respect, the sensations that the chapters detail – the taste for Americanized canteen food, mild curry sauces, fiery chillies – are entirely explicable aspects of the contemporary city's local culture. To say that these sensations are points of overlap for the city's inhabitants is not, however, to say that the whole city finds the same meaning in them. There is no explicit local 'sensed community' shored up through mere shared tastes (Vannini, Waskul and Gottschalk 2011: 104–121; Howes and Classen 2013: 84). Rather, the social forms that coalesce around the city's inter semiotic artefacts are conspicuously more 'transcultural' (Ortiz 1995; Berg 2010; Rhys-Taylor 2013a), signifying something of 'here' as well as 'there'.

Nevertheless, the chapters aim to demonstrate the ways in which partial overlaps between material cultures are crucial to what remains of the city's convivial multiculture (Gilroy 2004; Parham 2012). None of this is to say that a 'sense' of cosmopolitan community is always reflected in the ways city dwellers talk about, or even think about themselves. But it is to say that the remarkable cross cultural connections evident in the city are clearly co-extensive with its sensory landscape.

This is hardly the first treatise on the post-millennial city to note the hybridity of its culture. Such arguments have been honed over at least three decades chronicling and critiquing the post-modern city, particularly within critiques of the 'neo-liberal' city (Harvey 1989; Soja 1996; Ritzer 2004; Kumar 2009). Yet, as much as we might locate the city's transnational culture in the flows of neoliberal modernity, the first part of this book also sought to relate the current city's multiculture to its already transcultural history. Such histories are barely acknowledged as part of the city's formal 'cultural heritage'. Nor are such histories recognized in the more academic regional histories of taste that repeatedly take the nation state, and national culture, as their unit of analysis (Mennell 1996; Warde 2000; Burnett 2004; Panayi 2008). Widely under-acknowledged, the 'primal history' of modernity (Gilroy 1993: 55; Benjamin and Tiedemann 1999: 463) is, however, integral to the society and culture of the twenty-first-century city. And despite their apparent 'invisibility', a multitude of planetary 'non-histories' (Certeau, Giard and Mayol 1998: 7) can be made sensible through a consideration of the flavours, smells and textures of the culture that holds the inner city's social formations together.

In Chapters 4 and 5 the book's focus turned away from taste and processes of association, towards the visceral forms of distaste. Although the auspices of the whole book are a focus on the role of the senses with social formation through largely 'ethnographic' methods, the first of the chapters on distaste departed from this remit. Thinking directly against the fetishization of the 'non-discursive' 'affective' and ethereally 'non-representational' aspects of 'the senses' (Thrift 2008; Anderson and Harrison 2010; Pile 2010), the chapter looked at the relationship between the written word and the senses. More precisely, it moved through a series of discursively mediated 'moral panics'. As the reader will recall, each of the episodes of collective disquiet discussed in Chapter 4 was sparked by newspaper stories about the consumption of 'abject' forms of meat. Ruminating on a mezze of horse and bush-meat, the chapter explored the enduring efficacy of newspaper stories in shoring up sensory constructions of 'them' and 'us'. Crucially, the chapter contributed to amassing evidence that, while race is a visually and discursively constructed phenomenon, racism takes on particularly visceral, dangerously invisible manifestations through its investment in the other senses (Smith 2006; Obasogie 2013; Friedman 2015). As the journalistic rhetoric featured in the chapter revealed, affective narratives about the imagined food-scape of multicultural cities enable racist knowledge to burrow deep into urbanites 'self-evident' gut responses to one and other. As the growing scholarship on race and the senses is demonstrating, the liberal dream of 'colour blindness' is, then, far from a solution to the racism that continues to beset the millennium's otherwise remarkable urban multicultures (Smith 2006; Crang and Tolia-Kelly 2010; Obasogie 2013; Friedman 2015). At present, a number of the biggest changes to urban populations and city land, in the UK and US, clearly still have strong racial elements. If this is to be addressed with anything more than the most superficial of anti-racisms, it will require a deeply sceptical attitude toward the personal gut responses elicited by the city's variegated sensory landscapes.

In the second of the chapters dwelling on distaste the text honed in on what could provisionally be referred to as London's 'fried chicken problem'. Initially departing from the narrower focus on the relationship between the construction of race and distaste, the chapter considered an assortment of discourses that frame the city's fried chicken takeaways as a health and welfare problem. Picking through the bones of fried chicken's economic, nutritional and social 'problems', the text considered the power of textual discourses to piggy-back on the body's propensity to disgust. Again, the chapter argued Londoners' gut-felt reactions to the increasingly ubiquitous smell, sight and sound of the fried chicken takeaway – as personal as they feel – often had firm foundations in the promulgation of specific discourses.

The most obvious discourses configuring the mainstream gut-felt unease around fried chicken pertained to health and animal welfare; that is to say, they related to seemingly culturally neutral ideas about 'the good life'. At the same time, it is also clear that, by way of their association with urban youth cultures, fried chicken is reviled as part of a cultural assemblage perceived to be a threat to the moral order of the city. As the chapter detailed, the aforementioned 'rationales' have found a specific utility in current efforts to capitalize on the potential value of inner-city land in which fried chicken takeaways clustered. As a string of documents concerning planning and place-making in East London demonstrate, the perceived 'problems' of fried chicken have made takeaways a particularly potent symbol of degenerate inner cities. As such, references to such outlets are powerful tools with which to garner majoritarian consent for the displacement of the inner city's current residents, along with their unruly multiculture. While urban eugenics is not the explicit obsession of the city's powers, as it was a century before, efforts to capitalize on inner-city land value, and the need to appeal to majoritarian sensibilities in order to do so, have analogous consequences. While the racial codification of fried chicken in the UK is distinct from the meaning of the dish in the US, the dish is, nonetheless, deeply embroiled in the racialized construction of inner-city folk devils, and the demographic cleansing of the inner city.

The last of this book's empirical chapters took a diversion away from the more recent additions to the city's food court and turned toward a constellation of sensations more likely to be recognized as part of the city's cultural heritage. Widely referred to as an essence of East London's erstwhile 'cockney' culture, the city's remaining cockle, whelk and eel vendors cut lonely figures in the city's global food court. As the chapter's historical threads wove together, it became clear however, that the relationship between the city and its estuarine fauna is not as endogenous as often assumed. Less rooted in the *terroir* of the city, a taste *for* seafood within the city emerges out of an assortment of routes into and out of its port. A taste for molluscs and fish was introduced by Roman occupiers, cultivated by Norman invaders, expanded by the Hanseatic merchants, with eels proffered by Dutch fishermen in Elizabethan London, and massively popularized in the late nineteenth century by a collection of Italian, Dutch and Jewish-Russian migrants. Seafood is emblematic of East End culture if only in the worldly cast responsible for propagating the taste.

Moving away from the dish's continental history, the chapter drew on an ethnography of the final years of one of East London's remaining *alfresco* seafood stands to reveal the relationship between the city's local culinary traditions and its contemporary social life. Echoing the chilli peppers in

Chapter 2, a close attention to the sensoria of the seafood stand unearthed disparate cultures and biographies convening around what are – this time by virtue of the saline nature of our planet – 'intersemiotic' culinary artefacts (Ivor-Case in Taylor 2001; Rhys-Taylor 2014). In this respect, the space and sensations of the seafood stand were also part of the transcultural assemblages that continued to unfold in and around the area once associated with the city's port. Yet despite the remarkable everyday multiculture evidenced around the stand, it is also clear that for some of the seafood stand's patrons, the small white trailer was the last refuge amidst the rising tides of globalization. For many, the taste of the British Isles' near-shallows remained important to the ways in which, a 'sensed community' (Howes and Classen 2013: 84) of 'indigenous Londoners' is elicited. More than background texture in a harmless old story, the polystyrene cups of jellied eels and cockles became important props within the articulation of exclusive and xenophobic social forms.

Since the re-emergence of the senses as subjects of serious social scientific consideration some two decades or more ago, we have greatly increased our understanding of their sociological roles. We understand better their significance to individual biographies' culture, as well as their ongoing transformation through history. The preceding chapters of this book seek to hone this socio-sensory attention on the dynamic landscape of an inner city in an effort to understand more precisely the role that sensoria and sensibilities play within its urban processes. By taking a related set of inner-city locations, and moving through an assortment of sensations scattered through them, the aim has been more than simply to compile an index of a space's sensory texture as it changes. Rather, the purpose has been to unearth the role of the sensoria and particular forms of sensibility within the city's social dynamics. The result is somewhat contradictory.

Sensory Paradoxes

As Bourdieu and Bourdieusians have long recognized, albeit in other words, the ways in which modern humans make sense of the sensoria that engage our bodies fall into patterns that serve to articulate the boundaries between social groups. In cities, where 'individual' tastes and distastes aggregate, the interaction between sensate bodies and the city's variegated topography is particularly important to the ongoing spatialization of distinct socio-economic groups (Atkinson and Deeming 2015). However, while sensoria – the material sensory artefact – are a necessary part of this process, it is sensibilities – the bundle of formal and informal codes for interpreting sensoria – upon which the ossification of the social strata pivots. Like the proverbial tree falling in a forest, the fried chicken only 'stinks' if there is a very particular someone there to smell it. As we saw in the case of fried chicken takeaway, or the 'otherworldly' immigrants' street market, particular sensations attract some bodies and repel others depending on the sensibility of the individual concerned. The upshot of this is that, using particular sensoria as markers of insider and outsider status, the city's residents often can marshal themselves, and each other, into exclusive social niches.

The sensibilities of Londoner's are, as such, clearly embroiled in the formation of exclusive forms of association. Yet, at the same time, the previous pages have also detailed the extent to which specific sensoria can also be important to the creation of spaces across which some differences fade into the background and within which degrees of mutual understanding, affinity and obligation are achieved. Whether it was the bustle of the fried chicken shop, the huddles of regulars gathering around the seafood stand, the international grocer or the street market, each entailed constellations of sensoria through which disparate cultural histories, and the bodies carrying them, *potentially* converge. This potential is, however, only significant, if the material histories coincide with appropriate forms of sensibility, sensibilities able to accommodate the convergence of multiple identities, histories and cultures around a particular location. Notably, it seems that such sensibilities have a long pedigree in the city's historically poorer neighbourhoods, wherein 'being together', albeit if only 'rubbing along' (Watson 2006: 61) has been an enduring feature of everyday life. In a variegated urban environment, a modicum of community cohesion is nourished through residents' habituated familiarity with the sensory texture of one another's life worlds. Intersemiotic sensory artefacts with tangled histories could play an important part in this process. At the very least, a group of people with shared affinities for a particular sensation practice a form of 'civic inattention' (Goffman 2008: 87) when they physically meet around their shared tastes. At its most intense however, the senses are also clearly involved in actual smudging of the boundaries of culture that each city-dweller inhabits and the production of new identities and transcultural social forms. As divisive as gut feelings can be, the sensoria that fill the city's everyday spaces are also key players in the dynamic multiculture that has historically characterized London's East End.

Integral to both processes of social ossification, and cultural dissolution, paradoxes similar to those revealed through this book have been noted before. As Les Back observed of London as it approached the new millennium, 'within Europe's major conurbations, complex and exhilarating forms of transcultural production exist simultaneously with the most extreme forms of violence and racism' (Back 1996: 7). Yet, despite the apparent self-evidence of this paradox within many urban contexts, there remained, for a long time at least, a paucity of approaches with which to dissect the mechanisms through which such contradictions emerge. How and why, in one context, does a body allow changes to the culture that lives through it, while in another the senses police exclusive forms of social distinction? What are the historical, political and economic contingencies pertinent to these moments? And what is at stake for the future of the city in understanding the role of the senses in them?

Cities, Senses and 'Extensive Multiplicities'

In recent years, an assortment of urban scholars within anthropology, critical geography and sociology have explored concepts and diagrams sketched by continental thought-smiths, Gilles Deleuze and Felix Guattari (Kearney 1995; Back 1996; Cupers 2005; Cadman 2009; Dovey 2009; Wood 2009; McFarlane 2011; Rowe 2012). The concepts of 'territorialization', 'deterritorialization', and 'the fold' all found a particular degree of purchase within geography, not least because the analogies were taken from geography's dusty old uncle, geology. The Deleuzian biological analogy of the 'rhizome' – with its absence of linear, arboreal structures – also found utility for describing cultural patterns and new political movements in the increasingly densely interconnected world studied by sociologists and anthropologists. For urbanists (Cadman 2009; Dovey 2009; Wood 2009; McFarlane 2011; Rowe 2012), among the most fruitful of the concepts whittled by the continental philosophers might be their idealized binary of 'group formations'; namely the 'extensive multiplicity' and the 'intensive multiplicity', described elsewhere in their work as the 'subjugated' group and the 'subject-group'(Deleuze and Guattari 2003: 348). As ideal types existing in the mind of philosophers, the 'intensive and extensive multiplicity' are perhaps too abstract to have spoken directly to the contexts discussed in previous chapters. Nevertheless, they have use when retrospectively reflecting on the themes discussed over the previous pages.

Both extensive and intensive multiplicities refer, somewhat abstractly, to particular types of grouping (human, animal, mineral or molecular). What ultimately distinguishes the extensive multiplicity from the intensive multiplicity is the criteria through which a 'group' is developed. Crudely speaking, an 'extensive multiplicity' can be understood as a uniform group (Colebrook 2002: 59; Dovey 2009: 27): a droplet of water molecules; a bag of triangular orange candies; or a huddle of self-identifying Britons. Importantly, within an extensive multiplicity, there is an extensive limit through which the group is defined, to which it is 'subjugated': its wateriness, its triangular-orange-candy-ness or its 'Britishness'. The consistency of the group is not changed as long as additions to it conform to pre-determined criteria by which it is measured.

There are a number of ways in which the examples covered over the previous chapters could be taken as windows on the formation of 'extensive multiplicities'. Membership or participation in many spheres of the city's everyday life necessitate that an individual smells, sounds, eats and looks a particular way, and that they ascribe the correct meaning and interpretation to those sensations. This is nothing particularly new. Over half a century ago, Howard Becker's (1963) symbolic interactionism revealed the ways in which a subcultural formation of 'insiders' was developing through similar processes. Drawing on Becker's work, today's scholars have honed in on the 'sensory orders' (Classen 1990; Geurts 2002; Howes 2006; Vannini, Waskul and Gottschalk 2011) and concomitant set of 'somatic rules' (Waskul and Vannini 2008) through which 'sensed communities' (Howes and Classen 2013: 84) are achieved. In many instances, those sensed communities – especially when articulated with reference to ethno-nationalism – have clearly delimited 'sensory' parameters, with a relatively clear set of sensoria and sensibilities associated with them. Perhaps even more significantly, through the previous chapters' attention to 'distaste' we also see how the formation of a group of 'insiders' is also upheld through the identification of 'sensible' limits, and expulsion of sensoria and sensibilities that threaten the internal consistency of the group. In this respect, the formation of 'extensive multiplicities' or 'subjugated groups' is partially marshalled through what Julia Kristeva identifies in 'abjection,' and what Mary Douglas famously saw in the definition of 'dirt'. When Kristeva writes that the 'abject and abjection are my safe guards, the primers of my culture' (Kristeva 1982), or when Douglas writes that dirt is simply 'matter out of place' (Douglas 2002), they are – in a way – referring to the mediation of exclusive and extensive transpersonal group formations – through the sensory capacities of individual bodies.

Cities, Senses and 'Intensive Multiplicities'

The social orders through which opportunities, wealth and resources are distributed across London are then, partly reproduced through regimes of taste and distaste. But order is not *always* maintained. Social strata do not *always* remain intact, and neither cultural practices, nor meanings, nor social hierarchies, are *always* mimetically transmitted across generations or space. Across both the *long durée* of the gustatory and olfactory history of London, but also within the microscopy of the contemporary everyday, the previous chapters have touched on moments during which the internal consistency of the group, otherwise 'subjugated' to particular predicates, is broken down by the inclusion of a smell, a flavour, a texture, a cadence, or a way of seeing, hearing, tasting and feeling the world, that was never of the group. Such moments suggest that, despite the ways in which we think and talk about culture and multiculture, the city hosts something more than a mere mosaic of hermetic groups clearly marked by 'extensive' limits. Rather, the smudging of identities and culture through the senses suggests that the city is home to group formations that are perhaps better understood as 'intensive multiplicities'. In contrast to extensive multiplicities, Deleuze and Guattari write, 'intensive multiplicities' are characterized by the fact that their composition 'alters with each addition or subtraction' (Deleuze and Guattari 2004: 519). That is, the formation of intensive multiplicities is not subjugated to an 'external measure' or the adherence to a particular set of sounds, smells, textures, or flavours. On the contrary, the subject group is defined by the creative coming together of this *and* this *and* this. 'What characterises the [intensive multiplicity] is neither the set nor its elements;

rather it is the *connection*, the "and" produced between elements', which brings about changes to the 'group' (Deleuze and Guattari 2004: 519).

For some critical geographers, the 'intensive multiplicity' is the perfect concept for characterizing metropolitan areas; a gargantuan collective of material, human, mineral, vegetable and animal flows, constantly morphing with each addition. As Dovey argues, '[a] house, neighbourhood or city is an intensive multiplicity. When different people move in, new buildings or rooms are added, the sense of the larger place changes' (Dovey 2009: 27). What I hope to have conveyed, however, is that some cities, and urban spaces within them, are more 'intensive' than others.

Central Places and Global Junctions

Torrents, eddies and trickles of bodies, materialities and sensibilities meet in innumerable combinations at urban locales across the planet. The meeting of disparate entities is, after all, an inherent aspect of city-ness, even in the most isolated of cities. However, as urban historians have noted, over the centuries there have been certain cities that were amenable to far greater magnitudes and speeds of flows in culture, commodities, capital and people, and which have been more productive meeting points, than others (Redfield and Singer 1954; Braudel 1982; Hohnenberg and Lees 1995; Landa 1997). In the longer view the points through which the greatest volume and variety of materials and ideas have moved are generally port cities, inherently embedded in international networks (Braudel 1982: 27–31; Hohnenberg and Lees 1995: 59–73). At different moments in their history each of London, Hamburg, Yokohama, Shanghai, Amsterdam, Hong Kong, Venice, New York, Antwerp, Mumbai and Valencia have been cities, not of the bounded nation, but rather central nodes in vast globe-spanning networks.

To separate these cities out is, of course, to say that they exist in distinction to another type of city – the central place – with its command over the economy of its terrestrial region and a responsibility for reproducing regional cultures and traditions through time: New Delhi, Madrid, Baghdad and Beijing (Redfield and Singer 1954). In contrast to these 'central places', the cities at the junctions of maritime networks have historically been 'determinedly autonomous and more concerned with the world at large than their backyard' (Hohnenberg and Lees 1995: 70). With a historical *raison d'être* to bunch together dense bundles of transnational networks, the inevitable upshot for these intensive cities – at the scale of the everyday – was a heterogeneity and highly dynamic local culture (Redfield and Singer 1954; Hohnenberg and Lees 1995: 65). Importantly, such cultural melange would only be possible if it were facilitated by the sensibilities of the port city's residents. Rarely resulting in self-identification with hybridity or recognized in local folklore – especially in the wake of the 'invention of national traditions' (Hobsbawm and Ranger 2012) – such cross-cultural connections were once, nevertheless, integral to each port city's distinct-yet-hybridized local culture and social forms.

There is a delightful elegance in the ways in which historical economists have distinguished between cities that were 'central places' – controlling integrated regional hierarchies and uniform cultures – and the messy 'meshworks' (Landa 1997) of transnational maritime metropolises (Braudel 1982; Hohnenberg and Lees 1995). It is similar to, and in fact maps neatly on to, the elegance with which Deleuze and Guattari distinguish between two abstracted ideal types of group formation. In reality, however, historical empiricism reveals the 'ideal types' existing in continual tension with one and other, often side by side and sometimes within one another. Many powerful cities have, for instance, been hybrid cities (Landa 1997: 80) integrating both central control functions (shoring up patriotism and patronage over large colonial regions) *and* cosmopolitan cultural and commercial spheres (connecting disparate markets, sewing new tastes and mutating culture through connections of disparate markets). There is perhaps no better example of this hybrid city than London (Hohnenberg and Lees 1995: 6) wherein – for a few centuries at least – the two distinct functions were encapsulated in one city: the West End, the 'central place' of government, and of imperial power; heart of civility and home to hierarchical organizations setting clear limits to the (national) community in its backyard, dictating what does, and what doesn't, belong. The East End: a dynamic multiplicity comprised of multiple cultures, typical of a maritime metropolis.

The 'central place/network' binary might have a particular salience for historians of urban formation. For scholars of contemporary urban formations, however, the dualism is of less obvious use. The growth of rail, of air travel, the motor car, transoceanic cable and, latterly, fibre optics have amplified the intensity of all urban *and rural* forms. Technology has decentralized erstwhile central places, rendered old port cities obsolete, while turning what were once peripheral cities increasingly into focal points of activity and investment. The demise of the port of London started as early as the 1950s, as the British nation started shifting from a focus on export and manufacture to services and intellectual property. Yet despite this, London was a long way from fading into insignificance. Central to London's enduring role as a world city are the various types of capital and control derived from its position atop centuries of maritime empire. These inheritances abound in the wealthy neighbourhoods of West London, or in the financial institutions of the City. Equally significant among its inheritances, however, is the pragmatic amenability to difference that was once necessitated in the city's East, the crystallization of centuries of emotional and somatic labour. Embedded in ways of 'being together' and 'rubbing along', the steadfast sensibilities of local culture in the city's east have long enabled communities to withstand often rapid changes in the texture, cadence, smell and flavour of the city. Importantly, and unintentionally, the city's history has bequeathed many of its working class neighbourhoods with resources for the twenty-first century's increasing compulsion for us to live with difference (Hall 1993).

Even within transnational junctions such as East London, however, there are particular locations that stand out for the relationship between their sensuous everyday life, and the transcultural social formations that emerge out of them. As this book has detailed, the city's assortment of grocers, everyday hot-food vendors and high streets – particularly those in the historically poorer and more cramped spaces of the city – are important sites of contact through which a loose network of transcultural associations are established and through which community and identities are continually transformed. Among these sites, it is perhaps the peculiar form of the city's 'open-air street markets' – those such as Ridley Road (as featured in the bush-meat scandal) or Petticoat Lane (the location of Tubby Isaac's seafood stand and Tomo's katsu wrap stand) – that most tangibly facilitate transcultural processes through the sensory experience of its users. In distinction to the charcoal suits, brushed steel and mirrored glass for which the global city is perhaps better known, many of the actual market places of the city remain home to a very literal coming together of heterogenous people, smells, flavours, sounds and textures on a daily basis. Such has nearly always been the case with street markets; from medieval market towns to the improvised retail landscapes of post-Soviet Europe and the global south (Cunningham, Moore and Cunningham 1974; Bromley 1998a, 1998b; Czakó and Sik 1999; Sik and Wallace 1999; Zinkhan, Fontenelle and Balazs 1999; Stillerman 2006). With a shifting range of products, modulated by actual transactions between buyers and sellers, managed through decentralized mechanisms, fed by flexible supply chains and occupied through diversities of tenure, afforded through low entry costs, such locations have it in them to provide a range of functions to the city. Admittedly sometimes 'the market and the keeper of the market submitted economic activities to explicit cultural and religious definitions of the norms' (Redfield and Singer 1954: 58). At many other instances, however, market places have been sites of dialogue, genuine exchange, cooperation and cross-cultural productions (Watson and Wells 2005; Watson and Studdert 2006; Parham 2012, 2015; Hiebert, Rath and Vertovec 2015). Certainly this is true of the commercial spaces covered in this book, all of which play vital roles in the development of a 'convivial' multiculture (Gilroy 2004; Mandel 2008; Parham 2012, 2015; Rhys-Taylor 2013a). Of course, as many 'ethnic entrepreneurs' testify (Arrighetti, Bolzani and Lasagni 2014), it is rarely their intention 'to facilitate transcultural processes' and harbour 'multicultural conviviality' within their environs. But it is also the nature of such literally cramped space, in parts of the city where a pragmatic indifference to difference was often necessitated, that disturbances to the boundary between the body and the city are inevitable. As low-level as such experiences might seem, they are certainly not inconsequential.

It is perhaps because of their role as spaces of encounter and active transformation of culture that the muscular guardians of more exclusive forms of association have so often descended on the East End's markets and ramshackle high streets in order to shake them up. As discussed in Chapters 2 and 4, the British League of Ex-Servicemen, the British Union of Fascists, the National Front, the British Nationalist Party and more recently the English Defence League have all, at various times, marched into the East End. Armed with exaggerated stories about the city's disorderly immigrant neighbourhoods, a common feature of far-right incursions has been their efforts to identify and label various East End sensoria – such as the heat of chilli peppers (Hopkins 2015) – as markers of 'outsider' status. These have been some of the cruder efforts to stifle the East End's quiet acceptance of difference. However, despite the violence that they have caused, such efforts have generally fallen a long way short of actually transforming the culture that characterized the city's east. Less obvious than these ham-fisted efforts to sensorially demarcate 'them' from 'us', however, are a range of processes working across the city, far more successfully than muscular fascists, to spatialize exclusive social structures, by way of investment in the senses.

Subjugating the East End

Early in 2015, a video was released onto a streaming site advertising a new luxury housing development, No.1 Commercial Street. The flats were located at the boundary of the old East End and the City of London (Siciliano 2015) and were, in fact, just around the corner from Tubby Isaac's seafood stand. Controversially, the video promoting the apartments was shot in the style of movie trailer for the thriller *American Psycho*. The short, high-end production film followed a young, white, pin-striped city trader – his hair slicked back – on his commute home from work. Striking for the hyper-misanthropy of the inner-monologue narrating the film, the trader was shown squirming at the heterogenous masses on public transport, fantasizing about women he passed, and arguing with his girlfriend. Finally the short film concluded with the young man finding a sense of peace and calm as he entered the low-lit polished glass and granite surfaces of his new luxury flat. The film, somewhat predictably given its general tastelessness, caused a notable degree of upset and was eventually pulled (Finamore 2015; Siciliano 2015; Wainwright 2015). The controversy did not, however, end with the pulling of the video. Rather, it grew even further when the flats it was advertising finally opened to residents and buyers. It was at this point that it was revealed that the new flats had not one but two sets of entrance doors. One set of doors were glass fronted, softly lit and furnished with muzak and a concierge for residents paying the 'full rates'. The other entrance, it turned out, was a matt grey utilitarian portal, around the side near the bins, for the building's less wealthy residents, that is, for those that had bought into the small percentage of 'affordable' flats that the developers were mandated by law to provide. While a new phenomenon in this historically impoverished part of the city, the 'poor doors' had in fact started emerging across London in a number of locations over previous years. In each instance, the developers responded to critics by arguing that the reason for the 'poor doors' can be found in the difficulty of separating out the service charges of the subsidized residents from the costs of the higher-end residents. Regardless of the rationale, the consequences are that the buildings' wealthier residents are literally protected from encounters with the sensory life-worlds of their poorer neighbours. Instead they are treated to the familiar (for them at least) and, therefore, unobtrusive sensory surroundings of a transnational hotel chain.

Soon after the furore around the video marketing luxury homes, two new blocks of luxurious flats emerged immediately behind 'No.1 Commercial Street', on exactly the spot that a block of mid-century social housing had stood until 2011. After over two years of construction, the hoardings fell to reveal 'Kensington Apartments' and 'Sloane Apartments', after the famous neighbourhoods of *West* London. The erasure of the housing tenure, the communities and the cultural references historically associated with the city's east is telling. Certainly, for much of early modernity, London was a hybrid city, both a globally networked city with heterogenous culture (in the East End), and a regional administrative centre reproducing the national culture (in the West End). Today, however, the colonization of East London with the cultural symbols and sensoria generally associated with the city's wealthier west, marks the increasing subjugation of residual culture of a maritime metropolis – its sensoria and its sensibilities – to the uniformity and hierarchical control of the 'central place' historically manifest in the city's west.

In the twenty-first century, however, the West London that the city's east is being subjugated to is far from merely the 'central place' of a territorial nation. Over the last three hundred years, the seat of power in London's west became first, the control centre of nation, then an Empire and, latterly, one of a handful of command centres of global neoliberalism. As critical urbanists have repeatedly demonstrated (Harvey 1989; Soja 1996; Smith 2002; Edensor 2014), part of this latter political modality is a 'new urbanism' in which the entirety of urban space is put to use for the extraction of profit from and for private individuals and corporations. Near the very top of the new urbanist's shopping list are a number of locations that once were reviled as sites of intense pollution and industry. Within the political and economic framework of the Conservative government, East London's borough councils, faced with cuts to their funding, are working increasingly with housing developers and landowners to attract the capital of transnational elites. And they are achieving this in part by subjugating London's East End to the blandscapes of 'new urbanism's serial monotony' (Smith 2002; Harvey 2012: 13). Other than in the glass-curtained ground-floor restaurants of New London's gleaming towers, the chances that its wealthy residents will encounter sensoria and sensibilities outside of their own carefully calibrated tastes are, then, greatly reduced.

As much as these developments are driven by changes in the East End's residential tenure, they are mirrored, if not accelerated by changes in retail environments. Thus, the high-end 'experiential' mega-malls usurping high streets in Shepherds Bush, Stratford and Croydon are all notable for the calculation behind the ways in which, like earlier department stores (Featherstone 1990; Laermans 1993), they subtly teach shoppers how they ought to appear, sound and smell. They do this, not least, by carefully modulating the sensorium of the shopping space, alongside active efforts to keep out unwanted sensations and people. At the same time as London's retail spaces are subject to ever-increasing degrees of calculative mediation, in a direct correlate, the city's more established and incorrigibly disorganized open-air street markets – Chrisp Street Market, Kingsland Waste Market, Whitechapel High Street, Brixton Market, the Brixton Arches, Deptford Market and many more besides – are now in the sights of land speculators and property developers. The frequency with which such sites are targeted for development reveals the stakes to be gained in subjugating the city's more anarchic atmospheres to those tailored to, and productive of, more fastidious sensibilities. Through the replacement of the city's erstwhile market with more controllable spaces, the subsequent impact on surrounding land values enable huge chunks of the inner-city population to be relocated, while accruing significant profits for investors. Once the realm of serendipitous encounter, the sensoria of the city, and sensibilities of city dwellers are increasingly instrumentalized for the short term profits of property speculators. Rationalized in terms of the profits that such developments will deliver, such interventions in the city's sensory landscape, also have serious consequences for the types of social formation that are then afforded by the urban environment.

Of course regulating the amplitude and intensity of the urban sensorium serves to mitigate what some might see as the sensory excess of contemporary urban life. Despite the demise of the furnaces and smoke stacks, the sound, light and smell generated by the city still has an impact on urbanites' physical well-being. Countless studies have revealed that urban 'noise', for instance, continues to affect attention spans, coronary systems, circadian rhythms and hearing ability, as well as the 'mental life' of city dwellers (Melamed and Bruhis 1996; Stansfeld and Matheson 2003; Ising and Kruppa 2004; Moudon 2009). As the architectural critic Juhani Pallasmaa notes, the ways in which humans actually sense the world are the product of millennia of biological evolution and relatively slow changes in the surrounding environment. Our senses are not, Pallasmaa argues, well suited to the sort of post-human living that the urban assemblage has ushered in (Pallasmaa 2012). In efforts to sustain a healthy body, a coherent sense of self, neighbourhoods, community or city, there are certainly environments that are *too* intense. And, as we know, historically the most injurious of urban sensoriums have been allotted to its least affluent residents. Yet, significant advances were made in the mid-twentieth century in terms of relocating and regulating a number of the city's more intense locales. Today, then, for the main part, where sensory regimes are implemented to 'protect' urbanites, it appears to be less in terms of damage to physical health, than in ways that speak to particularly gendered, racialized and class-inflected ideas about what the good city looks, sounds and smells like.

The classed elements of these interventions become clear when, for instance, glancing at the formal guidance offered to planning departments by the Department for Environmental Health (DEFRA 2005: 95). At the top of their list of noxious odours is an assortment of working class smells (Bourdieu and Nice 1984): fried chicken, burgers, pubs and fish and chips. This is, as previously discussed, reflected in problems typically raised by the city's more affluent residents in reference to hot food takeaways. It is worth noting that at the other end of the DEFRA's 'problematic' aroma scale are an assortment of olfactory markers of suburban petit bourgeois lifestyles: Italian food, French food and steakhouses. Less greasy perhaps, but no less aromatic. The gendered aspects of sensory regimes regulating the city become clearer when considering the consistency with which particular scents, sights and sounds are enlisted into the performance of 'good' and 'bad' femininities (Largey and Watson 1972; Kane 1990; Braun and Wilkinson 2001; Barcan 2014). The sensory regimes regulating the everyday life of the city are conspicuously racialized when it is so clearly the sensoria associated with non-white working class cultures that are most explicitly, and frequently, reviled.

Coming to Our Senses (Reprise)

In an echo of Jane Jacobs' famous critiques of mid-century mass urbanism (Jacobs 1989), many are starting to see correctives to the ceaseless problems of North American and European urbanism in a new breed of spaces of encounter, particularly high streets and open-air markets (Parham 2015), but also wholesale markets (Mele, Ng and Chim 2015). Obviously appealing to the omnivorous middle class's love of alfresco dining and cultural agility, the proposals for more open and flexible urban spaces, however, also have weightier rationales behind them. Importantly, by physically exposing city dwellers to one another, and to one another's sensory life worlds, such spaces are believed to facilitate the maturation of genuinely cosmopolitan subjects, capable of dealing with the mess and vitality of contemporary urban life.

Alert to the re-evaluation of such spaces, planners of London's recent neighbourhood revivification schemes have also started incorporating various forms of 'post-mall' retail interventions: Broadway Market, Spitalfields Market, Brixton Village, Chatsworth Road Market (see also Jacobs 1996; Dines 2009; Parham 2012; Gonzalez and Waley 2013). Creating concrete spaces in which a diversity of materials and concomitant people *could* flow, and in which life-worlds *potentially* meet, would seemingly go some way to fostering genuinely convivial multiculture. However, the re-invention of the street market and the food hall are far from guaranteed to sooth the squeamish misanthropy that infuses London's spatial injustices. In fact, in every instance listed above – Brixton, Hackney, Spitalfields – the flexibility of the revived spaces ultimately only accelerated the colonization of inner-city space by those most able to tap into the majoritarian sensoria and sensibilities. Which is to say, areas that once housed healthily mottled retail environments, have increasingly become bougie farmers or fashion markets. To be blunt, while the type of space and the infrastructure it is embedded in makes a difference, the remarkable urban multiculture of London's most vital spaces does not exist without the bodies that actually made connections across cultures and geographies possible, without the sensoria that they dress in, without the sensibilities through which they make sense of themselves and each other. This is not just to say that the inner city's new residents are depriving the city of 'colour'. London's new majoritiarian classes are ostensibly as diverse, if not more so, than the communities that used to coalesce around the city's working class neighbourhoods. Rather, it is to say that, despite the global *connections* of 'New London', its new public spaces are devoid of bodies with requisite sensibilities – the multisensory nonchalance and 'blasé attitude' – that made the worldly *culture* of the old metropolis possible. In short, as working-class neighbourhoods are refigured as gated citadels of luxury, as dwellings become commodities, the city's pragmatic amenability to difference is being supplanted with a distinctly suburban squeamishness.

All is not, however, lost. As part of the city's post-industrial inversion, something important is also happening to its erstwhile suburban spaces. Therein, amidst the landscapes of cul-de-sacs, secondary shopping malls and franchise cafes, a number of recent studies have found convivial multiculture alive and well (Wise 2010; Jones et al. 2015). Apparently, under the cloak of mirrors, tiles and fordist sensations, cultural differences and individual auras are not entirely stultified. Rather, they are simply rendered 'part of the wall paper' (Wise 2010; Jones et al. 2015). Thus, in contrast to the new open-air markets of the bourgeois inner-city, it is the 'blandscapes' typically associated with suburbia, retail parks and identikit high streets that nurture the city's convivial multiculture. Further enquiry into these spaces and what makes them work is crucial.

In both the reinvented inner-city street market and the suburban mall, interventions in the material design of urban space are potentially useful in terms of potentializing various forms of conviviality. But even here, the material form of space might not be sufficient for responding to the moral and social challenges of urban life. Importantly, as each of the chapters here aimed to quietly demonstrate, it is the embodiment of particular sensibilities, particular ways of seeing, hearing, smelling and touching the world, of making sense of those sensations (rather than particular sensoria alone) that ultimately characterize, or at least characterized, East London's culture. While the material culture of London's East End has constantly changed, sensibilities that catalyzed that change were, for centuries, coextensive with the old metropolis' intensity. What is absent then, in an impulse to revive and reconstruct the material spaces for conviviality, by an obsession with the 'hardware' of urban life, are the sensibilities that have historically made intensive urban formations possible, the 'software' that ultimately brings cities to life. At the very heart of intervening in the displacement shaping many of Northern Europe and North America's cities is, then, a process of individual reckoning. That is, the ultimate corrective to the socio-sensory reproduction of spatial injustice, might require individual city-dwellers to actually engage in serious effort to question the veracity of their own gut feelings. This entails much more than learning liberal tolerance or cultivating omnivorous disposition. And it requires more than just a multisensory version of colour-blindness. What is required, is deep and unceasing scepticism of the way in which we feel about specific smells, sights, sounds and textures, an interrogation as to why we might feel that way, and an alertness to the potential consequence of those sensations.

To actually think more carefully about the kaleidoscope of low-level squirms and delights aroused as part of everyday life in the city might seem insignificant given the colossal economic geopolitical and ecological challenges posed and faced by contemporary cities. Doubtless, the close-up vignettes covered in this book were largely only of immediate significance for the individuals concerned, and even then of very little significance. As insignificant as everyday 'gut feelings' might seem amidst the processes of a gargantuan global city, they are nevertheless at the heart of social formation and cultural production and, as such, are integral to urban economies. It is above all else, the broader historical view of the city that highlights the importance of the senses within our everyday lives. Set against the broader histories out of which individual experiences emerge, and into which they plunge back, otherwise unremarkable moments are brimful of significance. It is the longer-run socio-historical attention to everyday experiences that uncovers a multitude of crossroads that lie beneath the city's local culture, and which highlight the pertinence of the ongoing meeting of disparate life worlds within the city.

As Saskia Sassen (2001) famously notes, twenty-first-century London is, first and foremost, a control centre atop a hierarchical network of locations that are overriding local culture and histories across the planet, primarily for the purposes of 'rationalized' profit extraction. A closer look at the everyday life of the city, however, reveals the ongoing meeting of heterogeneous bodies, commodities and culture, a heterogeneity that is more congruent with London's historical roles as a city. Importantly, this very heterogeneity and the remarkable forms of 'being together' that it generates, are increasingly threatened by the city's newer centralized global command functions, and especially its role as a 'land bank' for the global elite. Exactly how the 'global city' relates to its planetary connections, partly relates to how it values heterogeneity within its own geography. For the sake of peoples, cultures around the world, for the sake of a sense of whom 'we' are that actually fits with the material realties we are faced with, for the sake of developing sustainable forms of cohabitation, it is imperative that we 'come to our senses', question our gut feelings and understand the importance of the senses within urban lives. Hopefully, this book goes some way to starting that process.

8

Methodological Afterword

While it served the purpose of outlining how and where this book was researched, the brief 'formal statement' on methods at the start of the book belies some of the issues thrown up by the research behind the previous chapters. It also avoided a discussion of some of the decisions made with respect to 'research methods' as the book was being developed. Discussion of both of these has been reserved for a methodological afterword.

Before going on to discuss these matters I want to tentatively offer two 'rationales' for having reserved them for an afterword. The first relates to the specific 'multisensory' form of this ethnography. Less obliquely, it relates to a desire to avoid some of the methodological fetishism that waits at the sidelines of novel forms of empiricism. That is not to say that issues raised by novel methods are not important. Simply that the questions invited through the application of ethnographic methods, and multisensory methods in particular, often threaten to obfuscate what such methods yield. As stated previously, although 'coming to our senses' could be an end in itself (we understand so little about the senses themselves), for this book, a sensory attention was adopted primarily for more obviously sociological reasons: for developing more nuanced understandings of 'race', class, power, globalization and multiculture. The methodological afterword comprises an attempt to swerve premature entanglement in methodological debates, while at the same time giving due attention to some important issues regarding methods.

The second rationale for the 'afterword' relates to following William Foote Whyte's reflections on his own urban ethnography: 'I am convinced that the actual evolution of research ideas does not take place in accord with the formal statements we read on research methods. The ideas grow up in part out of our immersion in the data and out of the whole process of living' (Whyte 1993: 280). Put otherwise, of all the methodological issues that were thrown up by this study, the most salient concerns were not obvious until writing was nearly finished. Following Foote Whyte, an afterword constitutes an attempt to have the text mirror the chronological emergence of methodological concerns as the research and writing up were played out.

Accessing Ambient Experience

> What speaks to us, seemingly, is always the big event, the untoward, the extraordinary: the front page splash, the banner headlines. Railway trains only begin to exist when they are derailed . . . Aeroplanes achieve existence only when they are hijacked . . . What's really going on, what we're experiencing, the rest, all the rest, where is it? How should we take account of, question, describe what happens every day and recurs every day: the banal, the quotidian, the obvious, the common, the ordinary, the infra-ordinary, the background noise, the habitual? (Perec and Sturrock 1998: 210).

Perhaps the most significant practical difficulty when gathering data for this book was created by its intention to answer the type of question posed above by Georges Perec. How might we access and interrogate, not only the sensational foreground of people's lives, but also the multisensory ambient buzz out of which the 'everyday' emerges? As Perec seemed aware, people's experience of the sensational foreground of their lives – that which jumps out of the background – is in some respects relatively simple for writers and researchers to access, represent and translate. The 'sensational' is, after all, that which we are caused to remark upon by its distinction from the banality of the background. Accordingly, we are all generally well equipped to pronounce upon the sensational foreground of our lives, leaving verbal transcriptions of these experiences available for researchers and journalists. Ambience, on the other hand, refers to the realm of experiences that are 'felt' by the body – that regulate its mood and activate responses – yet never really register at a level we would formally define as 'discursive consciousness'. This leaves 'the ambient' as an aspect of experience that is rarely translated into verbal expression; whether that be interpersonal expression, or the silent intra-personal discursive consciousness. Accordingly, standard surveys, formal interviews and even advanced ethnographic methods, can be of little use to researching more commonplace everyday sensory experiences. As a result, the sociological valence of ambient experience has been particularly under-researched.

The unsuitability of direct questions for researching the ambient sensuosity of everyday lives was made plain relatively early on in the development of this book. In the first few weeks of field work I developed a pilot of questions and discussion topics for people hanging around in or passing through East London's street markets. These questions, I thought, would trigger verbal translations of their sensuous relationship with their environs. I soon discovered, however, that in nearly every instance the participant was unable to translate their experience of the immediate context. More often they looked at me with a very blank expression.

That is not to say, however, that after a couple of seconds evaluating what I had asked – and possibly my motivations for asking it – participants were unwilling to talk about their sensory experiences. On the contrary, nearly everybody interviewed over the course of this ethnography offered ready-made narratives describing some 'sensational' smell or flavour that they 'personally' found either particularly obnoxious, pleasurable or evocative. Unfortunately, however, these narratives were invariably about elsewhere and other times than those delimited by the coordinates of this study. It is not that that these contributions were unimportant. These personal statements – or rather the impersonal patterns within these statements – were important for building up an understanding of the relationship between power, narrative, discursive consciousness, sensation and urban formations. Notably, these statements also brought into relief the widespread absence of reflection on the more mundane, sensuosity of immediately lived experience.

In this respect, what was required was a set of methods that would enable the research to move beyond simply representing and interrogating the sensation that registers in people's 'discursive consciousness', towards a consideration of the low-level, semi-conscious experience of the body. In short, the discursive inaccessibility of 'the sensuous' necessitated a commitment to situating my own corporeality – or, more gandiosely, 'incarnate intelligence' – into the context of the ethnography (Wacquant 2007: 8). It was this – the reflexive and multisensory immersion in the everyday life of inner East London – that alongside discussions and observations, truly enriched this book's understanding of the traffic between cities, sociality and the senses.

Ultimately, although not providing me with anything like the opportunity to walk in another's shoes (contra Pink 2008: 175), the practice of being there alongside participants and reflexively experiencing the research context myself, enhanced an understanding of the relationship between the sensuosity of the everyday and the social formations developing within the research field. Below I offer a handful of examples, hitherto undiscussed, that I think make plain what multisensory ethnographic immersion yields, but also which make plain the limits of ethnographic immersion and the impossibility of understanding how others are 'emplaced in the world' (Pink 2008: 175) through their senses.

Acquiring Tastes

Before moving any further, it serves to know something about the 'I' that has featured occasionally in these pages. This 'I' was born to middle-income parents, my father (originally working-class) was a chef and restaurateur (amongst *many* other things) and my mother (from a more middle-class background) fiercely proud of her A-level in home economics. 'I' grew up surrounded by cooking, and inevitably moved into the catering industry, working in restaurants from the age of thirteen until the age of twenty-one. In more recent years 'I' occasioned as a restaurant reviewer for a well-known collection of city guides, and in fact came to know London first and foremost, through its food and restaurants. These aspects of my biography have a bearing on my sensibility, shaping both the things I am sensitive to, how I perceive them and, ultimately, feeding in to the particular mode of sociological attention behind the book. It did not, however, bequeath me with the full range of sensory literacies, or sensitivities, required for engaging the broad range of biographies and contexts captured in the previous pages. As with learning a language, interpreting the sensory order of other people's lives required engagement with them, primarily by way of shopping and eating alongside them, so as to open up a space of sensory translation (Stoller 2008).

Of course, within communal dining experience, discussions about smell and taste could be initiated. However, this was far from always the case. Nor need it have been. In many respects, I was learning about many of the relationships that I wanted to dissect, first hand. By 'first hand', I mean to refer to the personal acquisition of new sensory fluencies and affinities. To give an example, amongst these new affinities was the unexpected development of a real hunger for jellied eels. While I had been a lifelong consumer of seafood, eels were something that I had previously steered well clear of. I offer the acquired taste for eels as an example, not because developing the taste is remarkable or heroic in itself (although it *is*). Rather I include it only because this particular example crystallizes the process through which I came to understand the socio-sensory plasticity that I witnessed within the lives of many of the study's *other* participants. That is, it endowed me with the processual experience of a particular set of sensations enmeshing a body within a specific social context. It is primarily through the personal accruement of such experiences, and the cross-referencing of these with other people's, that I sought to develop an understanding of the relationships that exist between everyday sensations and the city's social forms.

Sensing Boundaries

The multisensory ethnographic immersion – through which sensory literacies and affinities were acquired – was not, in any sense, a straightforward process. In many instances, the ethnographic immersion also entailed running into the 'socio-sensory boundaries' constructed between people. In some respects, my initial unwillingness to try jellied eels was emblematic of such a boundary. While I was primarily happy to stand around the stand eating the oysters and cockles I knew from within my own culinary biography, this was not the same food that the majority of the stand's patrons ate. Moreover, my reluctance to try them precluded me from an understanding of the specific sensations that they valued, as well as marking me out as distinct. Remarkably, this particular obstacle was surprisingly easy to overcome. However, as the following examples will demonstrate, not all the barriers fortified by my own sensibility – nor others' perception of me – were as easy or even possible to navigate. In several instances, the uncompromising limits of placing my own 'organism ... and incarnate intelligence' (Wacquant 2007: 8) at the centre of the 'forces' I aimed to dissect were made painfully clear.

One especially vivid encounter with a social boundary, erected through the senses, emerged amidst my initial forays into the lock up units behind the main strip of Ridley Road Market. Having heard many stories about the market previously, I was pretty certain that if any of the sensational details featured in those narratives were in fact true, my own sensibility would inhibit me from situating my own 'incarnate intelligence' in the line of that particular fire. Yet, as I would also discover elsewhere, it was not merely my own sensibility that would obstruct me from this particular arena. Rather, it was also other people's; while I found nothing of any real 'sensational' significance in the market's recesses, a number of informants were adamant about the presence of illicit meat at the market, and suggested that such things were probably being made invisible to me, a white middle-class male with a notebook in my hand. Even if I had the personal capacity to acquire this particular sensory literacy or 'taste', informants insisted that others' perception of me would still prohibit access to it.

The fact of something being hidden from you is, of course, impossible to either prove or disprove. There is little denying, however, that being of a minority age, gender and skin tone amongst middle-aged Caribbean, South Asian, and West African female shoppers – let alone clutching a notepad, pen, sound recorder and camera – there were elements of the 'action' in the market that it was difficult for me to submit my body 'to the fire' of. The heat, it seemed would always dissipate as I approached it. While I cannot definitively say this is the case with bush-meat, the inaccessibility can be illustrated through another example, less sensational than a trade in primate meat although equally pertinent. The following is an excerpt taken from the earliest of my field notes. On one of my first days' ethnographic incursions to Ridley Road Market, I was:

[...] drawn into a particular stall off to the side of the main strip of the market by a display of pea aubergines – a foodstuff I was familiar with from my paternal domestic environment, but had not seen in this country for years, let alone braided and bunched up like beige grapes. Yet what seized my attention was the box I noticed at my feet; a brown cardboard container of glossy, light-brown, calcite and conical mollusc shells. At the first glance I identified these as conches – a shell shape I vaguely remembered from my childhood, perhaps a shell from my grandmother's collection of ornamental seashells. It certainly seemed plausible. Conch shells, I knew, contained a muscular, tasty food that was relatively common on menus in the Caribbean. Surprised to see these stashed in a corner of a vegetable grocer I wanted to see these uncanny artefacts with my hands. Picking one up, the shell was cold, larger than the palm of my hand and smooth, but not as smooth as I had expected. As I turned it around in my hand two antennae slowly unfurled from the hard spiralled shell, and a firm fleshy body started to uncurl and splay over my fingers. It was not, as I was starting to realize, what I understood a conch to be. I glanced back down at the box to see a small degree of movement in a number of the other molluscs. Not the shell on my grandmother's shelf, but rather the one from my cousin's glass tank – his childhood pet. A giant African snail. And they did not look as though they were for keeping as pets. I turned towards the stall holder, who had previously been busy stacking bottles:

'How do you cook these?' I asked nonchalantly.

This was a typical opener that I was using to start a rapport with traders. While on many occasions I was at feigning a partial degree of ignorance, on this occasion I was not.

Looking me up and down he paused for a second before stating abruptly, 'You don't even know if I eat them.'

This was followed by an excruciatingly long silence during which my heart sped up as my mouth dried out. My initial strategy seemed to be to assume that the stall holder was joking. I laughed, then turned to his friend, with whom he'd been conversing.

'*Do* you eat them?'

More silence. Then, 'Get out!' I'm not sure which of the two said this.

I moved to put the shell back down in its box on the floor and simultaneously pivoted to turn out of the stall. Another man, a trader from a neighbouring stall stepped in having heard the exchange. Before I could return the snail to its box the shell was taken out of my hands. 'You crack the shell and scoop up like this, then chop,' he said as he made a chopping motion with one hand perpendicular to the other, glancing at the stall holder. 'Then you fry 'em up. Soups as well.'

'Oh, thanks. Thanks. Ok.' I said, keen to leave as quickly as possible.

Over the next five minutes my heart rate returned to near normal rate.

While I was eventually offered a recipe for these particular molluscs, what I initially experienced here were some of the visceral limits of trying to know all aspects of life in the street market through my own corporeal experience. Doubtless, some aspects of my own sensibility had opened windows between my experience and that of my study participants, and provided numerous opportunities for discussion. Elsewhere, however, there were evidently chasms that could not be crossed through experiential knowledge alone, chasms created both by the forms of power invested in my own sensibility, but also, importantly, through others' correlated perceptions of me. It was not only, it must be noted here, while wandering around Ridley Road that my own body – and people's perceptions of it – precluded access to specific areas. An analogous response was initially experienced when first hanging around Petticoat Lane Market and its side streets. Therein I first set out dressed in a thick sweater, denim jacket, cargo pants, woolly hat and fingerless gloves, armed with the latest trivia on West Ham United; an ensemble I embarrassingly believed to be the signature of the market users and traders. As I have since realized through time spent at the market, the result of this ill-fitting costume was that I was initially perceived to be an undercover policeman, a devious undercover journalist, or perhaps even more regrettably, a naive ethnographer. In this instance, however, as well as within most areas of Ridley Road, the social distance was steadily overcome and the markets traders and myself integrated each other into our daily lives.

Yet despite the eventual access to the market's everyday life that I achieved, the exclusion enacted through both my perception of the world and the world's perception of me, is a powerful testament to the possible limits of placing the ethnographer's own 'organism [. . .] and incarnate intelligence' at the centre of the 'forces' he intended to dissect. It is also suggestive of the potential damage done to others through careless attempts at 'heroic immersion' within a specific field. Such experiences were not, however, entirely devoid of sociological value. On the contrary, the experience of my own multisensory squeamishness, combined with others perceptions of me, is also exemplary of the social barriers constructed, and social strata reproduced, through the embodiment of particular ways of sensing the world. Moreover, there are also other ways of accessing data pertaining to locations from which the author might otherwise be prohibited. As demonstrated in the use of Sanchita Islam's work with East London's Bangladeshi and Somali youth in Chapter 2, or the use of Nurul Islam's 'HoodForts' productions in Chapter 5, there are existing repositories of voices and texts, emerging out of other authors' and researchers' sustained efforts. While not emerging from my own primary research, such accounts tally with the general view derived through my own ethnographic work, and offer invaluable insights to contexts wherein this particular author's 'incarnate intelligence' might otherwise be excluded.

The Senses and Spaces of Translation

It must be noted that while many areas of the city's everyday life were either initially insensible to, or sequestered from, me many more soon became sensible to me. This shift is largely attributable to the development of a multisensory literacy. Such was the extent of this literacy and familiarity that after about eighteen months of regular visits to Petticoat Lane, the owner of the seafood stand commented, as he handed me my morning eels, 'You're like a bit of an old timer down here now, aren't you?' Indeed, through changes that I underwent in my own body, I had adopted the culinary rhythms analogous to those of an erstwhile generation of the stand's visitors. Yet, I remain conscious of the fact that such experiences do not in any way provide objective access to the lived experience of an 'old timer's' life, nor that of anybody else's. What multisensory ethnographic methods provide above all else – and this is not of any less social scientific value – is broader and higher resolution space of translation between one person and another. It is, above all, the increased definition with which the social world appears through a multisensory attention, that provides the strongest case for 'coming to our senses'. Through such methods and their correlated representational practices, it is possible to start answering important questions as to the endurance of struggles within banal everyday experiences, as well as the human potential that is secreted within them.

BIBLIOGRAPHY

Anon. (1854), 'The London Comissariat', *The Quarterly Review* XCV.

Anon. (1893), 'On Cockneys', *Dundee Evening Telegraph*.

Anon. (1947a), 'Abolition of the Petrol Ration', *Hackney Gazette*, August 10.

Anon. (1947b), 'The Economic Crisis', *Hackney Gazette*, August 27.

Anon. (1947c), 'Open-Air Politics', *Hackney Gazette*, September 10: 1.

Anon. (1947d), 'The Battle of Ridley Road', *Hackney Gazette*, October 13: 1.

Anon. (2013), 'Eating Out 1950–2000', *20th Century London*. Available at: http://www.20thcenturylondon.org.uk/eating-out-1950-2000, accessed August 17, 2016.

Abbots, Emma-Jayne and Benjamin Coles (2013), 'Horsemeat-Gate: The Discursive Production of a Neoliberal Food Scandal', *Food, Culture and Society: An International Journal of Multidisciplinary Research* 16(4): 535–550.

Achaya, Kongandra Thammu (1994), *Indian Food: A Historical Companion*, Oxford: Oxford University Press.

Adam, Barbara, Ulrich Beck and Joost Van Loon (2000), *The Risk Society and Beyond: Critical Issues for Social Theory*, London: Sage.

Adams, Mags, Trevor Cox, Gemma Moore et al. (2006), 'Sustainable Soundscapes: Noise Policy and the Urban Experience', *Urban Studies* 43(13): 2385–2398.

Adams, Mags D., Neil S. Bruce, William J. Davies et al. (2008), 'Soundwalking as a Methodology for Understanding Soundscapes'. Available at: http://usir.salford.ac.uk/2461, accessed February 17 2015.

Adorno, Theodor W. (2002), *Essays on Music*, Berkeley, CA: University of California Press.

Agamben, Giorgio (2004), *The Open: Man and Animal*, Palo Alto, CA: Stanford University Press.

Ainsworth, William Harrison (1826), *Letters from Cockney Lands*, London: John Ebers.

Alexander, Claire E. (2000), *The Asian Gang: Ethnicity, Identity, Masculinity*, Oxford: Berg Publishers.

Alleyne, Mervyn (2003), 'Language in Jamaican Culture'. In Roxy Harris and Ben Rampton (eds), *The Language, Ethnicity and Race Reader*, London: Psychology Press, pp. 54–69.

Anderson, Benedict (1991), *Imagined Communities: Reflections on the Origin and Spread of Nationalism*, London: Verso.

Anderson, Ben and Paul Harrison (2010), 'The Promise of Non-Representational Theories'. In B. Anderson and P. Harrison (eds), *Taking-Place: Non-Representational Theories and Geography*, London: Ashgate, pp. 1–36.

Anderson, Dave (2015), 'Fried Chicken?' Available at: http://foodtellsastory.tumblr.com/post/111641232733/fried chicken, accessed August 13, 2015.

Anderson, Nels (1961), *The Hobo: The Sociology of the Homeless Man*, Chicago: University of Chicago Press.

Andrews, Jean (1992), 'The Peripatetic Chili Pepper: Diffusion of the Domesticated Capsicums Since Colombus'. In Nelson Foster and Linda S. Cordell (eds), *Chilies to Chocolate: Food the Americas Gave the World*, Tuscon, AZ: University of Arizona Press, pp. 81–95.

Animal Welfare Act 2006. Available at: http://www.legislation.gov.uk/ ukpga/2006/45/contents, accessed August 7, 2015.

Appadurai, Arjun (1986), 'Theory in Anthropology: Center and Periphery', *Comparative Studies in Society and History* 28(02): 356–374.

Appadurai, Arjun (1996), *Modernity At Large: Cultural Dimensions of Globalization*, Minneapolis, MN: University of Minnesota Press.

Appadurai, Arjun (2009), *The Social Life of Things: Commodities in Cultural Perspective*, Cambridge: Cambridge University Press.

Arens, William (1980), *The Man-Eating Myth*, Oxford: Oxford University Press.

Arrighetti, Alessandro, Daniela Bolzani and Andrea Lasagni (2014), 'Beyond the Enclave? Break-Outs into Mainstream Markets and Multicultural Hybridism in Ethnic Firms', *Entrepreneurship and Regional Development* 26(9–10): 753–777.

Atkins, Peter and Ian Bowler (2000), *Food in Society: Economy, Culture, Geography*, London and New York: Routledge.

Atkinson, Will and Christopher Deeming (2015), 'Class and Cuisine in Contemporary Britain: The Social Space, the Space of Food and Their Homology', *The Sociological Review* 63(4): 876–896.

Back, Les (1996), *New Ethnicities and Urban Culture*, London and New York: Routledge.

Back, Les (2007), *The Art of Listening*, Oxford: Berg.

Back, Les (2009), 'Researching Community and Its Moral Projects', *Twenty-First Century Society* 4(2): 201–214.

Back, Les and Nirmal Puwar (2012), *Live Methods*, Hoboken, NJ: Wiley-Blackwell.

Bagwell, Susan (2011), 'The Role of Independent Fast-Food Outlets in Obesogenic Environments: A Case Study of East London in the UK', *Environment and Planning A* 43(9): 2217–2236.

Bailey, Geoff, James Barret, Oliver Craig and Nicky Milner (2008), 'Historical Ecology of the North Sea Basin'. In Rick Torben and Jon Erlandson (eds), *Human Impacts on Ancient Marine Ecosystems: A Global Perspective*, Berkeley, CA: University of California Press.

Baker, Paul T. (1958), 'Racial Differences in Heat Tolerance', *American Journal of Physical Anthropology* 16(3): 287–305.

Barcan, Ruth (2014), 'Aromatherapy and the Mixed Blessing of Feminization', *The Senses and Society* 9(1): 33–54.

Barrett, James H., Alison M. Locker and Callum M. Roberts (2004), 'The Origins of Intensive Marine Fishing in Medieval Europe: The English Evidence', *Proceedings of the Royal Society of London B: Biological Sciences* 271(1556): 2417–2421.

Barthes, Roland and Stephen Heath (1988), *Image, Music, Text*, New York: Hill and Wang.

Bates, Charlotte (ed.) (2014), *Video Methods: Social Science Research in Motion*, London and New York: Routledge.

Baudrillard, Jean and Chris Turner (2003), *Cool Memories IV*, London: Verso.

BBC News (2005), 'Witchcraft Case Sparks Abuse Fear', *BBC*. Available at: http:// news.bbc.co.uk/1/hi/england/london/4608943.stm, accessed July 25, 2014.

BBC News (2012), 'How the Daily Mail Stormed the US', *BBC*, January 27. Available at: http://www.bbc.co.uk/news/magazine-16746785, accessed August 6, 2014.

Beck, Ulrich and Natan Sznaider (2006), 'Unpacking Cosmopolitanism for the Social Sciences: A Research Agenda', *The British Journal of Sociology* 57(1): 1–23.

Beck, Ulrich, Anthony Giddens and Scott Lash (1994), *Reflexive Modernization: Politics, Tradition and Aesthetics in the Modern Social Order*, Palo Alto, CA: Stanford University Press.

Becker, Howard Saul (1963), *Outsiders: Studies in the Sociology of Deviance*, London: Free Press of Glencoe.

Behrmann-Godel, Jasminca and Reiner Eckmann (2003), 'A Preliminary Telemetry Study of the Migration of Silver European Eel (Anguilla Anguilla L.) in the River Mosel, Germany', *Ecology of Freshwater Fish* 12(3): 196–202.

Bell, Daniel (2008), *The Coming of Post-Industrial Society*, New York: Basic Books.

Bell, David and Gill Valentine (1997), *Consuming Geographies: We Are Where We Eat*, London and New York: Routledge.

Bell, David and Joanne Hollows (2005), *Ordinary Lifestyles: Popular Media, Consumption and Taste*, Maidenhead: McGraw-Hill Education.

Benjamin, Walter (1968), *Illuminations*, New York: Knopf Doubleday Publishing Group.

Benjamin, Walter (2009), *One-Way Street and Other Writings*, London: Penguin.

Benjamin, Walter and Rolf Tiedemann (1999), *The Arcades Project*, Cambridge, MA: Harvard University Press.

Bennett, Natalie (2013), 'Horsemeat Scandal's Origin Lies in the Heart of Our Economic Model', *The Guardian*. Available at: http://www.theguardian.com/environment/blog/2013/feb/22/horse-meat-scandal-tesco-food-supply-system, accessed June 6, 2014.

Bennett, Tony, Mike Savage, Elizabeth Silva, Alan Warde, Modesto Gayo-Cal and David Wright (2009), *Culture, Class, Distinction*, London and New York: Routledge.

Berendt, Joachim-Ernst (1992), *The Third Ear: On Listening to the World*, New York: Henry Holt & Co.

Berg, Mette Louise (2010), 'On the Social Ground beneath Our Feet: For a Cosmopolitan Anthropology', *Social Anthropology* 18(4): 433–440.

Bertrand, Gilles (2004), 'Cypriots in Britain: Diaspora(s) Committed to Peace?' *Turkish Studies* 5(2): 93–110.

Boissy, A., C. Arnould, E. Chaillou et al. (2007), 'Emotions and Cognition: A New Approach to Animal Welfare', *Animal Welfare* 16(Supplement 1): 37–43.

Booth, Charles and Jesse Argyle (1902), *Life and Labour of the People in London*, London: Macmillan.

Bourdieu, Pierre and Richard Nice (1984), *Distinction*, Cambridge, MA: Harvard University Press.

Bourgois, Philippe (2003), *In Search of Respect: Selling Crack in El Barrio*, Cambridge: Cambridge University Press.

Bowman, Shanthy A., Steven L. Gortmaker, Cara B. Ebbeling, Mark A. Pereira and David S. Ludwig (2004), 'Effects of Fast-Food Consumption on Energy Intake and Diet Quality among Children in a National Household Survey', *Pediatrics* 113(1): 112–118.

Boyd, William (2001), 'Making Meat: Science, Technology, and American Poultry Production', *Technology and Culture* 42(4): 631–664.

Boyd, William and Michael Watts (1997), 'Agro-Industrial Just-in-Time: The Chicken Industry and Postwar American Capitalism'. In *Globalising Food: Agrarian Questions and Global Restructuring*, London: Routledge, pp. 192–226.

Boyes, Steve (2012), 'Bush-meat: Every Man's Protein Until the Forest Is Empty', *News Watch*. Available at: http://voices.nationalgeographic.com/2012/02/09/ bushmeat-every-mans-protein-until-the-forest-is-empty/, accessed August 12, 2016.

Braddock, Kevin (2011), 'The Power of the Hoodie', *The Guardian*, August 9. Available at: http://www.theguardian.com/uk/2011/aug/09/power-of-the-hoodie, accessed November 25, 2015.

Braidotti, Rosi (1994), *Nomadic Subjects: Embodiment and Sexual Difference in Contemporary Feminist Theory*, New York: Columbia University Press.

Braudel, Fernand (1982a), *Civilization and Capitalism, 15th–18th Century, Vol. II: The Wheels of Commerce*, Berkeley, CA: University of California Press.

Braudel, Fernand (1982b), *Civilization and Capitalism, 15th–18th Century, Vol. III: The Perspective of the World*, Berkeley, CA: University of California Press.

Braun, Virginia and Sue Wilkinson (2001), 'Socio-Cultural Representations of the Vagina', *Journal of Reproductive and Infant Psychology* 19(1): 17–32.

Bridgland, D. R., D. C. Schreve, D. H. Keen, R. Meyrick and R. Westaway (2004), 'Biostratigraphical Correlation between the Late Quaternary Sequence of the Thames and Key Fluvial Localities in Central Germany', *Proceedings of the Geologists' Association* 115(2): 125–140.

Briggs, Daniel, Vicky Heap and Hannah Smithson (2012), 'Can and Should the Post-Riot Populist Rhetoric Be Translated into Reality?' *Safer Communities* 11(1): 54–61.

Brimblecombe, Peter (1987), *The Big Smoke*, London: Routledge.

Bromley, Rosemary D. F. (1998a), 'Market-Place Trading and the Transformation of Retail Space in the Expanding Latin American City', *Urban Studies* 35(8): 1311–1333.

Bromley, Rosemary D. F. (1998b), 'Informal Commerce: Expansion and Exclusion in the Historic Centre of the Latin American City', *International Journal of Urban and Regional Research* 22(2): 245–263.

Browne, Anthony (2002), 'A Monkey Species Was Eaten into Extinction Last Year – The Gorilla Could Be Next', *The Guardian*, February 24. Available at: http://www.theguardian.com/world/2002/feb/24/highereducation.biologicalscience, accessed July 24, 2014.

Bruijs, Maarten C.M. and Caroline M.F. Durif (2009), 'Silver Eel Migration and Behaviour'. In Guido Van Den Thillart, Sylvie Dufour and J. Cliff Rankin (eds), *Spawning Migration of the European Eel*, New York: Springer, pp. 65–95.

Buettner, Elizabeth (2008), '"Going for an Indian": South Asian Restaurants and the Limits of Multiculturalism in Britain', *The Journal of Modern History* 80(4): 865–901.

Bull, Michael (2000), *Sounding out the City*, Oxford: Berg.

Bull, Michael and Les Back (eds) (2003), *The Auditory Culture Reader*, Oxford: Berg.

Burgoine, Thomas, Nita G. Forouhi, Simon J. Griffin et al. (2014), 'Associations between Exposure to Takeaway Food Outlets, Takeaway Food Consumption, and Body Weight in Cambridgeshire, UK: Population Based, Cross Sectional Study', *British Medical Journal* 348: g1464.

Burnett, John (2004), *England Eats Out: A Social History of Eating Out in England from 1830 to the Present*, Harlow, New York: Pearson/Longman.

Büscher, Monika and John Urry (2009), 'Mobile Methods and the Empirical', *European Journal of Social Theory* 12(1): 99–116.

Buzz, Bumblery, Robert Desilver and Thomas Town (1819), *Ephemera Or, The History of Cockney Dandies; A Poem, in One Canto*, Saint Thomas: Robert Desilver.

Cadman, Louisa (2009), 'Nonrepresentational Theory/Nonrepresentational Geographies', *International Encyclopedia of Human Geography* 7: 456–63.

Callahan, Ed (1969), *Soul Food Cook Book*, Concord, NH: Nitty Gritty Productions.

Camden, William, Thomas Moule and Mark Antony Lower (1870), *Remains Concerning Britain*, London: J. R. Smith.

Cameron, David (2014), 'British Values Aren't Optional, They're Vital', *Mail Online*. Available at: http://www.dailymail.co.uk/debate/article-2658171/ DAVID-CAMERON-British-values-arent-optional-theyre-vital-Thats-I-promote-EVERY-school-As-row-rages-Trojan-Horse-takeover-classrooms-Prime-Minister-delivers-uncompromising-pledge.html, accessed July 5, 2014.

Campbell, Denis (2015), 'Fast Food Takeaway Shops Grow More Rapidly in Deprived Areas of UK', *The Guardian*. Available at: http://www.theguardian. com/society/2015/apr/02/fast-food-takeaway-shops-grow-more-rapidly-in-deprived-areas-of-uk, accessed July 28, 2015.

Camporesi, Piero (1989), *Bread of Dreams*, Chicago, IL: University of Chicago Press.

Caplan, Patricia (1992), *Feasts, Fasts and Famine*, London: Goldsmiths' College, University of London.

Certeau, Michel de (1988), *The Practice of Everyday Life*, Berkeley, CA: University of California Press.

Certeau, Michel de, Luce Giard and Pierre Mayol (1998), *The Practice of Everyday Life: Vol. 2*, Minneapolis, MN: University of Minnesota Press.

Chan, Tak Wing and John H. Goldthorpe (2007), 'Social Stratification and Cultural Consumption: Music in England', *European Sociological Review* 23(1): 1–19.

Channel 4 (2008), 'Hugh's Chicken Run', *Channel 4*. Available at: http://www. channel4.com/programmes/hughs-chicken-run, accessed August 1, 2015.

Chapman, William P. and Chester M. Jones (1944), 'Variations in Cutaneous and Visceral Pain Sensitivity in Normal Subjects', *Journal of Clinical Investigation* 23(1): 81–91.

Chappelle, Dave (dir.) (2012), 'Dave Chappelle Chicken'. Available at: https://www. youtube.com/watch?v=wJ4B7G8Rw3Q, accessed August 12, 2015.

Charles, Nickie and Marion Kerr (1988), *Women, Food, and Families*, Manchester: Manchester University Press.

Chau, Adam Yuet (2008), 'The Sensorial Production of the Social', *Ethnos* 73(4): 485–504.

Cheshire, Jenny, Paul Kerswill, Sue Fox and Eivind Torgersen (2011), 'Contact, the Feature Pool and the Speech Community: The Emergence of Multicultural London English', *Journal of Sociolinguistics* 15(2): 151–196.

Christie, Robert H. (1911), *Twenty-Two Authentic Banquets from India*, Mineola, NY: Dover Publications.

Clarke, John and Tony Jefferson (1973), *Working Class Youth Cultures*, Birmingham: Centre for Contemporary Cultural Studies, University of Birmingham.

Clarke-Howard, Brian (2011), 'Bush-meat from Endangered Animals Feeds Hungry: Study', *News Watch*. Available at: http://voices.nationalgeographic.com/2011/11/21/bushmeat-feeding-children-madagascar/, accessed August 12, 2016.

Classen, Constance (1990), 'Sweet Colors, Fragrant Songs: Sensory Models of the Andes and the Amazon', *American Ethnologist* 17(4): 722–735.

Classen, Constance (1992), 'The Odor of the Other: Olfactory Symbolism and Cultural Categories', *Ethnos* 20(2): 133–166.

Classen, Constance, David Howes and Anthony Synnott (1994), *Aroma: The Cultural History of Smell*, London: Routledge.

Classen, Constance, Jerry P. Toner, Anne C. Vila et al. (eds) (2014), *A Cultural History of the Senses*, London: Bloomsbury Academic.

Clifford, James and George E. Marcus (1986), *Writing Culture: The Poetics and Politics of Ethnography: A School of American Research Advanced Seminar*, Berkeley, CA: University of California Press.

Cloake, Felicity (2015), 'Can You Ever Have "Healthy" Fried Chicken?' *The Guardian*. Available at: http://www.theguardian.com/lifeandstyle/shortcuts/2015/mar/30/can-you-ever-have-healthy-fried-chicken-fast-food, accessed July 28, 2015.

Cohen, Phil (1997), *Rethinking the Youth Question*, Basingstoke: Palgrave Macmillan.

Cohen, Phil (1998), *The Last Island*, London: University of East London, Centre for New Ethnicities Research.

Cohen, Stanley (2011), *Folk Devils and Moral Panics*, London: Taylor & Francis.

Colebrook, Claire (2002), *Understanding Deleuze*, Sydney: Allen & Unwin.

Collingham, Lizzie (2010), *Curry: A Tale of Cooks and Conquerors*, London: Random House.

Collins, David (2013a), 'The Wild Bunch: Romanian Gangs Buy Horses for Just £10 and Send Them to Slaughter', *Mirror*. Available at: http://www.mirror.co.uk/news/uk-news/horse-meat-burger-scandal-mirror-1680230, accessed June 26, 2014.

Collins, David (2013b), 'Horse Meat Abattoir Revealed: We Track Down Romanian Slaughterhouse Suspected of Supplying Meat', *Mirror*. Available at: http://www.mirror.co.uk/news/world-news/horse-meat-scandal-mirror-tracks-1704552, accessed June 26, 2014.

Cook, Ian and Harrison Michelle (2003), 'Crossover Food: Re-Materializing Postcolonial Geographies', *Transactions of the Institute of British Geographers* 28(3): 296–317.

Coombs, Benjamin (2013), *British Tank Production and the War Economy, 1934–1945*, London: Bloomsbury.

Cooper, Michael (1971), *The Southern Barbarians: The First Europeans in Japan*, Tokyo: Kodansha International in cooperation with Sophia University.

Corbin, Alain (1988), *The Foul and the Fragrant*, Cambridge, MA: Harvard University Press.

Corbin, Alain (1998), *Village Bells: Sound and Meaning in the 19th-Century French Countryside*, New York: Columbia University Press.

Crang, Mike and Divya P. Tolia-Kelly (2010), 'Nation, Race and Affect: Senses and Sensibilities at National Heritage Sites', *Environment and Planning A* 42(10): 2315.

Craven, Nick and George Arbuthnott (2013), 'Thousands of Bulgarians and Romanians Plan to Flood UK in 2014 as Employment Restrictions Relax', *Mail*

Online. Available at: http://www.dailymail.co.uk/news/article-2268952/Thousands-Bulgarians-Romanians-plan-flood-UK-2014-employment-restrictions-relax.html, accessed June 13, 2014.

Cree, Viviene, Gary Clapton and Mark Smith (2015), *Revisiting Moral Panics*, Bristol: Policy Press.

Cressey, Paul Goalby (2008), *The Taxi-Dance Hall: A Sociological Study in Commercialized Recreation and City Life*, Chicago, IL: University of Chicago Press.

Cresswell, Tim (1999), 'Embodiment, Power and the Politics of Mobility: The Case of Female Tramps and Hobos', *Transactions of the Institute of British Geographers* 24(2): 175–192.

Crossley, Nick (1995), 'Merleau-Ponty, the Elusive Body and Carnal Sociology', *Body & Society* 1(1): 43.

Crossley, Nick (2001), *The Social Body: Habit, Identity and Desire*, London: Sage.

Cunningham, William H., Russell M. Moore and Isabella C. M. Cunningham (1974), 'Urban Markets in Industrializing Countries: The Sao Paulo Experience', *The Journal of Marketing* 38(2): 2–12.

Cupers, Kenny (2005), 'Towards a Nomadic Geography: Rethinking Space and Identity for the Potentials of Progressive Politics in the Contemporary City', *International Journal of Urban and Regional Research* 29(4): 729–739.

Curtin, Philip D. (1984), *Cross-Cultural Trade in World History*, Cambridge: Cambridge University Press.

Cwiertka, Katarzyna Joanna (2006), *Modern Japanese Cuisine: Food, Power and National Identity*, London: Reaktion.

Czakó, Ágnes and Endre Sik (1999), 'Characteristics and Origins of the Comecon Open-Air Market in Hungary', *International Journal of Urban and Regional Research* 23(4): 715–737.

Daily Mail (2004), '"Bushmeat" Shopkeepers Jailed', *Mail Online*. Available at: http://www.dailymail.co.uk/news/article-53681/Bushmeat-shopkeepers-jailed.html, accessed July 24, 2014.

Daily Mail (2008) 'Swan Bake: Carcasses and Piles of Feathers Found next to Cooking Pots at Migrants' Camp', *Mail Online*. Available at: http://www.dailymail.co.uk/news/article-521710/Swan-bake-carcasses-piles-feathers-cooking-pots-migrants-camp.html, accessed June 26, 2014.

Dance, S. Peter (1966), *Shell Collecting: An Illustrated History*, Berkeley, CA: University of California Press.

Datoo, Siraj (2014), 'The Number of Romanians Attacked in London Has Quadrupled Year-on-Year', *BuzzFeed*. Available at: http://www.buzzfeed.com/sirajdatoo/the-number-of-romanians-attacked-in-london-has-doubled, accessed June 26, 2014.

Davis, Mike (2006), 'Planet of Slums', *New Perspectives Quarterly* 23(2): 6–11.

Davis, Mike (2007), *Planet of Slums*, London: Verso.

Dawkins, Marian Stamp (2006), 'Through Animal Eyes: What Behaviour Tells Us', *Applied Animal Behaviour Science* 100(1): 4–10.

Deelder, C. L. (1954), 'Factors Affecting the Migration of the Silver Eel in Dutch Inland Waters', *Journal Du Conseil* 20(2): 177–185.

DEFRA (2005), *Guidance on the Control of Odour and Noise from Commercial Kitchen Exhaust Systems*, London: HMSO.

DEFRA (2006), 'The Structure of the United Kingdom Poultry Industry'. Available at: http://archive.defra.gov.uk/foodfarm/farmanimal/diseases/vetsurveillance/documents/commercial-poultry-ind.pdf.

DEFRA (2012), *Food Statistics Pocketbook 2012*, London: HMSO.

DEFRA (2013), *Family Food 2012*, London: HMSO.

DEFRA (2014), *Family Food Datasets – UK Household Purchases*, London: HMSO. Available at: https://www.gov.uk/government/statistical-data-sets/family-food-datasets, accessed August 19, 2015.

Degen, Monica Montserrat (2008), *Sensing Cities: Regenerating Public Life in Barcelona and Manchester*, London: Routledge.

Degen, Monica Montserrat (2014), 'The Everyday City of the Senses'. In Ronan Paddison and Eugene McCann (eds), *Cities and Social Change: Encounters with Contemporary Urbanism*, London: Sage.

DeHanas, Daniel Nilsson (2013), 'Elastic Orthodoxy: The Tactics of Young Muslim Identity in the East End of London'. In Nathal Dessing, Nadia Jeldtoft, Jorgen Nielsen and Linda Woodhead (eds), *Everyday Lived Islam in Europe*, Ashgate Publishing Group, 2013.

Deleuze, Gilles and Félix Guattari (2003), *Anti-Oedipus: Capitalism and Schizophrenia*, London: Continuum.

Deleuze, Gilles and Félix Guattari (2004), *A Thousand Plateaus*, London: Continuum.

Department for Education (2015), 'Statistics: School and Pupil Numbers', *GOV. UK*. Available at: https://www.gov.uk/government/collections/statistics-school-and-pupil-numbers, accessed August 30, 2015.

DeSoucey, Michaela (2010), 'Gastronationalism Food Traditions and Authenticity Politics in the European Union', *American Sociological Review* 75(3): 432–455.

Devlieger, Patrick, Frank Renders, Hubert Froyen and Kristel Wildiers (2006), *Blindness and the Multi-Sensorial City*, Antwerp: Garant.

Devlin, Ryan Thomas (2011), '"An Area That Governs Itself": Informality, Uncertainty and the Management of Street Vending in New York City', *Planning Theory* 10(1): 53–65.

DeWitt, David (2014), *Precious Cargo: How Foods From the Americas Changed The World*, Berkeley, CA: Counterpoint.

Dines, Nick (2009), 'The Disputed Place of Ethnic Diversity: An Ethnography of the Redevelopment of a Street Market in East London'. In Rob Imrie, Mark Raco and Loretta Lees (eds), *Regenerating London: Governance, Sustainability and Community in a Global City*, London: Routledge, pp. 254–272.

Diprose, Rosalyn (2002), *Corporeal Generosity: On Giving with Nietzsche, Merleau-Ponty, and Levinas*, New York: SUNY Press.

Dobney, Keith and Anton Ervynck (2007), 'To Fish or Not to Fish? Evidence for the Possible Avoidance of Fish Consumption during the Iron Age around the North Sea'. In Colin Haselgrove and T. Moore (eds), *The Later Iron Age in Britain and Beyond*, Oxford: Oxbow Books, pp. 403–418.

Dobson, Thomas (1798), *Encyclopædia: Or, A Dictionary of Arts, Sciences, and Miscellaneous Literature*, Philadelphia: Budd and Barton.

Dollinger, Philippe (1970), *German Hansa*, London: Macmillan.

Dorrian, Mark and Gillian Rose (2003), *Deterritorialisations: Revisioning Landscapes and Politics*, London: Black Dog Publishing.

Douglas, Mary (1994), *Risk and Blame: Essays in Cultural Theory*, London: Routledge.

Douglas, Mary (2002), *Purity and Danger*, London and New York: Routledge.

Douglas, Mary and Michael Nicod (1974), 'Taking the Biscuit: The Structure of British Meals', *New Society* 30(637): 744–747.

Dovey, Kim (2009), *Becoming Places: Urbanism/Architecture/Identity/Power*, London: Routledge.

Dowler, Elizabeth and Hannah Lambie-Mumford (2014), 'Communities and Culture Network+ Food Aid Call'. Available at: http://www.communitiesandculture.org/files/2013/01/Living-with-Food-Insecurity-CCN-Report.pdf, accessed April 9, 2014.

Drew, C. E. (1947), 'Local Political Disorders', *Hackney Gazette*, August 27.

Drobnick, Jim and Jennifer Fisher (2008), 'Odor Limits', *The Senses and Society* 3(3): 349–358.

Dubow, Saul (1995), *Scientific Racism in Modern South Africa*, Cambridge: Cambridge University Press.

Duffett, Rachel, Alain Drouard and Ina Zweiniger-Bargielowska (2012), *Food and War in Twentieth-Century Europe*, Farnham: Ashgate Publishing Ltd.

Duffin, Claire (2013), 'Princess Anne: We Should Consider Eating Horse Meat', *The Daily Telegraph*, November 14. Available at: http://www.telegraph.co.uk/earth/agriculture/meat/10449803/Princess-Anne-We-should-consider-eating-horse-meat.html, accessed June 12, 2014.

Duggins, Alexi (2013), 'Horses for Courses', *Now. Here. This. Time Out Blog*. Available at: http://now-here-this.timeout.com/2013/03/14/horses-for-courses-alexiduggins-flogs-a-dead-horse/, accessed June 12, 2014.

Duncan, Ian J. H. (2006), 'The Changing Concept of Animal Sentience', *Applied Animal Behaviour Science* 100(1): 11–19.

Duneier, Mitchell and Ovie Carter (2001), *Sidewalk*, New York: Farrar, Straus and Giroux.

Dyson, John (1977), *Business in Great Waters*, Sydney: Angus & Robertson.

Easton, Mark (2014), 'Dip in Romania and Bulgaria Workers', *BBC*, May 14. Available at: http://www.bbc.co.uk/news/uk-27407126, accessed August 17, 2016.

Edensor, Tim (2006), 'Sensing Tourist Spaces'. In Claudia Minca and Tim Oakes (eds), *Travels in Paradox: Remapping Tourism*, Lanham, MD: Rowland and Littlefield, pp. 23–45.

Edensor, Tim (2014), 'The Social Life of the Senses: Ordering and Disordering the Modern Sensorium'. In David Howes (ed.), *A Cultural History of the Senses in the Modern Age*, London: Bloomsbury.

Ehara, Ayako (2010), 'The Japanese Table', Kikkoman Food Forum. Available at: http://www.kikkoman.com/foodforum/thejapanesetable/29.shtml, accessed July 12, 2015.

Ehrlichman, Howard and Linda Bastone (1992), 'Olfaction and Emotion'. In Michael J. Serby and Karen L. Chobor (eds), *Science of Olfaction*, New York: Springer, pp. 410–438.

Elfic, Dominic (2008), *A Brief History of Broiler Selection: How Chicken Became a Global Food Phenomenon in 50 Years*, Huntsville, AL: Aviagen International.

Elias, Norbert, Eric Dunning, Johan Goudsblom and Stephen Mennell (2000), *The Civilizing Process*, Oxford: Wiley-Blackwell.

Emmett, Susie (2013), 'Secretive Industry that Rules the Roost: Chicken is Set to Become the Best-Selling Meat Globally', *The Independent*. Available at: http://www.independent.co.uk/life-style/food-and-drink/features/secretive-industry-that-rules-the-roost-chicken-is-set-to-become-the-bestselling-meat-globally-8485878.html, accessed July 28, 2015.

Engels, Friedrich (2012), *The Condition of the Working-Class in England in 1844 with a Preface Written in 1892*, London: Penguin.

Fahim, Kareem (2009), 'Brooklyn Restaurant's Name Hits a Sour Note'. *The New York Times*, April 4. Available at: http://www.nytimes.com/2009/04/04/nyregion/04chicken.html, accessed August 12, 2015.

Fearnley-Whittingstall, Hugh (2003), *The River Cottage Cookbook*, London: Collins.

Featherstone, Mike (1987), 'Intoduction to Special Issue on Norbert Elias and Figurational Sociology', *Theory Culture and Society* 4(2): 197–211.

Featherstone, Mike (1990), 'Perspectives on Consumer Culture', *Sociology* 24(1): 5–22.

Featherstone, Mike, Mike Hepworth and Bryan S. Turner (1991), *The Body: Social Process and Cultural Theory*, London: Sage.

Feld, Stephen (ed.) (1996), *Senses of Place*, Santa Fe, NM: School of American Research Press.

Fenger, J., O. Hertel and F. Palmgren (1998), *Urban Air Pollution – European Aspects*, New York: Springer Science & Business Media.

Finamore, Emma (2015), '"American Psycho" Luxury London Property Ad Is Pulled after Barage of Criticism', *The Independent*. Available at: http://www.independent.co.uk/news/uk/home-news/american-psycho-luxury-london-property-ad-is-pulled-after-barage-of-criticism-9960585.html, accessed February 4, 2016.

Fischer, David Hackett (1989), *Albion's Seed: Four British Folkways in America*, Oxford: Oxford University Press.

Fischler, Claude (2002), *L'Homnivor*, Berkeley, CA: University of California Press.

Florida, Richard, Charlotta Mellander and Tim Gulden (2012), 'Global Metropolis: Assessing Economic Activity in Urban Centers Based on Nighttime Satellite Images', *The Professional Geographer* 64(2): 178–187.

Food Standards Agency (2014), 'Don't Wash Raw Chicken'. Available at: https://www.food.gov.uk/news-updates/campaigns/campylobacter/fsw-2014, accessed August 3, 2015.

Forrest, Derek William (1974), *Francis Galton: The Life and Work of a Victorian Genius*, London: Paul Elek Publishers.

Foster Intelligence (2013), *Tackling the Takeaways: A New Strategy for Fast Food Outlets in Tower Hamlets*, London: Tower Hamlets Council.

Foucault, Michel (1999), 'Body and Governmentality'. In Gyan Prakash, *Another Reason: Science and the Imagination of Modern India*, Princeton: Princeton University Press, pp. 123–159.

Fox, Jon E., Laura Moroşanu and Eszter Szilassy (2012), 'The Racialization of the New European Migration to the UK'. *Sociology* 46(4): 680–695.

Francis, Nick (2012), 'The UK is Much Better than Romania, All My Mates Will Come in 2014', *The Sun*. Available at: http://www.thesun.co.uk/sol/homepage/news/4637926/Wave-of-Romanian-and-Bulgarian-immigrants-is-threatening-to-swamp-Britain.html, accessed June 13, 2014.

Fraser, Lorna K. and Kimberley L. Edwards (2010), 'The Association between the Geography of Fast Food Outlets and Childhood Obesity Rates in Leeds, UK', *Health & Place* 16(6): 1124–1128.

Fraser, Mariam (2006), 'Event', *Theory, Culture & Society* 23(2–3): 129–132.

French, Simone A., Mary Story, Dianne Neumark-Sztainer, Jayne A. Fulkerson and P. Hannan (2001), 'Fast Food Restaurant Use among Adolescents: Associations with Nutrient Intake, Food Choices and Behavioral and Psychosocial Variables', *International Journal of Obesity and Related Metabolic Disorders: Journal of the International Association for the Study of Obesity* 25(12): 1823–1833.

Friedman, Asia (2015), 'Blinded by Sight: Seeing Race Through the Eyes of the Blind', *Contemporary Sociology: A Journal of Reviews* 44(5): 688–689.

FSAI (2003), *Investigation of the Composition and Labelling of Chicken Breast Fillets from the Netherlands Imported into Ireland*, Dublin: FSAI.

Galton, Francis (1883), *Inquiries into Human Faculty and Its Development, London*, London: Macmillan. Available at: http://www.wwww4.com/read_book/inquiries_into_human_faculty_and_its_development_1660088.pdf, accessed August 21, 2015.

Gentle Author, The (2012), *Spitalfields Life*, London: Salt Yard Books.

Geurts, Kathryn Linn (2002), *Culture and the Senses: Bodily Ways of Knowing in an African Community*, Berkeley, CA: University of California Press.

Gibbons, Boyd (1986), 'The Intimate Sense of Smell', *National Geographic* 170(3).

Giddens, Anthony (1991), *Modernity and Self-Identity: Self and Society in the Late Modern Age*, Palo Alto, CA: Stanford University Press.

Gidley, Ben (1997), *The Proletarian Other: Charles Booth and the Politics of Representation*, London: Goldsmiths Sociology Occasional Papers.

Gill, Nick (dir.), Nick Brown (dir.) and Brown Fox (dir.) (2003) 'Hi-Fi'. Available at: https://www.youtube.com/watch?v=B-yG50MfCMU, accessed August 13, 2015.

Gill, Nick, (dir.) and Luke Scott (dir.) (2003) 'Soul'. Available at: https://www.youtube.com/watch?v=B-yG50MfCMU, accessed August 13, 2015.

Gilroy, Paul (1993), *The Black Atlantic: Modernity and Double Consciousness*, Cambridge, MA: Harvard University Press.

Gilroy, Paul (2004), *After Empire: Melancholia or Convivial Culture?* London: Routledge.

Ginzburg, Ralph (1962), *100 Years of Lynchings*, Baltimore, MD: Black Classic Press.

Godley, Andrew and Bridget Williams (2007), 'The Chicken, the Factory Farm and the Supermarket: The Emergence of the Modern Poultry Industry in Britain', *Economics & Management Discussion Papers* Em-dp2007-50, Henley Business School, Reading University, Reading, UK. Available at: http://www.reading.ac.uk/web/files/merl/andrew_godley_paper.pdf, accessed September 13, 2015.

Goethe, Johann Wolfgang von and Michael Hamburger (1996), *Roman Elegies and Other Poems and Epigrams*, London: Anvil Press Poetry.

Goffman, Alice (2015), *On the Run: Fugitive Life in an American City*, New York: Picador USA.

Goffman, Erving (2008), *Behavior in Public Places*, New York: Simon and Schuster.

Goldhill, Olivia (2014), 'Ebola Crisis: Why Is There Bush Meat in the UK?' *The Telegraph*, August 2. Available at: http://www.telegraph.co.uk/health/healthnews/11006343/Ebola-crisis-why-is-there-bush-meat-in-the-UK.html, accessed August 5, 2014.

Gonzalez, Sara and Paul Waley (2013), 'Traditional Retail Markets: The New Gentrification Frontier?' *Antipode* 45(4): 965–983.

Goodman, David and Michael Watts (1997), *Globalising Food: Agrarian Questions and Global Restructuring*, London: Psychology Press.

Goody, Jack (2002), 'Elias and the Anthropological Tradition', *Anthropological Theory* 2(4): 401–412.

Goody, Jack (2003), 'The "Civilizing Process" in Ghana', *European Journal of Sociology* 44(01): 61–73.

Goody, Jack (2009), *Renaissances: The One or the Many?*, Cambridge: Cambridge University Press.

Green, Candida Lycett (1996), *England: Travels through an Unwrecked Landscape*, London: Pavilion.

Green, Johnathon (2015), 'The Cockney Novelists', *Spitalfields Life*. Available at: http://spitalfieldslife.com/2015/07/11/the-cockney-novelists/, accessed July 25, 2015.

Griffith, D. W. (dir.) (1915), 'Birth of a Nation'. Available at: https://www.youtube.com/watch?v=vZ871wZd7UY, accessed December 6, 2015.

Griffiths, Ralph (1797), *The Monthly Review*, London: R. Griffiths Publishing.

Grosz, Elizabeth A. (1995) *Space, Time, and Perversion: Essays on the Politics of Bodies*, London: Routledge.

Grove, Peter and Colleen Grove (2008), *Curry, Spice and All Things Nice*, Surbiton: Grove Publications.

Guallar-Castillón, Pilar, Fernando Rodríguez-Artalejo, Nélida Schmid Fornés et al. (2007), 'Intake of Fried Foods is Associated with Obesity in the Cohort of Spanish Adults from the European Prospective Investigation into Cancer and Nutrition', *The American Journal of Clinical Nutrition* 86(1): 198–205.

Hackney Council (2006), *Review of Market Provision in Hackney*, London: Hackney Council.

Hackney Council (2007), *Summary of Accounts 2006/2007*, London: Hackney Council.

Hackney Council (2009), *Local Development Framework Supporting Documents to Dalston Area Action Plan – Masterplan*, London: Hackney Council.

Hackney Council (2015), *Dalston Conservation Area Appraisal*, London: Hackney Council.

Hall, Stuart (1990), 'Cultural Identity and Diaspora'. In Johnathon Rutherford (ed.), *Identity: Community, Culture, Difference*, London: Lawrence and Wishart, pp. 222–237.

Hall, Stuart (1993), 'Culture, Community, Nation', *Cultural Studies* 7(3): 349–363.

Hall, Stuart and Tony Jefferson (1993), *Resistance Through Rituals: Youth Subcultures in Post-War Britain*, London: Psychology Press.

Hall, Stuart, Chas Critcher, Tony Jefferson, John N. Clarke and Brian Roberts (1978), *Policing the Crisis: Mugging, the State and Law and Order*, London: Palgrave Macmillan.

Hamm, Jeffrey (1947), *The Battle of Ridley Road*, London: Raven Books.

Hancock, Lynn and Gerry Mooney (2013), '"Welfare Ghettos" and the "Broken Society": Territorial Stigmatization in the Contemporary UK', *Housing, Theory and Society* 30(1): 46–64.

Hannerz, Ulf (1980), *Exploring the City: Inquiries Toward an Urban Anthropology*, New York: Columbia University Press.

Harper, Douglas A. (2006), *Good Company: A Tramp Life*, Boulder: Paradigm Publishers.

Harrison, Hubert and Jeffrey B. Perry (2001), *A Hubert Harrison Reader*, Middletown, CT: Wesleyan University Press.

Harrison, Ruth (1964), *Animal Machines*, London: Vincent Stuart.

Harvey, David (1989), *The Condition of Postmodernity*, Oxford: Wiley-Blackwell.

Harvey, David (2012), *Spaces of Capital: Towards a Critical Geography*, London: Routledge.

Hawkes, Steve (2013), '99% Horse in Findus Lasagne', *The Sun*, February 8. Available at: http://www.thesun.co.uk/sol/homepage/news/4784465/Findus-beef-lasagne-up-to-99-horse-tests-show.html, accessed May 30, 2014.

Hawkins, Kathryn and Ian Garlick (2002), *The Food of London*, Rutland: Tuttle Publishing.

Hebdige, Dick (1979), *Subculture: The Meaning of Style*, London: Routledge.

Hemmings, Clare (2002), *Bisexual Spaces: A Geography of Sexuality and Gender*, London: Psychology Press.

Henshaw, Victoria (2011), 'The Role of Smell in Urban Design', Thesis, University of Salford. Available at: https://www.escholar.manchester.ac.uk/uk-ac-man-scw:122866, accessed February 17, 2015.

Henshaw, Victoria (2013), *Urban Smellscapes: Understanding and Designing City Smell Environments*, London: Routledge.

Henshaw, Victoria and Oliver T. Mould (2013), 'Sensing Designed Space: An Exploratory Methodology for Investigating Human Response to Sensory Environments', *Journal of Design Research* 11(1): 57–71.

Hesketh, Alan (2014), Development Management Local Plan (DMLP) – *Justification in Support of DM12 – Hot-Food Takeaways and Schools*, Hackney Council.

Hewitt, Roger (1990), 'Youth, Race and Language in Contemporary Britain: Deconstructing Ethnicity?' In Lynne Chisholm (ed.) *Childhood, Youth, and Social Change: A Comparative Perspective*, London: Routledge, pp. 185–196.

Hewitt, Roger (2003), 'Language and the Destabilisation of Ethnicity'. In Roxy Harris and Ben Rampton (eds), *The Language, Ethnicity and Race Reader*, London: Psychology Press, pp. 188–198.

Hicks, Cherrill (2014), 'Don't Wash Chicken Before Cooking, New Guidance Warns', *The Telegraph*, June 16. Available at: http://www.telegraph.co.uk/news/health/10899022/Dont-wash-chicken-before-cooking-new-guidance-warns.html, accessed August 3, 2015.

Hiebert, Daniel, Jan Rath and Steven Vertovec (2015), 'Urban Markets and Diversity: Towards a Research Agenda', *Ethnic and Racial Studies* 38(1): 5–21.

Hobbs, Dick (1988), *Doing the Business: Entrepreneurship, the Working Class, and Detectives in the East End of London*, London: Clarendon Press.

Hobsbawm, Eric and Terence Ranger (eds) (2012), *The Invention of Tradition*, Cambridge: Cambridge University Press.

Hodkinson, Stuart and Glyn Robbins (2013), 'The Return of Class War Conservatism? Housing under the UK Coalition Government', *Critical Social Policy* 33(1): 57–77.

Hoggart, Richard (1998), *The Uses of Literacy*, London: Transaction Publishers.

Hohnenberg, Paul and Lynn Hollen Lees (1995), *The Making of Urban Europe, 1000–1994*, Cambridge, MA: Harvard University Press.

Holloway, Lewis and Moya Kneafsey (2000), 'Reading the Space of the Farmers' Market: A Preliminary Investigation from the UK', *Sociologia Ruralis* 40(3): 285–299.

Home, Everard (1821), 'On the Black Rete Mucosum of the Negro, Being a Defence against the Scorching Effect of the Sun's Rays', *Philosophical Transactions of the Royal Society of London* 111: 1–6.

hooks, bell (1992), *Black Looks*, London: Turnaround.

Hope, Christopher, Steven Swinford and Gordon Rayner (2013), 'Scale of the Horse Meat Scandal Is "Breathtaking", MPs Say', February 14, *Telegraph, Food and Drink*. Available at: http://www.telegraph.co.uk/foodanddrink/foodanddrinknews/9869087/Scale-of-the-horse-meat-scandal-is-breathtaking-MPs-say.html, accessed June 2, 2014.

Hopkins, Stephen (2015), 'Tommy Robinson Explains the Making of an Alter-Ego Even His Wife Can't Stand', *The Huffington Post UK*. Available at: http://www. huffingtonpost.co.uk/2015/12/10/stephen-yaxley-lennon-describes-the-making-of-tommy-robinson_n_8747794.html, accessed February 13, 2016.

Horkheimer, Max, Theodor W. Adorno and Gunzelin Schmid Noerr (2002), *Dialectic of Enlightenment: Philosophical Fragments*, Palo Alto, CA: Stanford University Press.

Horn, Adrian (2009), *Americanisation and Youth Culture, 1945–60*, Manchester and New York: Manchester University Press.

Howes, David (1987), 'Olfaction and Transition: An Essay on the Ritual Uses of Smell', *Canadian Review of Sociology/Revue Canadienne de Sociologie* 24(3): 398–416.

Howes, David (2003), *Sensual Relations*, Ann Arbor, MI: University of Michigan Press.

Howes, David (ed.) (2005), *Empire of the Senses*, Oxford: Berg Publishers.

Howes, David (2006), 'Scent, Sound and Synaesthesia'. In Chris Tilley, Webb Keane, Susanne Kuechler, Mike Rowlands and Patricia Spyer (eds), *Handbook of Material Culture*, London: Sage.

Howes, David (2012), 'The Cultural Life of the Senses', *Postmedieval: A Journal of Medieval Cultural Studies* 3(4): 450–454.

Howes, David and Constance Classen (2013), *Ways of Sensing: Understanding the Senses in Society*, London: Routledge.

Hulkko, Sami, Tuuli Mattelmäki, Katja Virtanen and Turkka Keinonen (2004), 'Mobile Probes'. In *Proceedings of the Third Nordic Conference on Human-Computer Interaction*, ACM, pp. 43–51.

Hunt, Charlotte (2002), 'Eels, Pie and Mash'. In Kathryn Hawkins (ed.), *The Food of London*, Rutland: Tuttle Publishing, pp. 16–17.

Huntley, Victoria (2009), 'East End Bengali and Somali Street Gangs Clash with Guns', *The Docklands & East London Advertiser*. Available at: http://www. eastlondonadvertiser.co.uk/news/east_end_bengali_and_somali_street_gangs_clash_with_guns_669265, accessed September 13, 2014.

Iida, Junko (2010), 'The Sensory Experience of Thai Massage: Commercialisation, Globalisation and Tactility'. In Devorah Kalekin-Fishman and Kelvin E.Y. Low (eds), *Everyday Life in Asia: Social Perspectives on the Senses*, Farnham: Ashgate, pp. 139–156.

Illich, Ivan (2005), *H2O and the Waters of Forgetfulness*, London: Marion Boyars.

Ishige, Naomichi (2007), 'Eggs and the Japanese'. In Richard Hosking, (ed.) *Eggs in Cookery: Proceedings of the Oxford Symposium on Food and Cookery 2006*, Oxford: Oxford University Press, pp. 100–107.

Ising, H. L. and B. Kruppa (2004), 'Health Effects Caused by Noise: Evidence in the Literature from the Past 25 Years', *Noise and Health* 6(22): 5.

Islam, Nurul (dir.) (2015), 'HoodForts – Chicken', Vimeo. Available at: https:// vimeo.com/126395665, accessed December 1, 2015.

Islam, Sanchita (2007), *Avenues*, London: Chipmunkapublishing Ltd.

Issenberg, Sasha (2007), *The Sushi Economy: Globalization and the Making of a Modern Delicacy*, London: Penguin.

Jackson, Ruth (1978), *Ruth Jackson's Soulfood Cookbook*, Plains, TN: Wimmer Brothers Books.

Jacobs, Jane (1989), *The Death and Life of Great American Cities*, New York: Vintage Books.

Jacobs, Jane M. (1996), *Edge of Empire: Postcolonialism and the City*, London, New York: Routledge.

Jacobs, Marc and Peter Scholliers (2003), *Eating Out in Europe: Picnics, Gourmet Dining and Snacks Since the Late Eighteenth Century*, Oxford: Berg.

Jakle, John A. and Keith A. Sculle (1999), *Fast Food: Roadside Restaurants in the Automobile Age*, Baltimore: JHU Press.

Jay, Martin (1993), *Downcast Eyes: The Denigration of Vision in Twentieth-Century French Thought*, Berkeley, CA: University of California Press.

Jeffery, Robert W. and Simone A. French (1998), 'Epidemic Obesity in the United States: Are Fast Foods and Television Viewing Contributing?' *American Journal of Public Health* 88(2): 277–280.

Johnstone, Nick (2012), 'Malaysians Take Pole in Battersea Sale Process', *Property Week*, May 28. Available at: http://www.propertyweek.com/news/malaysians-take-pole-in-battersea-sale-process/5037349.article, accessed March 31, 2016.

Johnstone, Nick (2013a), 'Malaysian Set on Sun Street Site', *Property Week*, May 24. Available at: http://www.propertyweek.com/news/regions/london/malaysian-set-on-sun-street-site/5055284.article, accessed March 31, 2016.

Johnstone, Nick (2013b), 'Chinese Dive into London Hotels', *Property Week*, June 28. Available at: http://www.propertyweek.com/resi/chinese-dive-into-london-hotels/5056619.article, accessed March 31, 2016.

Jones, Hannah, Sarah Neal, Giles Mohan et al. (2015), 'Urban Multiculture and Everyday Encounters in Semi-Public, Franchised Cafe Spaces', *The Sociological Review* 63(3): 644–661.

Jones, Owen (2012), *Chavs: The Demonization of the Working Class*, London: Verso Books.

Kane, Kate (1990), 'The Ideology of Freshness in Feminine Hygiene Commercials', *Journal of Communication Inquiry* 14(1): 82–92.

Kdragonkwon (2013), 'Boy Group', *Kpopselca Forums*. Available at: http://kpopselca.com/forum/korean-artists/official-big-bang-thread-t137/page750.html#p140584, accessed July 15, 2015.

Kearney, Michael (1995), 'The Local and the Global: The Anthropology of Globalization and Transnationalism', *Annual Review of Anthropology* 24: 547–565.

Keith, Michael (1993), *Race, Riots and Policing*, London: UCL Press.

Keith, Michael (2005), *After the Cosmopolitan? Multicultural Cities and the Future of Racism*, London: Routledge.

Kelly, Daniel (2011), *Yuck! The Nature and Moral Significance of Disgust*, Cambridge: A Bradford Book.

Kiechle, Melanie (2015), 'Navigating by Nose: Fresh Air, Stench Nuisance, and the Urban Environment, 1840–1880', *Journal of Urban History* 42(4): 753–771.

Kim, Chul-Kyoo and James Curry (1993), 'Fordism, Flexible Specialization and Agri-Industrial Restructuring: The Case of the US Broiler Industry', *Sociologia Ruralis* 33(1): 61–80.

Knab, Timothy (1997), *A War Of Witches: A Journey into the Underworld of the Contemporary Aztecs*, Boulder, CO: Perseus.

Knowles, Caroline (2005), *Bedlam on the Streets*, London: Routledge.

Knowles, Caroline and Douglas Harper (2009), *Hong Kong: Migrant Lives, Landscapes, and Journeys*, Chicago, IL: University of Chicago Press.

Koneh, Amara (2014), 'The Economics of Ebola', *Wall Street Journal*. Available at: http://online.wsj.com/articles/amara-konneh-the-economics-of-ebola-1407709918, accessed August 14, 2014.

Koolhaas, Rem, Stefano Boeri, Sanford Kwinter et al. (2000), *Mutations*, New York: ACTAR.

Korsmeyer, Carolyn (2014), *Making Sense of Taste: Food and Philosophy*, Ithaca, NY: Cornell University Press.

Kress, Susan (1998), 'Can Sociology Be Literature? Laurel Richardson's Fields of Play', *Journal of Contemporary Ethnography* 27(2): 270–277.

Kristeva, Julia (1982), *Powers of Horror*, New York: Columbia University Press.

Kumar, Krishan (2009), *From Post-Industrial to Post-Modern Society: New Theories of the Contemporary World*, London: John Wiley & Sons.

Kurlansky, Mark (2000), *The Basque History of the World*, London: Random House.

Kurlansky, Mark (2003), *Salt: A World History*, London: Random House.

Kurlansky, Mark (2011), *Cod: A Biography of the Fish That Changed the World*, London: Random House.

Laermans, Rudi (1993), 'Learning to Consume: Early Department Stores and the Shaping of the Modern Consumer Culture (1860–1914)', *Theory, Culture & Society* 10(4): 79–102.

Lambie-Mumford, Hannah, Daniel Crossley, Eric Jensen, Monae Verbeke and Elizabeth Dowler (2014), *Household Food Security in the UK: A Review of Food Aid – Executive Summary*, Coventry: University of Warwick.

Lanchester, John (2011), 'Recession? What Recession?' *The Guardian*, December 2. Available at: http://www.theguardian.com/lifeandstyle/2011/dec/02/recession-proof-london-restaurants-lanchester, accessed April 8, 2014.

Landa, Manuel De (1997), *A Thousand Years of Nonlinear History*, New York: Zone Books.

Largey, Gale Peter and David Rodney Watson (1972), 'The Sociology of Odors', *American Journal of Sociology* 77(6): 1021–1034.

Lawrence, Felicity, Andrew Wasley and Radu Ciorniciuc (2014), 'Revealed: The Dirty Secret of the UK's Poultry Industry', *The Guardian*. Available at: http://www.theguardian.com/world/2014/jul/23/-sp-revealed-dirty-secret-uk-poultry-industry-chicken-campylobacter, accessed July 29, 2015.

Lemanski, Dominik (2013), 'Now There's Donkey Meat in UK Salami', *Dailystar.co.uk*, January 20. Available at: http://www.dailystar.co.uk/news/latest-news/294020/Now-there-s-donkey-meat-in-UK-salami, accessed May 30, 2014.

Leonard, Barry (2011), *USDA Agricultural Projections to 2017*, Collingdale, PA: Diane Publishing.

Lévi-Strauss, Claude (1997), 'The Culinary Triangle'. In Penny Van Esterik and Carole Counihan, *Food and Culture: A Reader*, London: Routledge, pp. 28–35.

Lévi-Strauss, Claude, John Weightman and Doreen Weightman (1992), *The Raw and the Cooked*, London: Penguin.

Lichtenstein, Rachel and Iain Sinclair (2000), *Rodinsky's Room*, London: Granta Books.

Lidin, Olof G. (2002), *Tanegashima: The Arrival of Europe in Japan*, Copenhagen: NIAS Press.

Liston, Katie and Stephen Mennell (2009), 'Ill Met in Ghana: Jack Goody and Norbert Elias on Process and Progress in Africa', *Theory, Culture & Society* 26(7–8): 52–70.

Loades, D. M. (2009), *The Making of the Elizabethan Navy, 1540–1590: From the Solent to the Armada*, Woodbridge: Boydell Press.

Locker, Alison (2007), '*In Piscibus Diversis*: The Bone Evidence for Fish Consumption in Roman Britain', *Britannia* 38: 141–180.

London Borough of Newham (2012), *Newham 2027 – Newham's Local Plan – The Core Strategy*, Newham Council.

London Borough of Newham (2013), 'Decision Notice Application 14/00954/FULL'. Available at: https://pa.newham.gov.uk/online-applications/appealDetails.do?activ eTab=externalDocuments&keyVal–IZOG1JY52R00, accessed August 12, 2015.

Longley, Paul A. (2002), 'Geographical Information Systems: Will Developments in Urban Remote Sensing and GIS Lead to "Better" Urban Geography?' *Progress in Human Geography* 26(2): 231–239.

Lorimer, H. (2008), 'Cultural Geography: Non-Representational Conditions and Concerns', *Progress in Human Geography* 32(4): 551–559.

Low, Kelvin E. Y. (2013a), 'Sensing Cities: The Politics of Migrant Sensescapes', *Social Identities* 19(2): 1–17.

Low, Kelvin E. Y. (2013b), 'Olfactive Frames of Remembering: Theorizing Self, Senses and Society', *The Sociological Review* 61(4): 688–708.

Lupton, Deborah (1996), *Food, the Body, and the Self*, London: Sage.

Lury, Celia and Nina Wakeford (2012), *Inventive Methods: The Happening of the Social*, London: Routledge.

Lymbery, Philip (2014), *Farmageddon: The True Cost of Cheap Meat*, London: Bloomsbury Publishing.

Lynn, Guy (2012), 'Cane Rat Meat "Sold to Public"', *BBC*, September 17. Available at: http://www.bbc.co.uk/news/uk-england-london-19622903, accessed July 24, 2014.

MacDougall, David (2006), *The Corporeal Image*, Princeton: Princeton University Press.

Mackenzie, Sophie (2013), 'Would You Eat Horsemeat?' *The Guardian*, January 16. Available at: http://www.theguardian.com/lifeandstyle/wordofmouth/2013/jan/16/would-you-eat-horsemeat, accessed June 12, 2014.

Macklin, Graham (2007), *Very Deeply Dyed in Black: Sir Oswald Mosley and the Postwar Reconstruction of British Fascism*, London: IB Tauris & Co Ltd.

Maddock, Jay (2004), 'The Relationship between Obesity and the Prevalence of Fast Food Restaurants: State-Level Analysis', *American Journal of Health Promotion* 19(2): 137–143.

Malone, Andrew (2010), 'Slaughter of the Swans: As Carcasses Pile up and Crude Migrant Camps Are Built on the River Bank, Peterborough Residents are Scared to Visit the Park', *Mail Online*. Available at: http://www.dailymail.co.uk/news/article-1261044/Slaughter-swans-As-carcasses-pile-crude-camps-built-river-banks-residents-frightened-visit-park-Peterborough.html, accessed June 26, 2014.

Malone, Andrew (2014), 'How Ebola Could Strike Britain Due to Secret Trade in Monkey Meat', *Mail Online*. Available at: http://www.dailymail.co.uk/news/article-2713707/Secret-trade-monkey-meat-unleash-Ebola-UK-How-appetite-African-delicacies-British-markets-stalls-spread-killer-virus.html, accessed August 5, 2014.

Manalansan, M. (2006), 'Immigrant Lives and the Politics of Olfaction in the Global City'. In Jim Drobnick (ed.), *The Smell Culture Reader*, Oxford: Berg, pp. 41–52.

Mandel, Ruth (2008), *Cosmopolitan Anxieties: Turkish Challenges to Citizenship and Belonging in Germany*, Durham, NC: Duke University Press.

Mansingh, Ajai and Laxmi Mansingh (1985), 'Hindu Influences on Rastafarianism'. In Rex Nettleford (ed.), *Caribbean Quarterly Monograph*, St Augustine: University of the West Indies, pp. 96–115.

Mansingh, Laxmi (1979), 'Cultural Heritage Among the East Indians in Jamaica'. In *Second University of West Indies Conference on East Indians in the Caribbean*, St. Augustine: University of the West Indies, pp. 16–22.

Mansingh, Laxmi and Ajai Mansingh (1999), *Home Away from Home: 150 Years of Indian Presence in Jamaica, 1845–1995*, Hanover Parish: Ian Randle Publishers.

Mariani, John F. (2013), *Encyclopedia of American Food and Drink*, New York: Bloomsbury USA.

Marion Young, Iris (1990), 'Abjection and Oppression: Dynamics of Unconcious Racism and Homophobia'. In Arleen B. Dallery, Charles E. Scott and P. Holley Roberts (eds), *Crises in Continental Philosophy*, Albany: State University of New York Press, pp. 201–214.

Mars, Valerie (1983), 'Spaghetti, but Not on Toast: Italian Food in London'. In *Food in Motion: The Migration of Foodstuffs and Cookery Techniques: Proceedings: Oxford Symposium 1983*, London: Progress Books, pp. 144–146.

Martens, Lydia and Alan Warde (1998), 'The Social and Symbolic Significance of Ethnic Cuisine in England: New Cosmopolitanism and Old Xenophobia', *Sosiolosgisk Arbok* 1: 111–146.

Marx, Karl (2012a), *Economic and Philosophic Manuscripts of 1844*, London: Courier Corporation.

Marx, Karl (2012b), *Capital, Volume One: A Critique of Political Economy*, London: Courier Corporation.

Marx, Karl and Friedrich Engels (1975), *Collected Works*, London: Lawrence and Wishart.

Matt, Susan J. (2007), 'A Hunger for Home: Homesickness and Food in a Global Consumer Society', *The Journal of American Culture* 30(1): 6–17.

Mayhew, Henry (1861), *London Labour and the London Poor*, London: G. Newbold.

McDowell, Linda (2009), 'Old and New European Economic Migrants: Whiteness and Managed Migration Policies', *Journal of Ethnic and Migration Studies* 35(1): 19–36.

McFarlane, Colin (2011), 'The City as Assemblage: Dwelling and Urban Space', *Environment and Planning – Part D* 29(4): 649.

McGuinness, Ross (2013), 'The Food Taboo . . . Why Don't Britons Want to Eat Horse Meat?' *Metro*. Available at: http://metro.co.uk/2013/01/17/the-food-taboo-why-dont-britons-want-to-eat-horse-meat-3355053/, accessed July 3, 2014.

McWilliams, Mark (2012), *The Story Behind the Dish: Classic American Foods*, Santa Barbara, CA: ABC-CLIO.

Melamed, Samuel and Shelly Bruhis (1996), 'The Effects of Chronic Industrial Noise Exposure on Urinary Cortisol, Fatigue, and Irritability: A Controlled Field Experiment', *Journal of Occupational and Environmental Medicine* 38(3): 252–256.

Mele, Christopher, Megan Ng and May Bo Chim (2015), 'Urban Markets as a "Corrective" to Advanced Urbanism: The Social Space of Wet Markets in Contemporary Singapore', *Urban Studies* 52(1): 103–120.

Meltzer, Tom (2011), 'Britain's Fried-Chicken Boom', *The Guardian*, February 18, sec. Life and Style. Available at: http://www.theguardian.com/lifeandstyle/2011/feb/18/britains-fried-chicken-boom, accessed May 15, 2014.

Mennell, Stephen (1996), *All Manners of Food*, Champaign, IL: University of Illinois Press.

Miles, Elizabeth (1993), 'Adventures in the Postmodernist Kitchen: The Cuisine of Wolfgang Puck', *The Journal of Popular Culture* 27(3): 191–203.

Miller, Joe (2013) 'Historic Nunhead Pub Revived as Community Co-operative', *BBC News*, April 7. Available at: http://www.bbc.co.uk/news/uk-england-london-22016830, accessed December 11, 2015.

Miller, John (2014), 'ArcelorMittal Blames Ebola for Delay in Liberia Mine Expansion', *The Wall Street Journal*. Available at: http://online.wsj.com/articles/arcelormittal-blames-ebola-for-delay-in-liberia-mine-expansion-1407522087, accessed August 14, 2014.

Mills, Roger and Clem Vallance (1989), 'Far East and Farther East' (Episode 6), 'Around the World in 80 Days', BBC Documentary.

Mintz, Sidney Wilfred (1986), *Sweetness and Power: The Place of Sugar in Modern History*, London: Penguin Books.

Mitchell, William Frank (2009), *African American Food Culture*, Santa Barbara, CA: ABC-CLIO.

Monbiot, George (2014), 'If You Must Eat Meat, Save It for Christmas', *The Guardian*. Available at: http://www.theguardian.com/commentisfree/2014/dec/16/perpetual-denial-food-meat-production-environmental-devastation, accessed August 1, 2015.

Monbiot, George (2015), 'Faeces, Bacteria, Toxins: Welcome to the Chicken Farm', *The Guardian*. Available at: http://www.theguardian.com/commentisfree/2015/may/19/chicken-welfare-human-health-meat, accessed August 1, 2015.

Montgomery, Janet, J. A. Evans, S. R. Chenery, Vanessa Pashley and Kristina Killgrove (2010), '"Gleaming, White and Deadly": Using Lead to Track Human Exposure and Geographic Origins in the Roman Period in Britain', *Journal of Roman Archaeology*, Supplementary Series 78: 199–226.

Morigi, Anthony N., Danielle Schreve and Mark White (2011), *The Thames Through Time: The Archaeology of the Gravel Terraces of the Upper and Middle Thames: Early Prehistory to 1500 BC*, Oxford: Oxford Archaeology.

Morley, David (ed.) (2002), *Home Territories: Media, Mobility and Identity*, London: Routledge.

Morrison, Arthur and Peter Miles (2012), *A Child of the Jago*, Oxford: Oxford University Press.

Morton, James (2001), *East End Gangland*, London: Sphere.

Moss, Michael (2013), *Salt Sugar Fat: How the Food Giants Hooked Us*, London: Random House.

Moudon, Anne Vernez (2009), 'Real Noise from the Urban Environment: How Ambient Community Noise Affects Health and What Can Be Done about It', *American Journal of Preventive Medicine* 37(2): 167–171.

Mukherjee, S. Romi (2014), 'Global Halal: Meat, Money, and Religion', *Religions* 5(1): 22–75.

National Obesity Observatory (2010), *The Economic Burden of Obesity*, London: Public Health England.

Newman, Martin (2014), 'Horse Meat Galloping off the Shelves in Spite of British Food Contamination Scandal', *Mirror*. Available at: http://www.mirror.co.uk/

news/uk-news/horse-meat-galloping-shelves-spite-3162605, accessed July 5, 2014.

Newsnight (David Starkey) (2011), 'The Whites Have Become Black', *Newsnight, BBC HD*. Available at: https://www.youtube.com/watch?v=OVq2bs8M9HM, accessed March 29, 2016.

Nicholson, Renton (1838), *Cockney Adventures, Or, Sketches of London Life*, London: W. M. Clark and A. Forrester.

Norwood, F. Bailey and Jayson L. Lusk (2011), *Compassion, by the Pound: The Economics of Farm Animal Welfare*, Oxford: OUP Catalogue.

Nsubuga, Jimmy (2015), 'MP Who's Spoken at Chicken Cottage Awards (Yes, They're Real) Says There are Too Many Chicken Shops', *Metro*. Available at: http://metro.co.uk/2015/08/07/labour-mp-sadiq-khan-said-there-are-too-many-chicken-shops-at-chicken-cottage-awards-5331814/, accessed December 6, 2015.

Obama, Barack (2008), *Dreams from My Father: A Story of Race and Inheritance*, London: Canongate Books.

Obasogie, Osagie K. (2013), *Blinded by Sight: Seeing Race Through the Eyes of the Blind*, Stanford, CA: Stanford University Press.

O'Connor, Brendon and Martin Griffiths (2007), *Anti-Americanism: Causes and Sources*, Westport, CT: Greenwood Publishing Group.

Oddy, Derek J. (2003), *From Plain Fare to Fusion Food: British Diet from the 1890s to the 1990s*, Woodbridge: Boydell Press.

Ohnuki-Tierney, Emiko (1995), 'Structure, Event and Historical Metaphor: Rice and Identities in Japanese History', *The Journal of the Royal Anthropological Institute* 1(2): 227.

Okihiro, Gary Y. (2009), *Pineapple Culture: A History of the Tropical and Temperate Zones*, Berkeley, CA: University of California Press.

Open Dalston (2008a), 'Hackney Council to "Redevelop" Ridley Road Market'. Available at: http://opendalston.blogspot.co.uk/2008/10/hackney-council-to-redevelop-ridley.html, accessed July 25, 2014.

Open Dalston (2008b), 'Hackney Bean-Counters Go Bananas in Dalston's Market'. Available at: http://opendalston.blogspot.co.uk/2008/03/hackney-beancounters-go-bananas-in.html, accessed July 25, 2014.

Open Dalston (2008c), 'Hackney's Mayor Pipe Smears Children's Laureate'. Available at: http://opendalston.blogspot.co.uk/2008/06/hackneys-mayor-pipe-smears-childrens.html, accessed July 25, 2014.

Open Dalston (2009), 'Ridley Road Market Plans – Make Your Views Known'. Available at: http://opendalston.blogspot.co.uk/2009/10/ridley-road-market-plans-make-you-views.html, accessed July 25, 2014.

Opie, Frederick Douglass (2013), *Hog and Hominy: Soul Food from Africa to America*, New York: Columbia University Press.

Ortiz, Fernando (1995), *Cuban Counterpoint: Tobacco and Sugar*, Durham, NC: Duke University Press.

Orwell, George (1958), *The Road to Wigan Pier*, Chicago: Houghton Mifflin Harcourt.

Page, Martin (2002), *The First Global Village: How Portugal Changed the World*, Alfrigade: Casa das Letras.

Pallasmaa, Juhani (2005), *The Eyes of the Skin: Architecture and the Senses*, 2nd Edition, London: John Wiley & Sons.

Pallasmaa, Juhani (2012), 'Newness, Tradition and Identity: Existential Content and Meaning in Architecture', *Architectural Design* 82(6): 14–21.

Panayi, Panikos (2008), *Spicing Up Britain*, London: Reaktion Books.

Panayi, Panikos (2012), 'The Anglicisation of East European Jewish Food in Britain', *Immigrants & Minorities* 30(2/3): 292–317.

Parham, Susan (2005), 'Designing the Gastronomic Quarter', *Architectural Design* 75(3): 86–95.

Parham, Susan (2012), *Market Place: Food Quarters, Design and Urban Renewal in London*, Newcastle Upon Tyne: Cambridge Scholars Publishing.

Parham, Susan (2015), *Food and Urbanism*, London: Bloomsbury.

Park, Robert E. and Ernest W. Burgess (2012) *The City*, Chicago, IL: University of Chicago Press.

Parker, Nick (2013), 'A Load of Old Pony', *The Sun*. Available at: http://www. thesun.co.uk/sol/homepage/news/4790318/The-Sun-goes-inside-Romanian-abattoir-that-produces-horse-meat.html, accessed June 12, 2014.

Penaloza, Lisa (1998), 'Just Doing It: A Visual Ethnographic Study of Spectacular Consumption Behavior at Nike Town', *Consumption Markets & Culture* 2(4): 337–400.

Perec, Georges and John Sturrock (1998), *Species of Spaces and Other Pieces*, London: Penguin Classics.

Peterson, Dale and Karl Ammann (2003), *Eating Apes*, Berkeley, CA: University of California Press.

Philpott, Carl M. and Duncan Boak (2014), 'The Impact of Olfactory Disorders in the United Kingdom', *Chemical Senses*: bju043.

Pieterse, Jan Nederveen (2009) *Globalization and Culture: Global Mélange*, Plymouth: Rowman & Littlefield.

Pieterse, Jan Nederveen (2011), 'Many Renaissances, Many Modernities?' *Theory, Culture & Society* 28(3): 149–160.

Pile, Steve (1993), *Place and the Politics of Identity*, London: Routledge.

Pile, Steve (2010), 'Emotions and Affect in Recent Human Geography', *Transactions of the Institute of British Geographers* 35(1): 5–20.

Pile, Steve (2013), *The Body and the City: Psychoanalysis, Space and Subjectivity*, London: Routledge.

Pink, Sarah (2008), 'An Urban Tour: The Sensory Sociality of Ethnographic Place-Making', *Ethnography* 9(2): 175–196.

Pink, Sarah (2009), *Doing Sensory Ethnography*, London: Sage.

Pink, Sarah (2012), *Advances in Visual Methodology*, London: Sage.

Pliny (1890), *The Natural History of Pliny*, London: G. Bell and sons.

Ponsford, Dominic (2003), 'Sun Accused of Swan Bake Myth-Making', *Press Gazette*. Available at: http://www.pressgazette.co.uk/sun-accused-of-swan-bake-myth-making/, accessed August 12, 2016.

Powell, Darren and Michael Gard (2014), 'The Governmentality of Childhood Obesity: Coca-Cola, Public Health and Primary Schools', *Discourse: Studies in the Cultural Politics of Education* 36(6): 1–14.

Preece, R. C. (1999), 'Mollusca from Last Interglacial Fluvial Deposits of the River Thames at Trafalgar Square, London', *Journal of Quaternary Science* 14(1): 77–89.

Proctor, Helen S., Gemma Carder and Amelia R. Cornish (2013), 'Searching for Animal Sentience: A Systematic Review of the Scientific Literature', *Animals* 3(3): 882–906.

Proust, Marcel (2006), *Remembrance of Things Past*, London: Wordsworth Editions.

Public Health England (2014), *Obesity and the Environment Fast Food Outlets*, London: Public Health England.

Pye, Michael (2015), *The Edge of the World – A Cultural History of the North Sea and the Transformation of Europe*, Cambridge: Pegasus.

Quinn, Sue (2013), 'Sriracha Shortage: Why Chilli Sauce Is Hot Property – and Getting Hotter', *The Guardian*, November 5. Available at: http://www.theguardian.com/lifeandstyle/wordofmouth/2013/nov/05/sriracha-shortage-chilli-sauce-hot-spice, accessed December 6, 2014.

Rabinow, Paul and Nikolas Rose (2003), *The Essential Foucault*, New York: The New Press.

Raento, Mika, Antti Oulasvirta and Nathan Eagle (2009), 'Smartphones an Emerging Tool for Social Scientists', *Sociological Methods & Research* 37(3): 426–454.

Raimbault, Manon and Daniele Dubois (2005), 'Urban Soundscapes: Experiences and Knowledge', *Cities* 22(5): 339–350.

Rampton, Ben (2014), *Crossings: Language and Ethnicity Among Adolescents*, London: Routledge.

Randolph, Mary (2004), *The Virginia Housewife or Methodical Cook*. Available at: http://www.gutenberg.org/ebooks/12519, accessed August 12, 2015.

Rayner, Jay (2013), 'Fried Chicken Fix: After-School Fast Food', *The Guardian*. Available at: https://www.theguardian.com/lifeandstyle/2013/oct/26/fried-chicken-fast-food-shop-schoolkids, accessed August 12, 2016.

Reaves, Erik J., Lyndon G. Mabande, Douglas A. Thoroughman, M. Allison Arwady and Joel M. Montgomery (2014), 'Control of Ebola Virus disease—Firestone District, Liberia, 2014', *MMWR Morb Mortal Weekly Report* 63(42): 959–965.

Red Hot Entertainment (Ft. Jaxor, Klayze Flaymz, Ray & Terra) (2007), 'Junior Spesh'. Available at: https://www.youtube.com/watch?v=Q6pbZLiLt30, accessed August 12, 2016.

Redfield, Robert and Milton B. Singer (1954), 'The Cultural Role of Cities', *Economic Development and Cultural Change* 3(1): 53–73.

Reid, Sue (2004), 'Butchered in Africa, On Sale in Britain'. *The Daily Mail*, November 30. Available at: http://www.iccservices.org.uk/downloads/health/bushmeat_butchered_in_africa.pdf, accessed August 12, 2016.

Reilly, Alan (2013), 'CEO Statement to the Joint Oireachtas Committee on Agriculture, Food and the Marine'. Available at: http://www.fsai.ie/news_centre/oireachtas_05.02.2013.html, accessed May 30, 2014.

Reilly, Jill (2013), 'The Great Horsemeat Scandal . . . of 1948: Archive Newsreel Shows UK Food Chain Was Rocked by the Same Crisis 65 Years Ago', *Mail Online*. Available at: http://www.dailymail.co.uk/news/article-2278692/The-great-horsemeat-scandal--1948-Archive-newsreel-shows-UK-food-chain-rocked-crisis-65-years-ago.html, accessed July 3, 2014.

Rhys-Taylor, Alex (2013a), 'The Essences of Multiculture: A Sensory Exploration of an Inner-City Street Market', *Identities* 20(4): 393–406.

Rhys-Taylor, Alex (2013b), 'Disgust and Distinction: The Case of the Jellied Eel', *The Sociological Review* 61(2): 227–246.

Rhys-Taylor, Alex (2014), 'Intersemiotic Fruit: Mangoes, Multiculture and the City'. In Hannah Jones and Emma Jackson (eds), *Stories of Cosmopolitan Belonging: Emotion and Location*, London: Routledge.

Riach, Kathleen and Samantha Warren (2014), 'Smell Organization: Bodies and Corporeal Porosity in Office Work', *Human Relations* 68(5): 789–809.

Richardson, Laurel (1988), 'The Collective Story: Postmodernism and the Writing of Sociology', *Sociological Focus* 21(3): 199–208.

Richardson, Laurel (1990), *Writing Strategies: Reaching Diverse Audiences*, Newbury Park: Sage.

Ridley, Matt (2004), *Nature via Nurture: Genes, Experience and What Makes Us Human*, London: Harper Perennial.

Rinehart, Robert (1998), 'Fictional Methods in Ethnography: Believability, Specks of Glass, and Chekhov', *Qualitative Inquiry* 4(2): 200–224.

Ritzer, George (2004), *The McDonaldization of Society*, Thousand Oaks: Sage.

Roberts, Julian V. and Mike Hough (2013), 'Sentencing Riot-Related Offending: Where Do the Public Stand?' *British Journal of Criminology* 53(2): 234–256.

Robinson, Martin (2012), 'Food Shops in East London Caught Selling DEAD RATS as Undercover Probe Reveals Illegal Meat Trade', *Mail Online*. Available at: http://www.dailymail.co.uk/news/article-2204579/Food-shops-east-London-caught-selling-DEAD-RATS-undercover-probe-reveals-illegal-meat-trade.html, accessed July 24, 2014.

Rodger, John (2012), *Criminalising Social Policy: Anti-Social Behaviour and Welfare in a De-Civilised Society*, London: Routledge.

Ross, Andrew and Final Draft Consultancy (2013), 'Obesity-Based Policies to Restrict Hot Food Takeaways: Progress by Local Planning Authorities in England', *Final Draft Consultancy*. Available at: http://www.medway.gov.uk/pdf/Obesity-based%20policies%20to%20restrict%20hot%20food%20takeaways-%20progress%20by%20local%20planning%20authorities%20in%20England.pdf, accessed July 28, 2015.

Rouse, Carolyn and Janet Hoskins (2004), 'Purity, Soul Food, and Sunni Islam: Explorations at the Intersection of Consumption and Resistance', *Cultural Anthropology* 19(2): 226–249.

Rowe, James E. (2012), 'The Case for Employing Deleuzian Philosophical Concepts for Understanding Local Economic Development', *Applied Geography* 32(1): 73–79.

Royle, Tony (2000), *Working for McDonald's in Europe: The Unequal Struggle*, London: Psychology Press.

Rozin, Paul and Deborah Schiller (1980), 'The Nature and Acquisition of a Preference for Chili Pepper by Humans', *Motivation and Emotion* 4(1): 77–101.

Rubin, Barry and Judith Colp Rubin (2004), *Hating America: A History*, Oxford: Oxford University Press.

Russell, Benjamin (2014), 'Man "Beheads" Protected Swan before Taking It Home to EAT', *Express.co.uk*. Available at: http://www.express.co.uk/news/nature/466646/Man-beheads-protected-swan-before-taking-it-home-to-EAT, accessed June 26, 2014.

Sahlins, Marshall (1976), *Culture and Practical Reason*, Chicago: University of Chicago Press.

Samuel, Raphael (2012), *Theatres of Memory: Past and Present in Contemporary Culture*, London: Verso Books.

Sasaki, Ken-Ichi (2000), 'For Whom Is City Design: Tactility versus Visuality'. In Iain Borden, Tim Hall and Malcolm Miles (eds), *The City Cultures Reader*, London and New York: Routledge, pp. 36–44.

Sassen, Saskia (1993), 'Rebuilding the Global City: Economy, Ethnicity and Space', *Social Justice* 20(3–4): 32–40.

Sassen, Saskia (2001), *The Global City: New York, London, Tokyo*, Princeton, NJ: Princeton University Press.

Scally, Gabriel (2013), 'Adulteration of Food: What It Doesn't Say on the Tin', *British Medical Journal* 346: f1463.

Schlosser, Eric (2012), *Fast Food Nation: The Dark Side of the All-American Meal*, Chicago, IL: Houghton Mifflin Harcourt.

Schou, Soren (1992), 'Postwar Americanisation and the Revitalisation of European Culture'. In Michael Skovmand (ed.), *Media Cultures: Reappraising Transnational Media*, London: Routledge, pp. 142–160.

Schwabe, Calvin W. (1979), *Unmentionable Cuisine*, Charlottesville, VA: University of Virginia Press.

Schwartz, H. (2003), 'The Indefensible Ear: A History'. In Michael Bull and Les Back (eds), *The Auditory Culture Reader*, Oxford: Berg, pp. 487–501.

Scollon, Ron, Suzanne Wong Scollon and Rodney H. Jones (2011), *Intercultural Communication: A Discourse Approach*, London: John Wiley & Sons.

Seeley, John R. (1967), *The Americanization of the Unconscious*, New York: International Science Press.

Seremetakis, C. Nadia (1996), *The Senses Still*, Chicago, IL: University of Chicago Press.

Serres, Michel, Margaret Sankey and Peter Cowley (2008), *The Five Senses: A Philosophy of Mingled Bodies*, London: Continuum International Publishing Group.

Sherrif, Abdul (2010), *Dhow Cultures and the Indian Ocean: Cosmopolitanism, Commerce and Islam*, Oxford: Oxford University Press.

Shimizu, Akira (2010), 'Meat-Eating in the Kojimachi District of Edo'. In Eric C. Rath and Stephanie Assmann (eds), *Japanese Foodways, Past and Present*, Champaign, IL: University of Illinois Press.

Siciliano, Leon (2015), 'Redrow's Luxury London Flat Advert Pulled after "Class War" Criticism', *The Telegraph*, January 5. Available at: http://www.telegraph. co.uk/news/newsvideo/weirdnewsvideo/11324969/Watch-Strange-advert-for-luxury-London-flats.html, accessed January 2, 2016.

Sik, Endre and Claire Wallace (1999), 'The Development of Open-Air Markets in East-Central Europe', *International Journal of Urban and Regional Research* 23(4): 697–714.

Simmel, Georg, David Frisby and Mike Featherstone (1997), *Simmel on Culture*, London: Sage.

Sinclair, Iain (2009), *Hackney, That Rose-Red Empire*, London: Hamish Hamilton.

Sloman, Larry (1998), *Reefer Madness: A History of Marijuana*, London: Macmillan.

Small, Stephen and John Solomos (2006), 'Race, Immigration and Politics in Britain: Changing Policy Agendas and Conceptual Paradigms 1940s–2000s', *International Journal of Comparative Sociology* 47(3–4): 235–57.

Smith, Alfred Emanuel and Francis Walton (1899), *New Outlook*, London: Outlook Publishing Company.

Smith, Andrew and Bruce Kraig (2013), *The Oxford Encyclopedia of Food and Drink in America*, Oxford: Oxford University Press.

Smith, Mark M. (2003), 'Making Sense of Social History', *Journal of Social History* 37(1): 165–186.

Smith, Mark M. (2006), *How Race Is Made*, Chapel Hill, NC: UNC Press.

Smith, Mark M. (2014), *The Smell of Battle, the Taste of Siege: A Sensory History of the Civil War*, New York: Oxford University Press.

Smith, Neil (2002), 'New Globalism, New Urbanism: Gentrification as Global Urban Strategy', *Antipode* 34(3): 427–450.

Smith, P. D. (2012), *City: A Guidebook for the Urban Age*, London: A&C Black.

Smith, Virginia (2008), *Clean: A History of Personal Hygiene and Purity*, Oxford: Oxford University Press.

Smith-Dawkins, Rebecca (2014), 'Horse Meat Back on the Shelves at Butchers in Nottingham', *Nottingham Post*, February 24. Available at: http://www.nottinghampost.com/HORSE-MEAT/story-20688714-detail/story.html, accessed July 5, 2014.

Smithers, Rebecca (2014), 'Don't Wash Chicken before Cooking It, Warns Food Standards Agency', *The Guardian*. Available at: http://www.theguardian.com/lifeandstyle/2014/jun/16/do-not-wash-chicken-advises-fsa, accessed August 3, 2015.

Sockmonkey (2012), 'Simply Foods on Anerley Hill – Application to Change to Hot Fast Food', *Virtual Norwood*. Available at: http://www.virtualnorwood.com/forum/topic/12368-simply-foods-on-anerley-hill-application-to-change-to-hot-fast-food-takeaway/, accessed August 4, 2015.

Soja, Edward W. (1996), *Thirdspace*, Oxford: Wiley-Blackwell.

Soriguer, Federico, Gemma Rojo-Martínez, M. Carmen Dobarganes et al. (2003), 'Hypertension is Related to the Degradation of Dietary Frying Oils', *The American Journal of Clinical Nutrition* 78(6): 1092–1097.

Spencer, Stuart, Eddy Decuypere, Stefan Aerts and Johan De Tavernier (2006), 'History and Ethics of Keeping Pets: Comparison with Farm Animals', *Journal of Agricultural and Environmental Ethics* 19(1): 17–25.

Spurr, Harry A. (1899), *A Cockney in Arcadia*, New York: F. P. Harper.

Stansfeld, Stephen A. and Mark P. Matheson (2003), 'Noise Pollution: Non-Auditory Effects on Health', *British Medical Bulletin* 68(1): 243–257.

Steinmüller, Hans (2011), 'The Moving Boundaries of Social Heat: Gambling in Rural China', *Journal of the Royal Anthropological Institute* 17(2): 263–280.

Sterne, Jonathan (2003), *The Audible Past: Cultural Origins of Sound Reproduction*, Durham, NC: Duke University Press.

Stewart, John O. (1989), *Drinkers, Drummers, and Decent Folk: Ethnographic Narratives of Village Trinidad*, Albany, NY: State University of New York Press.

Stillerman, Joel (2006), 'The Politics of Space and Culture in Santiago: Chile's Street Markets', *Qualitative Sociology* 29(4): 507–530.

Stoller, Paul (1989), *The Taste of Ethnographic Things: The Senses in Anthropology*, Philadelphia, PA: University of Pennsylvania Press.

Stoller, Paul (1997), *Sensuous Scholarship*. Philadelphia, PA: University of Pennsylvania Press.

Stoller, Paul (2002), *Money Has No Smell: The Africanization of New York City*, Chicago, IL: University of Chicago Press.

Stoller, Paul (2008), *The Power of the Between*, Chicago, IL: University of Chicago Press.

Stone, Harry Wallop (video by Chris) (2013), 'Video: Which Tastes Better: Horse or Beef?' *The Telegraph*, January 24. Available at: http://www.telegraph.co.uk/foodanddrink/foodanddrinkvideo/9806849/Which-tastes-better-horse-or-beef.html, accessed June 12, 2014.

Stott, Richard (2013), 'Homesick Blues', *Reviews in American History* 41(1): 19–24.

Striffler, Steve (2007), *Chicken: The Dangerous Transformation of America's Favorite Food*, New Haven, CT: Yale University Press.

Summers, Owen (1988), 'Yard Probe Black Disco Drug Gangs', *Daily Express*, January 8: 24.

Sutton, David E. (2001), *Remembrance of Repasts: An Anthropology of Food and Memory*, Oxford: Berg.

Swinburn, Boyd and Garry Egger (2002), 'Preventive Strategies against Weight Gain and Obesity', *Obesity Reviews* 3(4): 289–301.

Swinburn, Boyd, Garry Egger and Fezeela Raza (1999), 'Dissecting Obesogenic Environments: The Development and Application of a Framework for Identifying and Prioritizing Environmental Interventions for Obesity', *Preventive Medicine* 29(6): 563–570.

Swinford, Steven, Gordon Rayner and Christopher Hope (2013), 'Scale of the Horse Meat Scandal is "Breathtaking", MPs Say', *The Telegraph*, February 14. Available at: http://www.telegraph.co.uk/foodanddrink/foodanddrinknews/9869087/Scale-of-the-horse-meat-scandal-is-breathtaking-MPs-say.html, accessed May 30, 2014.

Tamari, Tomoko (2006), 'Rise of the Department Store and the Aestheticization of Everyday Life in Early Twentieth Century Japan', *International Journal of Japanese Sociology* 15(1): 99–118.

Taylor, D. (1991), 'The Social Psychology of Racial and Cultural Diversity: Issues of Assimilation and Multiculturalism'. In Alan G. Reynolds (ed.), *Bilingualism, Multiculturalism, and Second Language Learning: The McGill Conference in Honour of Wallace E. Lambert*, New York: Psychology Press, pp. 1–19.

Taylor, Matthew and James Meikle (2013), 'Cuts and Deregulation Fostered Horsemeat Scandal, Says Labour', *The Guardian*, January 18. Available at: http://www.theguardian.com/world/2013/jan/18/cuts-horsemeat-scandal, accessed June 12, 2014.

Taylor, Patrick (2001), *Nation Dance: Religion, Identity, and Cultural Difference in the Caribbean*, Bloomington, IN: Indiana University Press.

Ten, C. L. (2003), *The Nineteenth Century*, New York: Psychology Press.

Thornton, Sarah (2013), *Club Cultures: Music, Media and Subcultural Capital*, London: John Wiley & Sons.

Thorpe, Nick (2013), 'Romania Denies Horsemeat Charge', *BBC*, February 13. Available at: http://www.bbc.co.uk/news/world-europe-21436257, accessed June 26, 2014.

Thrift, Nigel (2008), *Non-Representational Theory: Space, Politics, Affect*, London: Routledge.

Tobin, Lucy (2014), 'Diane Abbott Is Right to Cry Fowl on Fried Chicken', *The Evening Standard*. Available at: http://www.standard.co.uk/comment/letters/lucy-tobin-diane-abbott-is-right-to-cry-fowl-on-fried chicken-9830954.html, accessed July 28, 2015.

Treaty of Lisbon (2007), 2007/C 306/01.

Tsukamoto, Katsumi and Mari Kuroki (2013), *Eels and Humans*, New York: Springer.

Tweedie, Neil (2015), 'How Fried Chicken Gobbled up the High Street', *Mail Online*. Available at: http://www.dailymail.co.uk/debate/article-3032984/NEIL-TWEEDIE-fried chicken-gobbled-High-street-dire-results-Britain-s-health.html, accessed July 28, 2015.

Twine, Richard (2002), 'Physiognomy, Phrenology and the Temporality of the Body', *Body & Society* 8(1): 67–88.

Tyler, Imogen (2013), *Revolting Subjects: Social Abjection and Resistance in Neoliberal Britain*, London: Zed Books Ltd.

Vannini, Phillip, Dennis Waskul and Simon Gottschalk (2011), *The Senses in Self, Society, and Culture: A Sociology of the Senses*, New York: Routledge.

Vasseleu, Cathryn (1998), *Textures of Light: Vision and Touch in Irigaray, Levinas, and Merleau-Ponty*, London: Routledge.

Venkatesh, Sudhir (2009), *Gang Leader for a Day*, London: Penguin.

Wacquant, Loïc (2007), *Body & Soul: Notebooks of an Apprentice Boxer*, Oxford: OUP USA.

Wainwright, Oliver (2015), '"American Psycho" Property Promo Pulled after Twitterstorm'. *The Guardian*, January 5. Available at: http://www.theguardian. com/artanddesign/architecture-design-blog/2015/jan/05/american-psycho-redrow-property-promo-pulled-after-twitterstorm, accessed February 4, 2016.

Walker, Marc (2013), 'Queen Eats Horse', *Dailystar.co.uk*. Available at: http:// www.dailystar.co.uk/news/latest-news/300239/QUEEN-EATS-HORSE, accessed May 30, 2014.

Wallach, Jennifer Jensen (2015), *Dethroning the Deceitful Pork Chop: Rethinking African American Foodways from Slavery to Obama*, Fayetteville, AR: University of Arkansas Press.

Wallerstein, Immanuel (1979), *The Capitalist World-Economy*, Cambridge: Cambridge University Press.

Walton, John K. (2000), *Fish and Chips and the British Working Class, 1870–1940*, London: Continuum International Publishing Group.

Warde, Alan (1997), *Consumption, Food and Taste*, London: Sage.

Warde, Alan (2000a), 'Eating Globally: Cultural Flows and the Spread of Ethnic Restaurants'. In Don Kalb et al. (eds), *The Ends of Globalization: Bringing Society Back*, London: Rowman and Littlefield, pp. 299–316.

Warde, Alan (2000b), *Eating Out: Social Differentiation, Consumption and Pleasure*, Cambridge: Cambridge University Press.

Waskul, Dennis D. and Phillip Vannini (2008), 'Smell, Odor, and Somatic Work: Sense-Making and Sensory Management', *Social Psychology Quarterly* 71(1): 53–71.

Waskul, Dennis D., Phillip Vannini and Janelle Wilson (2009), 'The Aroma of Recollection: Olfaction, Nostalgia, and the Shaping of the Sensuous Self', *The Senses and Society* 4(1): 5–22.

Watson, Sophie (2006), *City Publics: The (dis)enchantments of Urban Encounters*, London: Psychology Press.

Watson, Sophie and David Studdert (2006), *Markets as Sites for Social Interaction: Spaces of Diversity*, London: Policy Press.

Watson, Sophie and Karen Wells (2005), 'Spaces of Nostalgia: The Hollowing Out of a London Market', *Social & Cultural Geography* 6(1): 17–30.

Webb, Jonathan D. C. and G. Terence Meaden (2000), 'Daily Temperature Extremes for Britain', *Weather* 55(9): 298–315.

Webb, Sam (2013), 'Up to 70,000 Romanian and Bulgarian Migrants a Year "Will Come to Britain" When Controls on EU Migrants Expire', *Mail Online*. Available at: http://www.dailymail.co.uk/news/article-2263661/Up-70-000-Romanian-Bulgarian-migrants-year-come-Britain-controls-EU-migrants-expire. html, accessed June 13, 2014.

Webber, Richard (2013), 'Visual Images of Neighbourhoods – How Reliably Can They Predict Who Lives Where?' Goldsmiths, November 14. Available at: http://www.gold.ac.uk/calendar/?id=6853, accessed August 10, 2016.

Wessendorf, S. (2010), 'Commonplace Diversity: Social Interactions in a Super-Diverse Context', Göttingen MPI-MMG. Available at: https://cream.conference-services.net/resources/952/2371/pdf/MECSC2011_0004_paper.pdf, accessed September 17, 2012.

Westwood, Sallie and John Williams (2003), *Imagining Cities: Scripts, Signs and Memories*, London: Routledge.

Whyte, William Foote (1993), *Street Corner Society: The Social Structure of an Italian Slum*, Chicago, IL: University of Chicago Press.

Williams, Anna (2004), 'Disciplining Animals: Sentience, Production, and Critique', *International Journal of Sociology and Social Policy* 24(9): 45–57.

Williams, J., P. Scarborough, A. Matthews et al. (2014), 'A Systematic Review of the Influence of the Retail Food Environment around Schools on Obesity-Related Outcomes', *Obesity Reviews* 15(5): 359–374.

Williams-Forson, Psyche A. (2006), *Building Houses out of Chicken Legs: Black Women, Food, and Power*, Chapel Hill, NC: University of North Carolina Press.

Willis, Paul (1981), *Learning to Labor: How Working Class Kids Get Working Class Jobs*, New York: Columbia University Press.

Wintour, Patrick (2013), 'Diane Abbott Outlines Plan to Curb Fast Food Shops', *The Guardian*, January 3. Available at: http://www.theguardian.com/politics/2013/jan/03/diane-abbott-fast-food-curb, accessed December 6, 2015.

Wise, Amanda (2010), 'Sensuous Multiculturalism: Emotional Landscapes of Inter-Ethnic Living in Australian Suburbia', *Journal of Ethnic and Migration Studies* 36(6): 917–937.

Wise, Amanda and Selvaraj Velayutham (2009), *Everyday Multiculturalism*, Basingstoke: Palgrave Macmillan.

Witt, Doris (1999), *Black Hunger: Food and the Politics of U.S. Identity*, Oxford: Oxford University Press.

Wood, Stephen (2009), 'Desiring Docklands: Deleuze and Urban Planning Discourse', *Planning Theory* 8(2): 191–216.

Woodson, Carter Godwin (1990), *The Mis-Education of the Negro*, Trenton, NJ: Africa World Press.

Woodworth, R. S. (1910), 'Racial Differences in Mental Traits', *Science* 31(788): 171–186.

Wright, Jan and Valerie Harwood (2012), *Biopolitics and the 'Obesity Epidemic': Governing Bodies*, London: Routledge.

Wyatt, Caroline (2003), 'The Rich Smells of Paris', *BBC*, August 3. Available at: http://news.bbc.co.uk/1/hi/world/europe/3118231.stm, accessed April 10, 2015.

Xiang, Hai, Jianqiang Gao, Baoquan Yu et al. (2014), 'Early Holocene Chicken Domestication in Northern China', *Proceedings of the National Academy of Sciences* 111(49): 17564–17569.

YouGov (2012), 'Capital Cuisine. YouGov: What the World Thinks'. Available at: http://yougov.co.uk/news/2010/06/02/capital-cuisine/, accessed April 7, 2014.

Young, Michael and Peter Wilmott (2013), *Family and Kinship in East London*, London: Routledge.

Zinkhan, George M., Suzana de M. Fontenelle and Anne L. Balazs (1999), 'The Structure of São Paulo Street Markets: Evolving Patterns of Retail Institutions', *Journal of Consumer Affairs* 33(1): 3–26.

Zukin, Sharon (1998), 'Politics and Aesthetics of Public Space: The American Model'. Available at: http://www.publicspace.org/es/texto-biblioteca/eng/a013-politics-and-aesthetics-of-public-space-the-american-model, accessed November 19, 2014.

Zukin, Sharon (2009), *Naked City: The Death and Life of Authentic Urban Places*, Oxford: Oxford University Press.

Zukin, Sharon (2014), 'Theme V.4 The Street and the Urban Public Sphere: Diversity, Difference, Inequality', International Sociological Association Conference, Yokohama 2014. Available at: https://isaconf.confex.com/isaconf/wc2014/webprogram/Session4086.html, accessed November 25, 2015.

Zukin, Sharon, Scarlett Lindeman and Laurie Hurson (2015), 'The Omnivore's Neighborhood? Online Restaurant Reviews, Race, and Gentrification', *Journal of Consumer Culture*: 1469540515611203.

INDEX

9 781472 581167